CSCPRC REPORT NO. 10

U.S. Nuclear Science Delegation to the People's Republic of China.

Nuclear Science in China

Edited by D. ALLAN BROMLEY and PIERRE M. PERROLLE

Submitted to the Committee on Scholarly Communication
with the People's Republic of China

NATIONAL ACADEMY PRESS
Washington, D.C.   1980

NOTICE: The exchange visit of the Nuclear Science Delegation to the People's Republic of China was supported by a grant from the National Science Foundation. This visit was part of the exchange program operated by the Committee on Scholarly Communication with the People's Republic of China, founded jointly in 1966 by the American Council of Learned Societies, the National Academy of Sciences, and the Social Science Research Council. Sources of funding for the Committee include the National Science Foundation, the International Communication Agency, the National Endowment for the Humanities, the Ford Foundation, and the National Institutes of Health.

The Committee represents American scholars in the natural, medical, and social sciences, as well as the humanities. It advises individuals and institutions on means of communicating with their Chinese colleagues, on China's international scholarly activities, and on the state of China's scientific and scholarly pursuits. Members of the Committee are scholars from a broad range of fields, including China studies.

Administrative offices of the Committee are located at the National Academy of Sciences, Washington, D.C.

The views expressed in this report are those of the members of the Nuclear Science Delegation and are not necessarily the official views of the Committee on Scholarly Communication with the People's Republic of China or its sponsoring organizations.

Library of Congress Cataloging in Publication Data

U.S. Nuclear Science Delegation to the People's Republic of China.
Nuclear science in China.

(CSCPRC report; no. 10)
1. U.S. Nuclear Science Delegation to the People's Republic of China. 2. Nuclear physics–Study and teaching (Higher)–China. 3. Nuclear research–China. I. Bromley, David Allan, 1926- II. Perrolle, Pierre M. III. National Academy of Sciences, Washington, D.C. Committee on Scholarly Communication with the People's Republic of China. IV. Title. V. Series: National Academy of Sciences, Washington, D.C. Committee on Scholarly Communication with the People's Republic of China. CSCPRC report; no. 10.

QC792.78.C6U56   1980   539.7'0951   80-19616
ISBN 0-309-03086-2

Available from:
NATIONAL ACADEMY PRESS
2101 Constitution Avenue, N.W.
WASHINGTON, D.C. 20418

Printed in the United States of America

Preface

The visit upon which this report is based was undertaken under the aegis of the Committee on Scholarly Communication with the People's Republic of China, which is jointly sponsored by the U.S. National Academy of Sciences, the Social Science Research Council, and the American Council of Learned Societies. The delegation was in China from May 21 through June 9, 1979. Our formal host in the People's Republic was the Chinese Academy of Sciences, and the Institute of Atomic Energy also played an essential role in organizing and expediting our activities.

Obviously in only 3 weeks it is impossible to obtain more than superficial impressions of as large and complex a society as that of China. However, as a result of the warm welcome, open cooperation, and enthusiastic reception that the delegation received in each of the many research and educational institutions it visited, we believe that we have been able to develop a general overview of the current status of Chinese nuclear science activity. And as a consequence of our hosts' generous hospitality and willingness to discuss any and all topics, we have returned with what we hope is a sound impression of some of the major thrusts in contemporary Chinese society.

After a 10-year hiatus during the Cultural Revolution, science, technology, and education in China are undergoing rapid reconstruction. The Chinese have set themselves extremely ambitious goals in all three areas; it is our impression that with assistance from the United States, Japan, and Western Europe these goals are attainable, but a vast amount of dedicated hard work will be required on the part of the Chinese people themselves.

During the period since renormalization of Chinese-U.S. relations, there has been time for reappraisal by China's leaders of the modernization goals

Preface

originally announced in 1978, which featured very major investments to be made in technology both within China and from foreign sources. The plans called for large numbers of Chinese scientists and technologists to be sent abroad to gain related training and experience. Chinese planners have stated that the full original program will not be economically achievable at least on the initial optimistic timetable.

Chinese political, scientific, and technological leaders are currently addressing two very difficult but very important sets of decisions. In order to utilize available economic and trained manpower resources most effectively, it will be necessary to make hard priority decisions among a great many *possible* programs and projects—each individually with high merit and strong claim to the necessary support—in order that the programs of highest priority can proceed expeditiously. And decisions must be made concerning the extent to which the selected programs will draw upon foreign experience and hardware, as opposed to stimulating development of such experience and hardware within China itself. These questions have been highlighted in the area of nuclear science, central to our visit, but are in no way unique to it. It is our impression that these difficult questions are being addressed in realistic and timely fashion.

We are especially grateful to our Chinese hosts for all their efforts toward making our brief visit such a productive and informative one. We would especially mention Qian Sanqiang, Vice President of the Chinese Academy of Sciences and President of Zhejiang University; Qin Lisheng, Deputy Secretary-General of the Chinese Academy of Sciences; Zhao Dongwan, Deputy Director of the State Science and Technology Commission; Wang Ganchang, Director of the Institute of Atomic Energy, Vice Minister, Second Ministry of Machine-Building, President, Chinese Nuclear Energy Society, and Vice President of the Chinese Physical Society; Yang Chengzhong, Vice Director of the Lanzhou Branch of the Chinese Academy of Sciences and Director of the Institute of Modern Physics; Feng Yinfu, Director of the Foreign Affairs Bureau of the Chinese Academy of Sciences; Hu Yungchang, Deputy Director of the Shanghai Branch of the Chinese Academy of Sciences; Jin Houchu, Director of the Institute for Nuclear Research in Shanghai; and Yang Shilin, Deputy Director of the Zhejiang Science and Technology Commission and Vice President of Zhejiang University. Zhang Xiaoyang of the Foreign Affairs Branch of the Chinese Academy of Sciences and Ding Dazhao of the Institute of Atomic Energy traveled with us throughout our visit. Their untiring and effective efforts on our behalf contributed enormously to making our travel productive and pleasant; we are much indebted to them.

We also express our thanks to the U.S. Committee on Scholarly Communication with the People's Republic of China for their support of the

Preface

delegation and for making our visit possible. We have benefitted greatly from briefings, arranged by the Committee, from Michel Oksenberg of the National Security Council, Anne Keatley of the Office of Science and Technology Policy, and Mary Brown Bullock and Pierre Perrolle of the Committee staff.

No eight-person group can possibly represent the many dimensions and diversity of U.S. nuclear science, but to a remarkable degree the Nominating Committee established by the CSCPRC brought together individuals whose expertise, experience, and interests in this broad field were truly complementary.

As Chairman of the delegation, I would be remiss indeed were I not to express to each member of the group my deep appreciation of his enthusiasm, hard work, and good humor in the face of sometimes unexpected situations, all of which contributed so much to making our travels both rewarding and often memorable.

P. K. Kuo not only translated for us over long hours and talks, but also drew on his personal knowledge of China, and things Chinese, to provide us with often essential background information and perspective. And, as Chairman, my particular thanks go to Pierre Perrolle for continuing help, insight, and support throughout the trip and the subsequent production of this report. Without his broad background, experience, and common sense we would have accomplished vastly less than we did.

And finally my special thanks go to Frances DeGrenier and Mary Anne Thomson Schulz, my Secretary and Executive Assistant, respectively, at Yale, for all their help in the production of this report.

D. ALLAN BROMLEY, *Chairman*

The delegation together with Zhang Xiaoyiang of the Chinese Academy of Sciences at the Summer Palace in Beijing. Left to right: (front row) P. K. Kuo, A. Zucker, D. A. Bromley, P. M. Perrolle, Zhang Xiaoyang; (back row) E. M. Henley, R. Middleton, B. Harvey, A. K. Kerman, S. S. Hanna, T. A. Tombrello.

U.S. NUCLEAR SCIENCE DELEGATION TO THE PEOPLE'S REPUBLIC OF CHINA

D. ALLAN BROMLEY, Yale University, *Chairman*
  Henry Ford II Professor of Physics and Director,
  A. W. Wright Nuclear Structure Laboratory
PIERRE M. PERROLLE, National Academy of Sciences, *Secretary*
  Professional Associate, Committee on Scholarly Communication with the
  People's Republic of China
PAO-KUANG KUO, Wayne State University, *Interpreter*
  Associate Professor of Physics
STANLEY S. HANNA, Stanford University,
  Professor of Physics and Director,
  Tandem Accelerator Laboratory
BERNARD G. HARVEY, Lawrence Berkeley Laboratory,
  Associate Director and Director, Nuclear Science Division
  Vice Chairman, American Physical Society (APS) Nuclear Physics Division
ERNEST M. HENLEY, University of Washington,
  Professor of Physics
  Chairman, APS Nuclear Physics Division
ARTHUR K. KERMAN, Massachusetts Institute of Technology,
  Professor of Physics and Director,
  Center for Theoretical Physics
ROY MIDDLETON, University of Pennsylvania,
  Professor of Physics and Director,
  Tandem Accelerator Laboratory
THOMAS A. TOMBRELLO, California Institute of Technology,
  Professor of Physics and Director,
  W. K. Kellogg Radiation Laboratory
ALEXANDER ZUCKER, Oak Ridge National Laboratory,
  Associate Director, Physical Sciences

Contents

1 Introduction   1

2 Organization of Research and Higher Education Activities in China   10

3 Overview of Current Trends in Science and Education Policy   24

4 Overview of Chinese Nuclear Science Activities   33

5 Visits to Educational Institutions   38
    Beijing University, 38
    Qinghua University, 50
    Lanzhou University, 58
    Fudan University, 66
    Zhejiang University, 73

6 Visists to Research Institutes   79
    Institute of Physics (Beijing), 79
    Institute of Theoretical Physics (Beijing), 83
    Institute of High-Energy Physics (Beijing), 86
    Institute of Atomic Energy (Beijing), 87
    Institute of Geology of the State Bureau of Seismology (Beijing), 100
    Institute of Modern Physics (Lanzhou), 102
    Institute for Nuclear Research (Shanghai), 131

7 Visits to Industrial Institutions   145
   Vanguard Factory (Shanghai), 145
   Silk and Dye Factory (Hangzhou), 152
   Shanghai Industrial Exhibition, 153

8 General Comments on Industrial Development
   and Miscellaneous Impressions   155
   Industrial Development, 155
   Miscellaneous Impressions, 157

9 Concluding Remarks   173

APPENDIXES

A Itinerary   175
B Talks Given in China by the U.S. Nuclear Physics Delegation   183
C Hotel Accommodations   187
D Names of Hosts and Scientists Met at Institutions Visited   189
E Technical Materials Received in China by Members of the Delegation   201

1

Introduction

Prior to normalization of relations between the United States and the People's Republic of China in January 1979, and beginning in 1972, the Committee on Scholarly Communication with the People's Republic of China (CSCPRC) had arranged for 33 U.S. scholarly delegations to visit the People's Republic of China; other organizations had arranged a limited number of similar exchange visits. And, since normalization of relations, a very large number of U.S. groups have visited and interacted with their Chinese counterparts.

The early CSCPRC delegations, in their reports, quite rightly devoted substantial space to general description and discussion of Chinese society generally, quite apart from matters of the discipline involved. As such, they provided a vital and early window into what had been an essentially closed and enigmatic country. In view of the major expansion in Sino-U.S. interactions in the intervening period and the many general publications devoted to Chinese life and people, we shall not repeat much of this material herein. Rather our focus will be on educational and nuclear science research activities, together with some slight insight that we have gained into Chinese industrial practice in related areas.

We must begin, however, by emphasizing again the warm, friendly hospitality rendered to us by all the Chinese groups with whom we came into contact. The exchange of information was marked throughout by openness and candor. At no time did any of us have the sense of surveillance or reluctance to discuss either scientific or political issues that many of us have encountered previously in centrally planned and administered societies.

At the same time, China is still far from being an open society. Military checkpoints prevent travel for more than 12 km from major cities without permission; guards (sometimes armed with fixed bayonets!) were present at the entrance to hotels to prevent entrance by any Chinese citizen lacking specific business or permission; similar guards are ubiquitous—but in a sporadic fashion not understood by any of us—in a number of the research institutes and in the hydroelectric plant we visited. We also gained the distinct impression that interaction between Chinese citizens and foreigners in the absence of specific well-defined business is still frowned upon by Chinese authorities. With the exception of formal banquets, it was required that the delegation members have their meals apart from Chinese friends and colleagues, and with only two exceptions we met no wives of our hosts during the entire trip—Middleton had dinner one evening in a restaurant with his Liverpool classmate, Dai Chuanzeng, and Mrs. Dai, and, during our visit to the Institute of Atomic Energy, we met the wife of Zhuo Yizhong, who also worked at the Institute.

Throughout this report we relay what were described to us as the detrimental effects of the Cultural Revolution and what has come to be called the influence of the "Gang of Four" on higher education and scientific research. The reader should bear in mind that we have no firsthand evidence of these processes and that our report largely paraphrases what we were told by Chinese officials. It is clear that the decade between 1966 and 1976 was one of turmoil in China and that conditions there were not conducive to education or research. But this report is primarily concerned with the state of nuclear research in China, and it is not intended to be a resource on the effects of the Cultural Revolution on university education and research.

Our itinerary, given in Appendix A, was sufficiently open that we had time for detailed discussions in the many institutions visited and time to gain some broader impression of contemporary Chinese society. We had originally requested that two additional cities be added to this itinerary—Xi'an, where we spent a short period at the airport en route from Beijing to Lanzhou, and Chengdu, from where we had hoped to travel to the Southwest Institute of Physics in Leshan—and we argued strongly on our arrival in Beijing for retention of these cities. These arguments had very clearly been transmitted immediately to the highest levels of both the Chinese Academy of Sciences (CAS) and the State Scientific and Technological Commission (SSTC), inasmuch as they were the opening topics in our discussions the following day with leaders of these two organizations. We became convinced that every effort was being made to accommodate our wishes, but that the internal Chinese transportation system was simply inadequate to make our requested itinerary feasible. In retrospect, it may well be that inclusion of Xi'an and Leshan would have been counterproductive in the sense of overloading our schedule. As it was, we concentrated on those cities and institutions having the major Chinese nuclear science activities.

Introduction

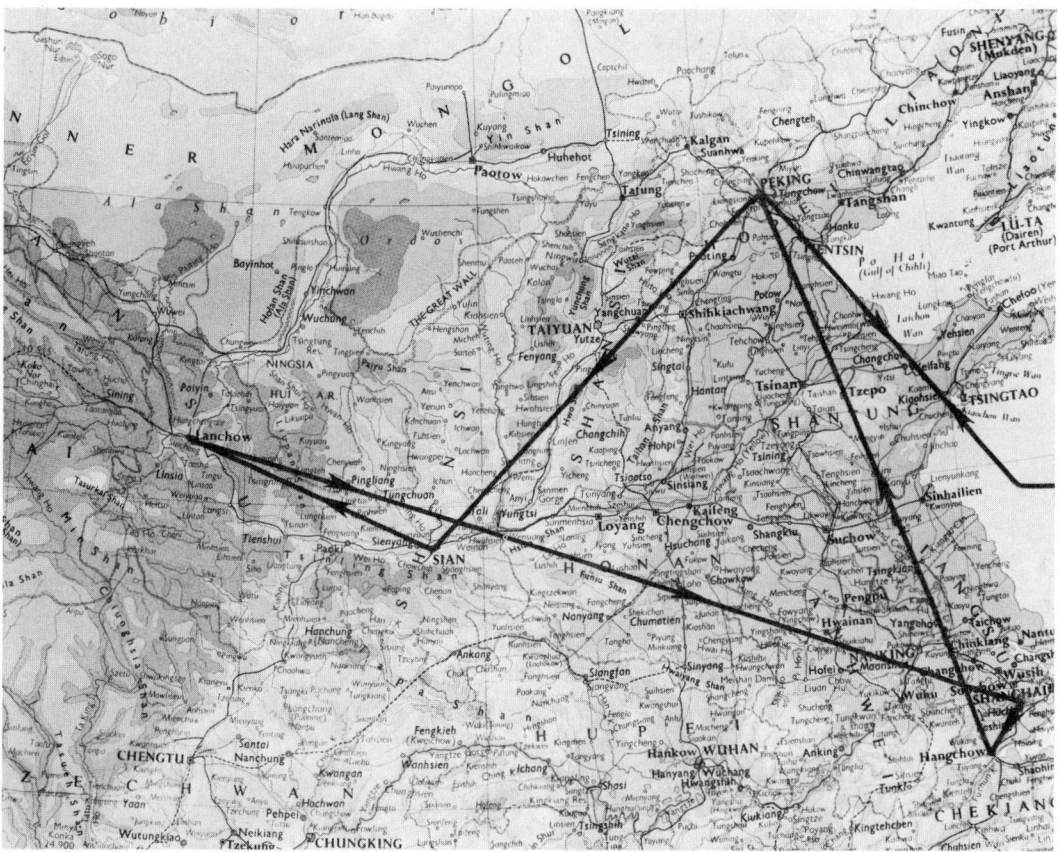

The delegation's itinerary superimposed on a map of China. The flight from Tokyo to Beijing is somewhat circuitous in order to avoid Korean territorial waters. Travel to and from Beijing was via Japan Air Lines; with the exception of the travel from Shanghai to Hangzhou, which was by train, all other travel indicated in this figure was via the Civil Air Administration of China (CAAC).

As is evident from our itinerary, our hosts made every effort to enable us to see as much of China as our time permitted. Moreover, we were singularly fortunate with respect to weather; although several heavy rainfalls occurred, they always did this during the night and the subsequent days were bright and clear. In addition to the tourist attractions listed for each city we visited, we were taken, for example, to the relatively new hydroelectric development at the Liu Jia Gorge on the Yellow River some 100 km upstream from Lanzhou.

Entirely Chinese in origin, equipment, and execution, this project was a striking contribution to a general impression that we gained throughout China. If a problem is considered important, the Chinese people appear never to have thrown up their hands in defeat, but rather have faced up to the challenges; and, although often starting from scratch, they have carried

NUCLEAR SCIENCE IN CHINA

The female lead in the Lanzhou martial arts group at the conclusion of a spectacular sword dance. The sword was only too real!

through the necessary design, development, and production necessary for its solution. Those members of the delegation with electrical engineering background and experience were particularly impressed with what had been accomplished in Liu Jia Gorge. Unfortunately, as a result of a prolonged drought in the Yellow River watershed, the reservoir above the dam had a water level 40 m lower than normal, and the plant was operating at only 20 percent of installed capacity.

Many of the delegation members had hoped to visit the Dun Huang caves in northern Gansu Province—with their spectacular cave paintings—but inasmuch as a 10-hour train and 2-hour automobile trip was required each way, it was not possible to fit this into our itinerary.

We were delighted, however, to find that classical Chinese dance and opera has returned and had the opportunity to see several examples; in Lanzhou we had the great pleasure of meeting the director, choreographer, and author of a classical dance drama featuring the Dun Huang paintings and legends.

Some of us were fortunate in visiting the White Pagoda Park in Lanzhou on June 1, recognized throughout China as "Children's Day." In addition to seeing thousands of remarkably well-behaved, happy children at both organized and spontaneous play, we were privileged to witness an impromptu performance by a Lanzhou martial arts group. Although its members were in the 10-13-year-old bracket, they were extraordinarily able and professional.

Although foreigners attract no attention whatever in Beijing or Hangzhou, in Shanghai (surprisingly) and Lanzhou (not surprising since it has long been a "closed" city) members of the delegation attracted substantial crowds of both adults and children whenever they appeared in public. Without exception these crowds were curious and friendly.

Our visits to each of the institutions listed in our itinerary followed the same general pattern. With unfailing politeness and genuine warmth, our hosts were always waiting for us at the entrance to the institution. After formal introductions the senior host present gave a brief introduction describing the history, structure, and plans of the institution and then asked for questions from the delegation. These were generally answered fully and in quantitative detail; those of us who had the advantage of having visited China previously within the past 2 or 3 years were particularly struck by the greatly increased openness with which political issues were now discussed. Following these sessions the delegation members normally split up into smaller groups to tour teaching and research laboratories and facilities, and in several instances, at the specific request of those in charge, reconvened following these visits for discussion of our impressions and suggestions. Although each group asked very seriously for our criticisms of their work and plans, we felt it prudent, given the vastness of our general ignorance of things Chinese, to limit our comments in these sessions to specific responses to scientific or technical questions or to general recommendations in which the entire delegation concurred.

Clearly the Chinese scientists recognize that they must increase their interactions with the international scientific community manifold if they are to achieve their stated goals. Indeed, everyone with whom we spoke was enthusiastic about such interactions.

On several occasions the question of formal membership for the scientific community of the People's Republic of China in the International Union of Pure and Applied Physics (IUPAP) was raised. (Bromley's position as Vice President of the Union was generally known at the time of the visit.) These discussions always began with the assertion that such membership was impossible until the "Taiwan issue" was settled. But contrary to such discus-

NUCLEAR SCIENCE IN CHINA

Our host while in China was Professor Qian Sanqiang, Vice President of the Chinese Academy of Sciences and President of Zhejiang University.

sions in the past, the representatives of the People's Republic no longer insist that they will not attend international meetings, for example, as long as representatives of the Taiwanese scientific community are present. Indeed, representatives of both communities attended the last large Type A IUPAP Conference in particle physics held 2 years ago in Tokyo and several subsequent conferences. We believe that this situation will continue and that eventually the People's Republic of China will become a member of IUPAP and similar unions without requesting the expulsion of Taiwanese representatives. But what the PRC representatives continue to insist upon is that the Taiwanese representatives make no claim to represent "China." Inasmuch as the Taiwanese have already agreed that in IUPAP, for example, their membership covers only those scientific activities within Taiwan, it should be possible to accommodate both the PRC and Taiwan as separate scientific entities within the ICSU family of scientific unions.

Introduction

A few of the some 250 members of the Lanzhou branch of the Chinese Physical Society that attended the lectures given by Bromley and Harvey at the Lanzhou Hotel. One of the audience at the right taped those lectures using a Chinese-made portable cassette unit.

We have recently learned that at a recent meeting of the International Union of Biology (IUB), held in Toronto, Canada, such an agreement was reached whereby there would be two adhering bodies to IUB, one representing scientific activities in Taiwan and one representing those in the People's Republic of China.

We anticipate, from all our discussions, that the Chinese will soon play a significant role in all major international scientific activities.

An interesting example of the ability to bend the rather centralized Chinese bureaucracy was presented by our visit to the Vanguard (Xianfeng) factory in Shanghai, a major manufacturer of electrostatic accelerators, motors, and other electrical equipment. During the course of our visits in Beijing and Lanzhou, we heard repeated references to "a factory in Shanghai" as a source of various accelerators—Van de Graafs, Cockcroft-Waltons, and small electron linacs. We asked repeatedly whether we could arrange to visit this factory, but no clear answer was forthcoming. On pressing the issue on our arrival in Shanghai, the magnitude of the bureaucratic problem involved became clear.

All nuclear research and development in China falls under the purview of either the Academy of Sciences or the Second Ministry of Machine-Building,

NUCLEAR SCIENCE IN CHINA

The old planetarium in Beijing was substantially damaged during the 1976 earthquake, and, although it is now in the process of repair, it is still closed to all visitors. A number of the ancient sighting instruments, however, are visible on the planetarium roof. In the immediate foreground is one of the major roadways now under construction to relieve some of the growing traffic congestion in the Beijing area.

both of which report directly to the State Council. The (Vanguard) factory, on the other hand, falls under the administration of the First Ministry of Machine-Building, in charge of heavy machinery. Various ministries appear to have little influence on one another except through the State Council—the highest government body in China—and the State Scientific and Technological Commission.

Our first request to visit the factory, transmitted and considered at the local Shanghai level, was denied out of hand: We were told that not only had no foreigners ever visited the factory, but also that it would be impossible to obtain such permission. At this point, no reason was given—and we were unclear as to whether it reflected security, an unwillingness to allow foreigners to see a facility of which the Chinese were not proud, bureaucratic difficulties in obtaining the necessary permission for the visit, or something entirely unknown to us.

Introduction

At this point we enlisted the assistance of Wang Ganchang, Director of the Institute of Atomic Energy and Vice Minister of the Second Ministry of Machine-Building, and later of Qian Sanqiang, Vice President of the CAS. Zhao Dongwan, the Deputy Director of the SSTC, also became involved and the decision to grant us permission to visit the factory, after 2 days of intense discussion, was ultimately made at that level!

As it turned out, the problem had been purely bureaucratic; the Chinese have every reason to be proud of the factory, and no security matters were involved. We were received graciously by the Vanguard factory management, given an excellent tour and description of the facility, and came away very much impressed. Had we not had this opportunity to see Chinese high-technology manufacturing capabilities and been forced to draw our conclusions from much of the equipment we had seen during our visits, we would have formed quite different ones.

In the following sections of this report, we begin with a general discussion of the organization of research and educational activities in China as a framework for subsequent discussion of details. Following overview sections on Chinese science and education policy and on nuclear science activities, we present more detailed reports on our visits to five quite different universities and to seven different research institutes. We follow this with brief sections on our visit to the Vanguard factory, to the silk and dye factory in Hangzhou, and to the Shanghai Industrial Exhibition. The report concludes with impressions of Chinese industrial development, general impressions in a number of topical areas, a few overall conclusions, and finally a number of appendixes pertaining to our travel.

2
Organization of Research and Higher Education Activities in China*

Scientific research and technological development in China fall entirely within the purview of government administration and planning: Policies toward research, such as setting priorities, planning, and financing, as well as research activity itself, are all carried out by governmental units (many of them operating at the national level), which will be described in detail below. Similarly, China's educational system is managed entirely by the State. The development of professional and skilled manpower, particularly in science and technology, is an important component of the overall economic plans. The entire system of education, including higher education, is under the general jurisdiction of the Ministry of Education and of the local education bureaus (at the provincial level and below), which are directly subordinate to the Ministry, although, as will be described below, other sectors of the State bureaucracy also play an important role in the management of higher education. The current Minister of Education, Jiang Nanxiang, who assumed the position in February 1979, was formerly Minister of Higher Education in

---

*This and the following chapter are based partly on information monitored by the CSCPRC Reference and Information Center and on the basis of previous conversations with Chinese officials in China and in the United States. The information presented here is also drawn from conversations held by the delegation on May 22, 1979, with two separate groups of officials from the State Scientific and Technological Commission (SSTC) and from the Chinese Academy of Sciences (CAS). Present at the SSTC meeting were Zhao Dongwan, Deputy Director of the SSTC; Wei Zhaolin, Head of the SSTC's Fifth Bureau; and Huang Kunyi, of the Foreign Affairs Bureau of the SSTC. Present at the meeting of the CAS were Professor Qian Sanqiang, Vice President of the CAS; Qin Lisheng, Deputy Secretary-General of the CAS; Wang Ganchang, Director of the Institute of Atomic Energy (IAE); Li Shounan, Deputy Director of the IAE; and Feng Yinfu, Deputy Director of the Foreign Affairs Bureau of the CAS.

Organization of Research and Higher Education Activities in China

Zhao Dongwan, Deputy Director of the State Scientific and Technological Commission, and Allan Bromley, during the delegation's introductory meeting with Zhao Dongwan and other representatives of the Commission.

the mid-1960's, when such a separate Ministry existed. His recent appointment suggests the importance of higher education in China's educational policy.

Professor Qian Sanqiang, Vice President of the Chinese Academy of Sciences, and Qin Lisheng, Deputy Secretary-General of the Chinese Academy of Sciences, with Allan Bromley during the introductory meeting between the delegation and representatives of the Chinese Academy of Sciences.

NUCLEAR SCIENCE IN CHINA

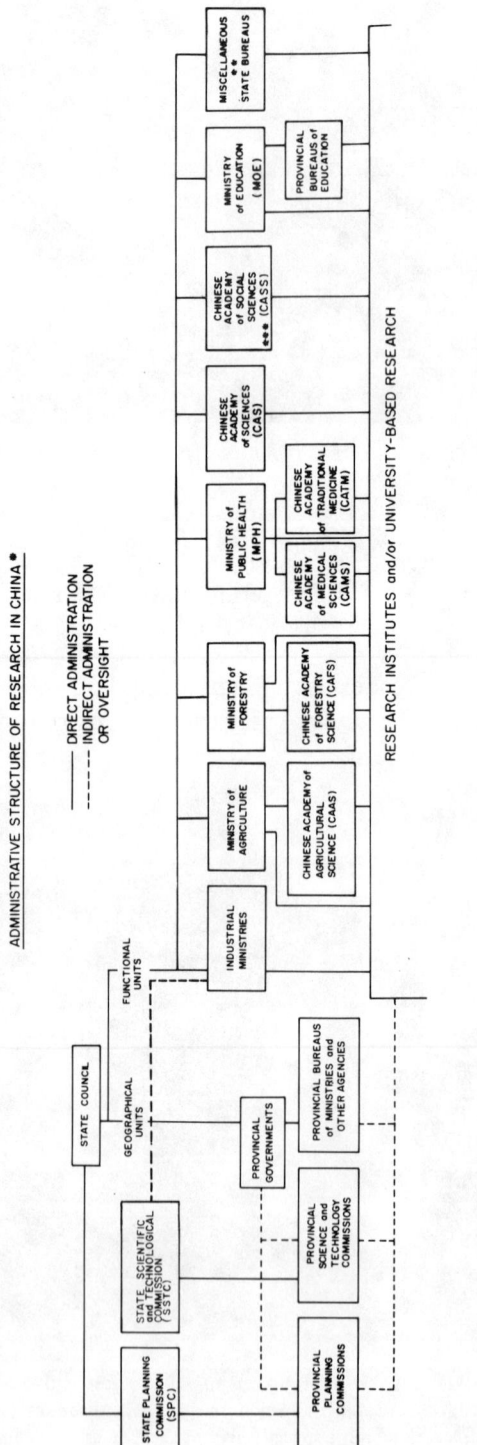

Administrative structure of research in China.

STATE SCIENTIFIC AND TECHNOLOGICAL COMMISSION (SSTC)

The most important national bureau involved in the formulation of science policy is the State Scientific and Technological Commission (SSTC). Nominally subordinate to the State Council (cabinet), it is a fairly powerful policy-making and coordinating body, which works in conjunction with the State Planning Commission (which both initiates and ultimately approves broad long-range economic policies), especially now that science policy has been identified as a key to the overall policy of modernization. The SSTC was originally established in 1958 to perform this policy function, but ceased to operate during the Cultural Revolution. It was restored in late 1977 and is now headed by Vice Premier Fang Yi, whose earlier career had been in the area of foreign economic and technical aid. Fang Yi's elevation to Politburo status in the Communist Party in August 1977 is a further reflection of current importance of science policy and of the SSTC.

Research in China is conducted within three main areas of China's vast institutional structure: under the jurisdiction of the Chinese Academy of Sciences (CAS) and the academies of agricultural sciences, of medical sciences, and of social sciences; under the various industrial ministries and special agencies; and within the higher-education system. Even though all the research units are governmental, because the peculiarities of bureaucratic politics in China are such that various functional "systems" or bureaucratic hierarchies are extremely compartmentalized, there is a strong need for coordination among their activities. This task of coordination, on a broad national scale at least, is the main function of the SSTC.

In conversations with officials of the SSTC, members of the delegation were told that while all the institutes and universities have discretionary funds for normal operations, all research units submit to the Commission for approval research plans and requests for funding of major new research projects. (It was not clear whether this meant each individual research institute or major administrative units such as ministries or research academies—our guess is the latter—nor was it clear whether nonscientific research is included in the purview of the SSTC—our guess is that it is not.) The SSTC then "balances" these requests in accordance with annual or longer-range plans (such as the current 8-year, 1978-1985, plan). Both short- and long-range plans, we were told, are subject to continuous readjustment. At the time of our visit, China's scientific plans, as well as economic plans, were undergoing major readjustments and the current phase, as described to us by one official of the CAS, is marked by sober realism in the face of economic constraints, in sharp contrast to the extreme optimism of 1978.

The Commission has a staff of around 500 administrators, very few of whom have backgrounds in science, engineering, or economics. In making their important priority decisions, they hold only informal consultations with certain scientists, but use no formal equivalent of the American peer review process. We know from recent visits to the United States that China's science administrators are well informed about peer review and other aspects of American management of science and its development. The officials to whom we spoke said that foreign science management systems are being studied, suggesting some interest in modifying China's current approach, but gave no hint of any opinions on the subject. We sensed that any attempt to make major changes in the existing system in China faces major political and cultural obstacles. The Commission, we were told, also generally monitors the implementation of research by requesting reports, holding meetings, or carrying out on-site inspection tours.

The SSTC is organized into bureaus reflecting various important (but not all) areas of science. The Fifth Bureau, for instance, is primarily concerned with nuclear science research. The Second Bureau deals with energy research, marine and earth sciences, natural resource development, and materials sciences. The Third Bureau is in charge of research in communications, space, and new technologies, and the Fourth Bureau with agriculture and forestry. We were told that the SSTC does not oversee any defense-related research; such research is apparently all coordinated by the National Defense Science and Technology Commission.

Few details were given concerning the process or criteria according to which priority decisions are made by the SSTC. This is, of course, a subject of political sensitivity, but the tone of the responses to questions on the matter suggest that even the Chinese planners themselves do not lay out decision-making principles very explicitly, but deal, rather, with each decision on an ad hoc basis, depending on the particular political circumstances and short-run constraints of each case. While the SSTC attempts to strike a balance between pure and applied research, among various fields and among demands from various geographical areas of China, by adopting a "national perspective," the officials we spoke with admitted, for instance, that the Shanghai area was definitely favored in the current plans. While there is a long-run desire to correct the geographical imbalances that benefit the coastal regions of China and Shanghai especially (this has long been an overtly stated issue in economic planning in China), in the short term, we were told, Shanghai has a competitive edge because of its strong scientific manpower base and research infrastructure.

In our discussions, we raised the problem of the inherent conflict between planning and the basic nature of scientific research, which includes unanticipated discoveries and developments. The SSTC officials generally acknowledged that this might be a problem, but they seemed to indicate that planning in science was a necessary consequence of economic planning, that discretionary funds allocated for "seed" research projects could only be very limited, and that virtually all funding had to be cleared by the SSTC. In later discussions with CAS officials, however, we found that there may be a considerable gap between the theoretical model, according to which the SSTC approves all research projects and funding, and reality, at least with respect to the CAS. Bearing in mind that the Academy is an institution of enormous prestige and power and, as was pointed out to us, has a much longer institutional history than the SSTC, it appears that the CAS submits its overall research budget directly to the State Council for approval, without first going through SSTC channels. It was strongly implied that the SSTC is not in a position to block the wishes of the CAS, and, in any case, the overlap in high-level administrative personnel of the CAS and of the SSTC make it unlikely that the two institutions would hold conflicting positions on issues.

THE CHINESE ACADEMY OF SCIENCES (CAS)

The CAS is the most prestigious and influential agency in China in charge of scientific research. It has quasi-ministerial status and administers about 100 major research institutes scattered around China, the majority of which are located in Beijing and Shanghai. While its activities are nominally coordinated with those of other research organizations by the State Scientific and Technological Commission (SSTC), as was indicated in the previous section, it is in fact, we were told, accountable directly to China's State Council.

The Academy was founded in November 1949 on the basis of its two predecessors, the Beijing Academy and the Academia Sinica, both founded in the late 1920's. According to the historical overview we were given in Beijing, the CAS initially administered 17 research institutes (including some in the social sciences) with a total research staff of about 200. By 1955, the CAS encompassed more than 40 institutes with a total staff of about 2,000. The current total staff of CAS institutes is about 10 times that number. Until the predecessors of the SSTC were formed in 1956 (State Technological Commission and Science Planning Commission), the CAS held the important responsibility for overall science policy planning for China, derived at the time from the model of the Soviet Academy of Sciences. While the overall planning and policy coordination role has formally been shifted to the reestablished SSTC, it is clear that historical antecedents have left the CAS with a high degree of policy influence. Interlocking directorates, of course, provide an additional dimension to the institutional relationships. This was pointed out to us in our discussions, and we were cited the

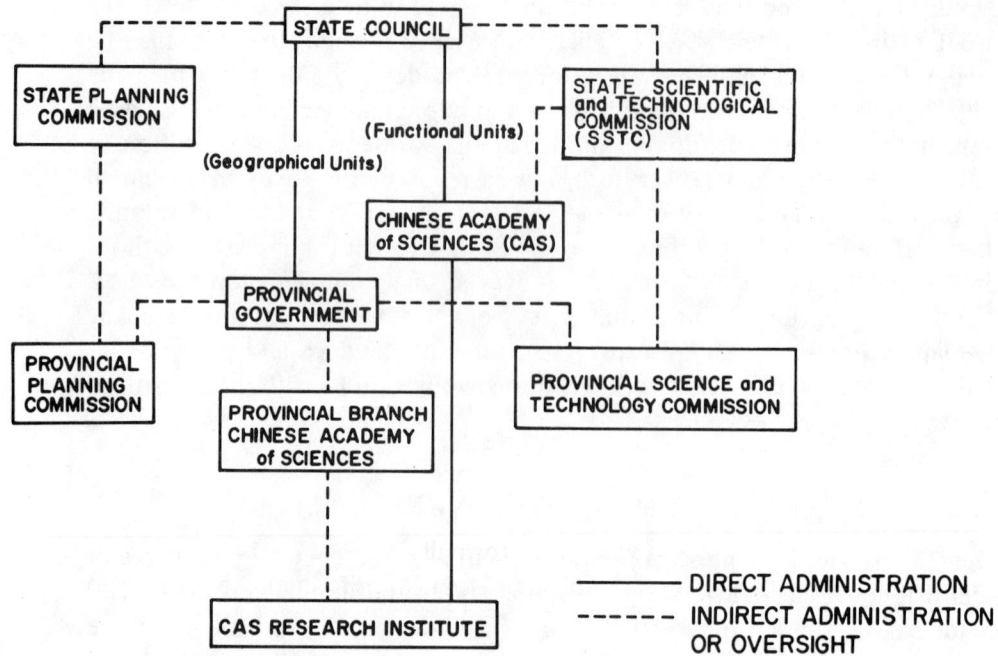

Administration of a research institute in the Chinese Academy of Sciences.

prime example of Fang Yi, who is concurrently Vice Premier (hence in the top leadership of the State Council), Minister-in-Charge of the SSTC, and, now, President of the CAS.

In one conversation, later confirmed by Chinese press reports, Professor Qian stated that the Academy currently has a membership of about 200 (dating from before the Cultural Revolution) and that the election of about 200 new members is in progress, with an approximate goal of expanding the number of academicians to about 1,000 in the next 5 to 10 years. Because of the very active role played by the CAS in the actual management and direction of the nation's research, Professor Qian noted that the current small membership was heavily overextended.

As described to us, the major substantive responsibilities of the CAS in the development of science in China lie in the three areas of basic research, new technology development, and multidisciplinary research. This counterbalances the second major organization sector for research in China, that of the industrial ministries. Research sponsored by the ministries are, understandably, closely related to production goals. The specific and immediate need of serving production in industry probably tends to preclude research that does not have immediate applications; furthermore, the extreme compartmentalization of the industrial sectors probably causes difficulties in much interdisciplinary work.

In the area of nuclear physics research, the CAS began in earnest in 1955 with the establishment of the Institute of Atomic Energy (called the Institute of Modern Physics until 1958) and the establishment of a cooperative relationship with the Soviet Union.* The Institute of Atomic Energy (IAE) is administratively different from most CAS institutes, since its management (and budget) is shared jointly with the Second Ministry of Machine-Building (in charge of nuclear energy and perhaps nuclear weapons as well). It was pointed out to us that, at the time of its inception, the IAE included only a handful of researchers, among them Qian Sanqiang, Vice President of the CAS, and Wang Ganchang, currently Director of the IAE. Other major research installations are the Institute of Modern Physics in Lanzhou, built in the late 1950's and formally opened in 1962 (after the cooperation with the Soviet Union had ceased), and the Institute for Nuclear Research in Shanghai, which was also developed with Soviet assistance and opened in 1959. Related work is also carried out at the Institute of Physics and at the Institute of Theoretical Physics (spun off from the Institute of Physics in 1978). (Details on the above institutions, all visited by members of the delegation, appear later in this report.) Fusion research is being carried out at the Institute for Plasma Physics (until 1978 part of the Institute of Physics, but now developing institutions of its own in Hefei, Anhui Province) and at the Southwest Institute of Physics in Leshan County, Sinchuan Province (previously commonly assumed in the West to be a CAS institute but actually solely run by the Second Ministry of Machine-Building).

The CAS also manages some important educational institutions. In 1958 the Chinese University of Science and Technology (CUST) was established in Beijing for the purpose of training research scientists for the various institutes of the CAS. During the Cultural Revolution, the CUST was moved to the town of Hefei in Anhui Province, in a move now alleged to have been an act of banishment by the "Gang of Four." The CUST has recently reopened its graduate school in Beijing, although its undergraduate campus (a new one is planned) will remain in Hefei as part of a decentralization policy under which Hefei will become a major center of scientific research.

---

*The present Institute of Physics was called the Institute of Applied Physics until 1958.

(The Institute of Plasma Physics will relocate there, for instance.) In the past year, the CAS has assumed, in addition, the administration of three other educational institutions. These are the Harebin University of Science and Technology in Manchuria, the Chengdu University of Science and Technology in Sichuan, and Zhejiang University in Hangzhou, an old and prestigious engineering school now charged with the training of engineers for the CAS institutes. The delegation visited the latter, and details on Zhejiang University appear elsewhere in this report. Manpower shortage has been identified as one of the most critical problems in China's scientific and technological development. In addition to managing the universities, the CAS plans to add about 1,000 new researchers of the associate professor or professor level to its ranks by 1985. Most of these are to receive advanced training abroad.

OTHER CHINESE ACADEMIES

Although the delegation did not interact with other scholarly academies in China, a brief institutional overview is provided here to round out the perspective on the organization of science and education in China. The best-known academies, other than the CAS, are the Chinese Academy of Medical Sciences, which is under the purview of the Ministry of Public Health, and the Academies of Agricultural Sciences and of Forestry Sciences, under the jurisdiction of the Ministries of Agriculture and of Forestry, respectively. (Until 1979, there was only one Ministry of Agriculture and Forestry and the related academies were also combined.) In addition, the Ministry of Public Health runs an Academy of Chinese Traditional Medicine. Like the CAS, these academies oversee a large network of research institutes and organizations.

Other academies, apparently recently established, exist in such fields as space technology, geological sciences, meteorological sciences, electric power sciences, and coal mining sciences, and most of these are thought to be subordinate to relevant ministries.

Scholarly research in China, while overwhelmingly emphasizing natural scientific research and technological development, is not confined to those areas alone. In late 1977, the Chinese Academy of Social Sciences (CASS) was established, marking the resumption of scholarly work in the social sciences and the humanities in China after a virtually complete halt that began in 1966. This research had, prior to 1966, been coordinated by one of the subdivisions of the CAS. The establishment of an academy of social sciences in its own right suggests an unprecedented concern for research in those fields. It is not known what part of the top-level administrative structure in China oversees the CASS, but the Academy, because of the immediate political implications of social research, is believed by Western analysts to be closely tied to Chinese Communist Party organs.

INDUSTRIAL MINISTRIES AND OTHER CENTRAL AGENCIES

Regardless of whether or not "academies" have been established under them, every industrial ministry in China runs a series of research institutions whose concerns, one might surmise, are production-oriented and therefore generally of an "applied" nature. Until very recently, these institutions have had limited interaction with the international scholarly community, and their activities and functions are therefore less well known than those of the CAS and other major academy institutes. Their numbers exceed those of CAS institutes perhaps by almost as much as one order of magnitude. The major industrial ministries are those of coal, petroleum, electric power, metallurgical industry, chemical industry, light industry, textile industry, water conservancy, post and telecommunications, railways, communications (highways and waterways), and machine building. There are eight machine-building ministries: One of these, which was recently established, is the Ministry of Agricultural Machinery; the others are referred to by their numbers (First, Second, etc.) and cover such areas as heavy machinery, atomic energy, shipbuilding, aircraft manufacture, and various aspects of military technology. In addition, China has a series of State bureaus that are of ministerial level and that include the Bureaus of Seismology, Oceanography, Meteorology, and Standardization and Metrology. These bureaus also oversee research organizations.

UNIVERSITY-BASED RESEARCH

Beside research promoted and administered by the CAS and various ministries, there has been a recent resurgence of university-based research, and this sector appears to be assuming an importance that exceeds past levels of activity, even those of the mid-1950's. While some research at the universities appears to be generated from within the faculty (and accordingly funded out of the university budget), the bulk of research is contracted out to the universities by outside agencies, such as ministries.

Since research at the universities seemed, on the basis of what the delegation was told, to have suffered a great deal more during the past decade than research at the institutes, university work is necessarily being completely rebuilt and is at a rather early stage. It is therefore difficult to clearly discern research patterns and directions at this point. We were told that the universities engage in both applied and basic research and it appears that those universities with close ties to ministries focus on the applied problems of industry and that the broader comprehensive or polytechnic universities devote relatively more time and resources to fundamental research. It is also

THE CHINESE SYSTEM of EDUCATIONAL ADMINISTRATION

For Colleges and Universities solely under Ministry of Education (MOE) Administration only, the right hand side of this chart does not apply.

——— Direct Administration

- - - Indirect Administration or Oversight for "Provincial Colleges" - For "National Colleges" there is direct Administration by either MOE or by another central agency.

* Includes Ministry of Agriculture and Forestry, Ministry of Public Health, various Industrial Ministries, State Bureaus such as those of Oceanography, Seismology, Meteorology, and the Chinese Academy of Sciences.

** Includes Provincial Level-equivalent municipalities of Beijing, Shanghai, and Tianjin

The Chinese Educational Administration.

probable that the 100-odd institutions of higher learning that have been designated (as was the custom prior to the Cultural Revolution) as "key universities" will be placing more emphasis on research (on the basis of more generous funding and perhaps a generally more advanced caliber of faculty and students) than will the other institutions.

INSTITUTIONAL RELATIONSHIPS AND THE DISSEMINATION OF INFORMATION

The organization of scientific research in China is, as noted above, very compartmentalized, and the delegation sensed that this characteristic is accentuated by the habits and attitudes of both scientists and administrators. These attitudes at times manifest themselves in tendencies toward institutional rivalry, the guarding of information, and activities aimed at bureaucratic self-preservation. We have the feeling that cooperative arrangements between research institutions are not easily arrived at in China and occur more as exceptions based on personal friendships and interactions than as a rule. Frequent instances of duplication of effort suggest strongly that there are obstacles to interinstitutional cooperative relationships.

In spite of these characteristics, however, we also gained the impression that genuine efforts are being made to overcome long-standing barriers of compartmentalization. One very positive example of these efforts is the current flourishing of professional societies. There are, at present, dozens of such societies, some of them well established and being reinstated after a decade of inactivity and some newly formed in response to current needs and priorities. They are under the general umbrella of the Chinese Scientific and Technical Association (STA), which is led by the theoretical physicist and President of Beijing University, Zhou Peiyuan. These professional organizations are currently very active in organizing meetings, workshops, and symposia; in publishing professional journals; and in developing international ties with foreign counterparts. The Chinese Physical Society is one of the older organizations, to which has been recently added the Chinese Nuclear Energy Society. These organizations were all involved to some degree in our visit.

HIGHER EDUCATION

Institutions of higher education in China are imbedded in the wider state bureaucratic structure, which is structured "vertically" into "sectors" (such as the various industries) and "horizontally" into administrative levels, the relevant ones here being the national level and the provincial level.* There are some 600 institutions of higher education in China, substantially more than the 400 or so that existed prior to the Cultural Revolution or even the 460 that were operating in the fall of 1978.† A relatively small number of these (35 to be exact) are run entirely by the Ministry of Education (MOE). These are primarily China's comprehensive universities (such as Beijing University or Fudan University) or polytechnic universities (such as Qinghua University). Others are run by various other "sectors," such as the industrial ministries, financed by them and responsible for producing manpower primarily for those sectors, although some of their activities (selection of students, curricular standards, placement of graduates, etc.) are coordinated across the board by the MOE.

---

*China has 30 "provincial"-level units, which include 22 provinces (including Taiwan), 5 autonomous regions (in outlying areas populated by minority ethnic groups), and the 3 major cities of Beijing, Shanghai, and Tianjin.
†One hundred and sixty-nine institutions of higher education, most of them totally new, were established in January 1979.

All colleges and universities are simultaneously under the immediate supervision of a provincial-level bureau of education and (except in the case of exclusively MOE institutions) of the local bureau of a ministry (or equivalent governmental agency). In the majority of cases, their principal administrative ties do not extend upward beyond the level of these provincial bureaus, and they are termed provincial colleges and universities. In other cases, which cover China's most prestigious institutions, national-level control is dominant, involving the MOE or another ministry or central agency (such as the CAS) directly. These major distinctions aside, a certain ambiguity remains in the overall situation, resulting from the fact that there is a complex division of labor between levels and sectors (such as the involvement of the MOE noted above) and from the fact that the local bureaus are simultaneously the implementing arm of both the provincial government and of national-level ministries and agencies.

Educational activities, along with research and economic activities, are all planned. The number of students enrolled, the placement of graduates, the size, recruitment, promotion of faculty, and college budgets are all part of a governmental plan, meaning both a national plan and local (i.e., provincial) plans. Therefore, the processes by which research institutes can acquire requisite manpower, or by which universities acquire desired teaching and research personnel, or by which universities teach certain subjects to a certain number of students, or, in fact, by which individual students attempt to pursue certain career interests, are extremely complex both in theory (drafting, readjusting, and implementing the plan involves an enormous number of participating institutions) and in practice (circumventing the rigidity of the system). This feature of the educational system is likely to add considerably to the time it will take for China's research and education establishment to boost itself out of the relative stagnation of the past decade or more.

In late 1977, Chinese educational authorities resumed the pre-Cultural Revolution practice of designating a number of "key" universities. These elite institutions, which now number about 100, are being given priority in terms of development and are expected to be the objects of relatively generous funding and allocation of manpower and other resources for teaching and research. It is primarily at the "key" institutions that substantial university-based research can be expected and where major graduate-level programs will be based. These are also the institutions that are the most likely to develop extensive ties with foreign institutions and individuals.

Graduate education was reinstated in China for the most part in the fall of 1978, when more than 10,000 graduate students were enrolled in more than 200 schools and 160 research institutes. In the fall of 1979, an additional 8,500 graduate students were enrolled, the bulk in university programs. At first, there was little indication that graduate programs would grant formal degrees, but, by the time of our delegation's visit, we were told that most graduate schools would now award doctoral or associate doctoral (i.e., master's) degrees. The graduate students are recruited on the basis of examinations given (in multiple locations) by each graduate school and that include a general section and a "specialty" section.

The major feature of the undergraduate educational system as it was reinstated in late 1977 is the recruitment of students through a nationwide standardized entrance examination. Although the dossiers of prospective students, which contain information on such matters as political attitude are ultimately introduced, academic achievement and ability as measured by the entrance examination are now the primary factors in the initial winnowing of candidates during the selection process. This is a dramatic shift from the recruitment patterns of the early 1970's, when middle school graduates, who were first required to engage in at least 2 years of industrial or agricultural work before being considered for higher education, were recruited almost exclusively on the recommendations of their work units, which are said to have greatly emphasized attitudinal factors and social class background (e.g., workers and peasants) over other factors.

The last "worker-peasant" class completed its 3-year curriculum (the norm of the early 1970's) this year. The new classes are following a 4-year curriculum, with a few exceptions such as the 5-year curriculum of the Chinese University of Science and Technology. The first of the new classes was enrolled in the spring of 1978 on the basis of exams given in late 1977, with 278,000 students selected from an applicant pool of about 5,700,000. The second class, consisting of about 400,000, was chosen in the summer of 1978 from about 6,000,000 examinees. The third class was selected in the summer of 1979, when 270,000 additional students were selected from among 4,600,000 applicants. It will take another year, therefore, before the college population in China reaches its steady state.

3

Overview of Current Trends in Science and Education Policy*

In terms of the advancement of scientific research in China, the past 2 years have been the most dramatic in the nearly 3-decade-long history of the People's Republic. The watershed in science policy areas in China began with the sudden downfall of the "Gang of Four"† in the fall of 1976, shortly after the death of Mao Zedong. For the past 3 years, the "Gang" and their followers have been repudiated as architects of a decade of policies, which began with the Cultural Revolution in 1966 and which included an attack on scientists and their work as self-serving, parasitic, elitist, and contrary to the interests of China's working classes. In the first year following the fall of the "Gang," new broad policy directions were clearly set: Science and technology would be given full play in a major effort to place China among the modern nations of the world by the end of the twentieth century. It has taken more than 2 full years, however, on this new path to resolve many of the specific issues related to modernization and to put into action the major components of science and technology policy. Although outside observers of China have often been surprised by sudden policy shifts in China, the confidence currently exuded by China's scientific and technical leaders suggests nevertheless that the priority now being given to scientific and technological development is likely to remain a basic national policy for at least the near future.

What specifically happened to individual scientists and institutions in China between 1966 and 1976 seems to have varied greatly. Accounts that

---

*See footnote at the beginning of the previous chapter.
†Mao's widow, Jiang Qing, and three other powerful radicals, Zhang Qunqiao, Yao Wenyuan, and Wang Hongwen.

members of our delegation heard were often impassioned, but, at the same time, generally sketchy and seemingly prone to some generalization and overstatement. Nevertheless, two things are clear about that period. First, in terms of prevailing policy and popular moods, high-level scholarship in all fields was on the defensive. Regardless of whether scientists were sent to the countryside for 2 months or 2 years or not at all, their positions were insecure, they became personally demoralized, and their work suffered accordingly. Any research that was done in that decade was accomplished more in spite of rather than supported by the prevailing atmosphere and intellectual conditions of the time. Second, the material support for extensive research was severely reduced (obviously more in some cases than others), and, under those conditions, both human minds and physical equipment fell into disuse. But there are two sides to the consequences of a decade of political turmoil and uncertainty. On one hand, the state of knowledge and the state of research equipment fell an additional 10 years behind the times, while science and technology in the rest of the world did not stand still. At the same time, however, the opportunity has now arisen for fresh beginnings. It is an opportunity, albeit at a considerable initial cost, to begin with new equipment and new facilities, with a new physical plant for research. It is also an opportunity to begin to catch up with the state of world scientific and technical knowledge of the late 1970's and not of the mid-1960's, leapfrogging the steps that were taken by others in those years.

NEW DIRECTIONS IN SCIENCE

The "Four Modernizations," referring to the areas of agriculture, industry, national defense, and science and technology, is the slogan affixed to China's current overall national plan. This policy was first enunciated by the late Premier Zhou Enlai in January 1975, a year before his death, but was then thwarted for 2 years by his political opponents in a struggle that combined fundamental ideological differences with a race for power surrounding the impending death of Mao Zedong. Now the "Four Modernizations" policy has been firmly anchored, and science and technology have been identified as the key to the other three areas of modernization. What this has meant in concrete terms has been, first of all, a rather thorough reshuffling of political and administrative personnel ranging from the highest levels of government to individual research and academic institutions and economic enterprises. Followers of the "Gang of Four" have been and, in some instances, are still in the process of being removed from positions of authority, leaving in their place individuals who support the current emphasis on scientific work. Secondly, a massive publicity effort has been launched to promote the importance of scientists and technical personnel and their work. For instance, a major national newspaper, *Guangming Ribao*, has, since May 1978, been devoted exclusively to science and education matters. In the Chinese press in general, there has been extensive coverage of scientific achievements and activities, both domestic and international; denunciation of the repressive influence exerted in the past by the "Gang"; and theoretical discussions of the role of science. Particularly important in these discussions has been the characterization of scientists and technicians as part of the "productive forces" of society, which means that their work must be valued rather than viewed as counterproductive to the revolutionary transformation of the class structure of society.

The role of scientific personnel in Chinese society has been redefined. In the more "radical" policy phases, such as most of the 1966-1976 decade, there was a deliberate attempt to minimize the differences and potential conflict between "red" and "expert" and between those who perform manual and mental labor by merging those roles. The "experts," i.e., intellectuals in general, were subjected to political education and required to engage in productive labor, while workers and peasants were deemed capable of making scientific achievements equal to those of the "experts" and political cadres were placed fully in charge of science policy. Now it is being argued that modern society requires a division of labor between "red" and "expert" and between manual laborer and intellectual, with each making his unique contribution to the advancement of the society. Scientists and technicians are thus being promoted to a position of respect rather than denigrated as in the recent past. Their roles as researchers, creators of new technology leading to modernization, and as teachers and diffusers of technical knowledge is being sought in relation to policymaking. This trend has, for instance, manifested itself in the establishment of academic councils in research institutes and universities, made up of scientists whose function is to advise these institutions' administrations on policy matters. There has also been a call in the Chinese press for bringing more intellectuals into the ranks of the Chinese Communist Party. It is worthy of note that 75 percent of the "scientific workers" present at the 1978 National Science Conference were Party members.

The institutional structure of scientific activity, which was discussed in the preceding section, has been strengthened. Administrative and research units that had been phased out during the Cultural Revolution have been reinstated, and new institutions have been created in response to expanding needs. There is also every indication from the Chinese press and from individual contacts that scientific research budgets are being increased substantially. Unfortunately, at the time of this writing the Chinese had not published budgetary figures in nearly 20 years, and research expenditures are simply not known.

THE NATIONAL SCIENCE CONFERENCE AND ITS AFTERMATH

Many of the policy decisions that were made after Mao's death were widely publicized in a national conference on science of unprecedented scale. More than 6,000 delegates attended the meeting, which was held in Beijing, March 18-31, 1978. The convening of the conference was first called for in a September 18, 1977, circular by Premier Hua Guofeng, which led to an intensive preparatory meeting of 1,200 scientists, convened in October, to discuss science policy. In the months that followed, a draft 8-year national plan for scientific work, covering the period 1978 to 1985, was put together for discussion at the March conference. A more general 23-year plan (to the year 2000) has apparently also been formulated.

The main purpose of the science conference was to announce formally the new governmental commitment to science and to mobilize national resources on behalf of the scientific and technological work, which would launch China on a new "Long March" toward becoming a "modern socialist state" by the year 2000. While the draft 8-year plan was not made public, major speeches by China's top leaders, Premier Hua Guofeng, Vice Premier Deng Xiaoping, the driving figure behind the modernization policy, and Vice Premier Fang Yi, China's leading science and technology administrator, stressed the following points:

- China's scientists would be given free reign in carrying out research according to national priorities.
- Priority sectors would receive funding and logistical support commensurate with national goals.
- Research priorities would include basic research that had been neglected in the past, while applied research would continue to play an important part.
- Priority areas would include both those in which China is currently approaching "advanced world levels" and areas in which China is currently weak.
- China's scientists would be given wide access to foreign technology through international scientific exchange and purchases of foreign technology.
- The number of research institutions would increase in key areas by establishing new centers and developing centers where research had lapsed during the Cultural Revolution.
- China's scientific and technical manpower would be substantially increased. The initial target figure is 800,000.

- Scientific learning would be widely diffused through mass education at all levels and popularization programs.
- Scientific achievement would be encouraged through recognition and material rewards.
- Nonscientific activities would not intrude substantially on research activities. Scientists and other professionals would be ensured that at least five-sixths of their time would be devoted to their professional work.
- Administrative and political leadership would encourage rather than hinder the activities of scientists.

While research funding will be allocated to a variety of sectors beyond those listed below, such as transportation and communication, oceanography and environmental protection, eight major areas have been given first priority in the 8-year plan for the development of science:

1. Agricultural Science and Technology: soil improvement and erosion control; irrigation; improvement of seed strains; fertilizers; forestry; animal science; fisheries; sideline production; agricultural biology and mechanization
2. Energy Research: petroleum geology and exploration and exploitation techniques; mechanization of coal extraction; atomic power generation; solar, geothermal, wind, tidal, and controlled thermonuclear energy production
3. Materials Science and Technology: iron ore mining and beneficiation; copper and aluminum production; cement and building materials; mining and dressing of nonmetallic ores; catalysts; plastics and synthetic rubber and fibers
4. Computer Science and Technology: large-scale and ultra-large-scale integrated circuits; large-scale computers; computer software and applied mathematics
5. Laser Science and Technology: for use in isotope separation, catalysis, information processing, and controlled thermonuclear reaction; laser physics; laser spectroscopy and nonlinear optics
6. Space Science and Technology: remote sensing; building and launching of skylabs and space probes
7. High-Energy Physics: building a large proton accelerator and developing its applications
8. Genetic Engineering: basic research in molecular biology; molecular genetics and cell biology; pharmaceutical applications; nitrogen fixation

Scientific activities reported since the conference, such as the convening of scholarly meetings and international exchanges, have underscored the set of priorities enunciated at the science conference.

In the late spring of 1979, when our delegation visited China, however, the ambitious plans enunciated at the 1978 National Science Conference were undergoing some retrenchment. Since late 1978, both economic planners and science planners in China, in working out specific plans for coming years, have had to face the realities of manpower shortages and the limits on the availability in China of development funds and especially of foreign exchange and credits with which to acquire technology from abroad. As we visited universities, for instance, little mention was made of the ambitious projections for student enrollments that had been cited to earlier visitors and in the Chinese press in 1978. Officials both of the State Scientific and Technological Commission and of the Chinese Academy of Sciences admitted to us that the optimism of 1978 had been excessive and that they were soberly reassessing the situation.

In addressing the members of our delegation, these officials stressed that the pinpointing in 1978 of eight priority areas for science and technology development does not imply that other areas of research, such as nuclear physics, are to be ignored: Physics is considered a key component, we were told, of scientific research and education in China, and nuclear physics is an important subfield of physics. It was explained to us that high-energy physics was selected as one of the priority areas for development because it represents a major field of basic research, is at the forefront of world science, and is one where—in contrast to almost all other areas of physics—China had no experimental research activity whatever. It was concluded, therefore, at the highest political levels, and we suspect with some very pointed advice from several early scientific visitors, that if China is to be a major world scientific power, high-energy research needs a substantial boost from its currently inadequate theoretical base. Some officials, indeed, were quite frank in confirming that the decision concerning high-energy physics was a very high (and therefore very political) decision. It was also acknowledged that China had received very contradictory advice on the matter from foreign scientists visiting China and that China's own scientists were rather divided on the issue. As to the implications of retrenchment in physics, we were told that major projects in high-energy physics (namely the plans for a 50-GeV proton accelerator in Beijing), in nuclear physics (namely the Lanzhou heavy ion accelerator complex and the purchase of the HVEC electrostatic accelerator by the Institute of Atomic Energy), and in plasma physics (plans for a large Tokamak to be built in Hefei) were not likely to be affected by cutbacks, although many lesser projects may have to be postponed indefinitely.

NEW DIRECTIONS IN HIGHER EDUCATION

In their efforts to develop science and technology, China's leaders have been acutely aware of shortages of technical manpower. Their short-run solution is to "rationalize" utilization of personnel, improving the "fit" between tasks at hand and available manpower. At one level, this may be seen as an attempt to put to an end the practice of the past 10 years of sending technical personnel and potential students and trainees to rural and industrial production sites. Cast earlier in terms of priority needs of production and an attempt to blur distinctions between mental and manual labor, that policy is now being denounced as a punitive measure taken against intellectuals by the followers of the "Gang of Four." Beyond reversing that policy, however, current efforts can also be seen as an attempt to fine tune the matching of personnel supply and demand. In order to guide the current effort, as well as planning for the future, the State Scientific and Technological Commission, in collaboration with the State Statistical Bureau, completed a nationwide manpower survey in 1978. Unfortunately, the details of that survey have not been accounced. While we were told that great efforts were being devoted to the development of research manpower in physics, none of the officials we talked to were able to cite any specific figures reflecting the current national situation or trends in that field.

The higher-education system in China is once again moving forward aggressively after a more than 10-year lapse involving school closures, abridged curricula, and limited allocation of funds to the educational sector. Recruitment of students has returned to a pre-Cultural Revolution system that features direct matriculation from upper middle schools (high schools), without the mandatory 2-year minimum hiatus for production work after middle school, which had characterized the early 1970's. Furthermore, as in the early 1960's, selection of college students is once again based almost entirely on academic criteria through use of a nationwide entrance examination, rather than on a system of work-unit recommendation stressing political attitude over academic qualifications.

The total college population will stand at somewhat more than 1 million after the fall 1979 enrollment. By the fall of 1980, Chinese colleges will have a full complement of four classes, totaling around 1.5 million students. In late 1978, projections had been cited for total college enrollments of about 4 million by 1985, but in mid-1979, Chinese officials with whom we discussed this were uncertain about the enrollment levels they might expect within the next 5 or 6 years.

As indicated in the previous chapter, however, the Chinese have already made sound new beginnings in graduate education. The initial enrollment in the fall of 1978 of more than 10,000 graduate students already far exceeds, on an annual basis, the level of graduate education prior to the Cultural Revolution. By the mid-1960's, a total of only about 15,000 Chinese students had studied at the graduate level (since 1949), and about 3,000 of these had done so in the Soviet Union and Eastern Europe. The burden of graduate instruction necessarily falls on the more senior faculty, many of them aging. But the dedication of these senior scholars, combined with reliance on education abroad, if sustained for some time to come, may eventually compensate effectively for the long lapse in high-level education in China during the Cultural Revolution. As in the case of undergraduate enrollments, the visions of 1978 for the future of graduate education in China were extremely ambitious and probably totally unrealistic—10 to 20 percent of the total enrollments in at least half of China's colleges and universities. Our impression in visiting universities in mid-1979 is that graduate enrollments will, more realistically, be allowed to fall within the framework of what is possible in terms of available resources of teaching manpower and research facilities at the universities and research institutes.

The year 1978 was also marked by ambitious statements with regard to overseas education for Chinese students. As overseas programs have been initiated, however, it is clear that the initial target, however vague, of having roughly 10,000 students overseas by 1985 will probably not be reached. The major constraints are the shortage of funds and foreign currencies for the programs and the overriding need for the existing manpower on research projects at home, even at their current levels of education and experience. The ultimate result will probably consist of fewer students, training at fairly advanced levels (i.e., doctoral-level research for personnel in their late thirties) for limited periods of time and relying where possible on direct or indirect financial support of the host countries or institutions to which the Chinese graduate students may be sent. This represents a more realistic expectation, albeit far less ambitious than the initial plan; overseas education will still, however, have a very significant impact on China's needed manpower base development.

China's scientists, it was clear to us, are devoting considerable time and effort to foreign language study, particularly English. Several mid-level scientists we spoke with had been studying English full-time for up to 8 or 9 months. This investment of time, like the investment in the construction and acquisition of new research equipment and facilities, will necessarily delay the development of research activities, but it is likely to yield a valuable pay-off in later years. The older generation of foreign-educated scientists seemed to be those who were best attuned to scientific developments in the rest of the world, and it is only through foreign language study and visits overseas that the new generation can be effective participants in China's drive to catch up with and become integrated with the international scholarly community.

Finally, mention should be made of China's major efforts to develop new teaching materials. The reference libraries we visited are a complex mixture of very old and very new materials, and periodical collections from abroad (both originals, photocopies of originals, and translations of originals) are impressive. Teaching materials are also a combination of old and new, and most new material is still in draft form. We have noted elsewhere in this report the process by which lectures by a visiting scientist from abroad will eventually form the basis of new textbooks. It was interesting for us to hear, on several occasions and in no uncertain terms, that, in spite of the efforts devoted to language study, Chinese education and science officials feel it essential to develop teaching materials in Chinese. For students to struggle with materials from abroad in a foreign language is considered both ineffective, a hindrance in education, and a process that is much too reminiscent of the "(semi-) colonial" past. At the very least, it is felt that foreign materials should be translated into Chinese as a first step, while in the long run, more books will be written by Chinese scholars themselves. Both the translation and the writing of textbooks are currently being generously rewarded in China today.

4

Overview of Chinese Nuclear Science Activities

For the past several decades, the delegation was told, nuclear science activities in China have been closely related to research and development of nuclear weapons; as such they have enjoyed relatively high priority. This work drew heavily upon the skills of Chinese scientists who had received nuclear science training in Western Europe and in the United States and on technology transfer from the Soviet Union.

Initially nuclear science research institutions were established in Beijing, Xi'an, Haerbin, and Tianjin in the mid-1950's. The first experimental reactor was constructed in Beijing, a gaseous diffusion isotope separation plant was built in Lanzhou, and initial uranium mining operations were undertaken in Xinjiang. We were told that more than 1,000 Chinese scientists and technicians were trained in the Soviet Union during the period of Sino-Soviet collaboartion at the Joint Institute for Nuclear Research (JINR) in Dubna and elsewhere. During the period of collaboration, China contributed one-third of the operating budget of JINR.

The first Chinese nuclear weapon was detonated in 1964 and the first Chinese hydrogen weapon in 1967, with continuing atmospheric testing of both fission and fusion weapons thereafter.

Obviously, therefore, China has the experience and technology in hand for the development of a nuclear energy program; but for obvious reasons such a program has low priority in China. Blessed with abundant hydroelectric power (only 2 percent of the estimated 500,000 MW of hydroelectric potential has been tapped thus far), as well as very large reserves of coal, oil, and natural gas, China is in an enviable position with respect to energy generally.

Repeatedly, however, the delegation was told that the Chinese consider combustion of fossil fuels as a source of heat energy to be an unconscionable waste of their chemical sophistication and that a determined effort will be made to conserve their reserves for use as feedstock for petrochemical, plastic, drug, and other industrial processes. Given this, they are clearly committed to developing what they consider to be the nuclear energy technology best suited to ultimate Chinese needs; in particular, they are working actively on both light and heavy water moderated fission reactors, and, at a lower level of activity and an earlier technological stage, on the technology of both magnetic and inertial confinement fusion reactors. Light water reactors have already been purchased from France, and negotiations concerning possible purchase of Canadian heavy water reactors are in progress.

Nonenergy applications of nuclear science appear to be growing rapidly in China. We saw examples in nuclear medicine (apparently growing very rapidly); in ion implantation in the fabrication of semiconductor integrated circuits and devices; in use of nuclear techniques in both petroleum and uranium mining and in the characterization of iron and other ores (the latter not yet pursued in the United States to our knowledge); in activation and other nuclear analysis techniques in environmental science, in archaeology, and in a wide range of technological applications; and in the detection of precursors to earthquakes and other geological applications.

In all of such work the need for well-trained nuclear scientists and engineers is clearly recognized, and, given the head start that nuclear science received both in the universities and in the Chinese Academy of Sciences' research institutes for military reasons, it is clear that there is both a tradition and a momentum that will ensure that Chinese nuclear science will grow substantially during the coming decade.

It is also clear, however, that particle physics has been established, at the very highest political levels, as the primary vehicle for China's reentry into the international scientific community; it has been selected, for example, as one of the eight major areas targeted in 1978 for development under the "four modernizations" program promulgated as official Chinese governmental policy. Given that visibility and emphasis, it is not surprising that there has already been a quite discernable shift from nuclear to particle physics in several of the theoretical groups with whom we had contact; we also suspect that the 50-GeV proton accelerator to be constructed at the Institute for High-Energy Physics in Beijing will have a very high relative priority for both human and material resources.

It bears repeated emphasis that effectively all Chinese research and, to a lesser extent, development was in stasis during the decade of the Cultural Revolution—a decade during which impressive change and progress characterized the world scientific community—so that beginning in 1977, and drawing upon what they had been able to preserve through this decade, the Chinese scientists in all fields have had to reestablish their research activities afresh, and with a staggering amount of catching up to do.

In the universities this rebuilding of research activity has been assigned a very obvious, and entirely reasonable, second priority after the rebuilding of the teaching function. With minor exceptions, therefore, research activity in nuclear science, as in other fields, is now still at a low level in Chinese universities. In the research institutes, however, the rebuilding program is being pursued aggressively, limited at present primarily by the availability of trained manpower. We saw no evidence of funding limitations at the research institutes visited, while at both Qinghua and Fudan universities, for example, it was clearly recognized that funding limitations would preclude any early acquisition of the desired tandem accelerator. In part, of course, this reflects the fact that hard currency required for foreign purchases (as in the case of these particular tandems) is in very short supply throughout China and that all such purchases are severely restricted.

The major research institutes active in nuclear science that we visited—the Institute of Atomic Energy (IAE) in Beijing, the Institute of Modern Physics (IMP) in Lanzhou, and the Institute for Nuclear Research (INR) in Shanghai—all have ambitious plans for major new accelerator projects and are making good progress toward their realization. The most ambitious plans, in part a reflection, no doubt, of the enthusiasm and drive of its Director, are those of the Institute of Modern Physics in Lanzhou. As currently planned, the three coupled accelerator complex—a sector focussed cyclotron, a separated sector cyclotron, and a 20-MV tandem accelerator—will provide this laboratory with research capability at least matching that of the world's foremost laboratories in this field.

Realization of these plans in timely fashion will depend critically upon the availability of adequately trained scientific and technical manpower and upon the extent to which the Chinese groups can capitalize upon experience already gained in laboratories outside of China in related problems. Already, we gather that the scientific manpower resources of most of the Chinese research institutes visited have been drawn away from actual research to focus on the rebuilding of facilities; this has the inevitable and unhappy consequence that when the facilities are completed these same scientists will be even farther removed from the intellectual frontiers of their science. And it is our impression that the Chinese groups often seem to "reinvent the wheel"—to work their way through problems that have already been solved elsewhere. They simply cannot afford to repeat past mistakes of others if their programs are to proceed at a reasonable pace.

It should be emphasized that all Chinese groups with which we came into contact were eager for suggestions and help from foreign scientists. The motivation is clearly present, but we are concerned about the effectiveness of present mechanisms of information and experience transfer that appear to center on relatively brief visits of relatively senior scientists to foreign laboratories. During the course of our visit, we repeatedly urged that a broader spectrum of Chinese scientific talent be sent abroad for periods of a year or longer to gain hands-on experience, both in nuclear instrumentation and its use in modern frontier research to which the Chinese facilities will be eminently suited. We consider this particularly important, since it is our impression that little actual basic nuclear science research has been accomplished since the Cultural Revolution other than what might be considered as training repetition of foreign measurements. We found little current expertise in experimental work either in nuclear structure or dynamics; strikingly, this was not the case in theory and in applied nuclear science where the Chinese groups appeared to be cognizant of the latest foreign work.

In part this difference reflects the fact that the existing Chinese accelerator facilities are not competitive in an international sense in basic research, whereas they are entirely adequate for a wide variety of applied studies; but in fact we believe that it also reflects a residue of Cultural Revolution pressures for relevance.

It may simply be that the Chinese consider that they cannot spare any significant number of their current scientists from the work in which they are now engaged for the foreign exposure that we have strongly recommended; and it is clear that the original optimistic Chinese statements of 1978 concerning the number of students and scientists expected to be sent abroad in the near future were based on serious misunderstandings concerning the costs of the announced training programs and the drain that they would represent on Chinese foreign currency supplies.

We must emphasize, however, that the Chinese manpower situation will change dramatically in a few years. From what we have seen in the universities—and described elsewhere in this report—the post-Cultural Revolution students who have now completed 2 years of their undergraduate program have been selected via a highly competitive mechanism clearly based on ability, are receiving an excellent scientific and technical education, and, following completion of their undergraduate programs 2 years hence, might be expected to be competitive with the best graduates anywhere.

Further selection from these graduates for foreign graduate study can lead to a truly outstanding new group of scientists, some 6 to 8 years hence, that could be expected to use the new Chinese facilities in nuclear and other science in very effective fashion in both fundamental and applied research.

It is on this time scale, then, that we look to major emergence of Chinese fundamental nuclear science; given what we have seen of the planning for new facilities and the education of new scientists, we find ourselves optimistic about the eventual competitiveness of the Chinese contribution to world nuclear science.

It is important that we emphasize this matter of time scale; it is one with which the Chinese themselves would generally not disagree. Currently we do not consider that extended visits of foreign nuclear scientists to China would be particularly productive scientifically—either for the scientists involved or for China—as long as China lacks the scientific and technological infrastructure that is now in the process of being rebuilt. Rather, and we cannot emphasize this too strongly, if the Chinese are to achieve their goals in nuclear and other sciences, it will be essential that a broad spectrum of their scientists spend extended periods in foreign laboratories. Only in this way, coupled with their ambitious facility rebuilding program already in place, do we foresee that the Chinese can overcome the major handicap represented by the lost decade of the Cultural Revolution.

5

Visits to Educational Institutions

BEIJING UNIVERSITY*

Beijing University was founded in 1898 and is clearly one of the most prestigious universities in China. The campus is an extremely large and pleasant one, blending traditional Chinese architecture with more modern, and less pleasant, buildings having obvious Soviet parentage.

The delegation was initially greeted by Professor Wang Zhuqi, Vice President of the University, in the absence of the President Zhou Peiyuan, whom we subsequently met at the banquet we hosted but who was in Shanghai on the day of our visit. Professor Wang was joined by a number of his colleagues both from the University administration and from the Departments of Physics and Technical Physics.

During the introductory briefing, which ranged over the entire Chinese educational system inasmuch as this was the delegation's first visit to a Chinese university, the discussion was open, candid, and quantitative whenever we asked specific questions.

Currently, Beijing University has 2,700 teaching staff, including 400 professors and associate professors, as well as 8,000 students, including 460 graduate students. Three thousand of these entered in the fall of 1976. Currently, neither undergraduate or graduate degrees are being awarded, but we have learned from Professor Qian Sanqiang, Vice President of the Academy, that both doctoral and associate doctoral (equivalent to U. S.

---

*The entire delegation toured the University on the morning of May 23. On May 25 and 26, several members (Bromley, Henley, Kerman) returned to give lectures and hold discussions with faculty members. In addition, Tombrello made a follow-up visit to the Technical Physics Department.

master's) degrees will soon become part of the formal educational system with requirements nominally similar to those now standard in American universities.* Currently the undergraduate program is a 4-year one and the graduate program a 3-year one.

A major problem remains as a legacy of the Cultural Revolution. There are two quite distinct types of Chinese undergraduates: students primarily of peasant-worker or soldier background admitted prior to 1977 without examinations or formal qualifications but on the basis of their work-unit recommendations, and those admitted since 1977 following rather rigorous competitive examinations. They have little in common, we were told.

Strangely enough the three formal criteria for admission to university training have remained the same throughout the entire period; they are simply: intellectual ability, physical health, and political behavior. What has changed, however, is the relative weighting assigned to each. While intellectual ability is now the dominant criterion, acceptable political behavior remains a necessary if not sufficient criterion for admission. Its assessment is based on peer and teacher evaluations, beginning at the earliest level of formal schooling, together with other unspecified evaluations. We were told that acceptable behavior involved maturity; observation of discipline; and demonstration of love of country, Party, physical labor, and study. We gathered that any physical handicap weighed heavily against a student's admission.

Intellectual ability is measured by a national, competitive examination taken at the end of high school. Last year 7,000,000 students graduated from high school, 5,000,000 took the college entrance examination, and about 400,000 were ultimately accepted for admission somewhere. Of these, 24,000 were in the Beijing area.

At the time of the examination, the students list their choices of universities and of professions separately. Of the roughly 600 Chinese universities and colleges, about 100 are recognized as "key" institutions, and the most able students clearly compete for admission to them. We were assured that the massive task of matching, sorting, and assigning as many students as possible—on the basis of their grades on the national examination—to the university and profession of their choice was entirely manual, i.e., no computer assistance was involved. We were told that Beijing University normally accepts students who score at least 400 out of a possible 500 on the national examinations and that in general the University was able to obtain its top choices from among the students listing it as first choice. (Students can list up to 10 universities and two specialties as preferences in registering for the national college entrance examination, so the sorting job is enormous.)

*Since this report was written, Chinese authorities announced that academic degrees (bachelor's, master's, and doctorates) would be awarded beginning in 1981.

Beijing University is fortunate in having an extremely attractive campus that includes a small lake and beautifully landscaped grounds. It is marked by many strange and surprising contrasts. The pagoda-like structure in the background is the water tower serving the campus, while the radio telescope in the foreground is operated by the Electrical Engineering Department of the University.

At present Beijing, and the other universities that we visited, are essentially running two parallel programs—one for the remaining "peasant-worker" students and one for the more recent students. In the case of the "peasant-worker" students, many have already been transferred directly to factories or to what we would recognize as 2-year technical schools; the most able ones, however, are being salvaged and, as in U.S. open-admission situations, are being given the necessary remedial training to bring them into the mainstream of current students. We gathered, however, that this latter fraction is rather small.

At Beijing University, as elsewhere, the major problem is that of restructuring both undergraduate and graduate programs that have been essentially moribund for the decade of the Cultural Revolution. Thus far, emphasis has properly been placed on developing text material, laboratory apparatus, and laboratory manuals for the first and second undergraduate years. Next year the emphasis will be on the third undergraduate year, and the following year on the fourth year, until the educational system has been rebuilt. This reconstruction has taken priority over the reestablishment of research activity and will continue to do so for the next several years. Although about 12 contact hours per week appears to be the Chinese university teaching standard, a very large amount of work is involved in the preparation of adequate texts and teaching materials. The Chinese are extremely sensitive concerning the need to use all Chinese language material, and we heard frequent disparaging references to the older period or "semi-colonial era" (prior to 1949), when foreign textbooks had been used.

Currently, the first 2 years of the physics curriculum include general physics, mathematics, differential and integral calculus, and theoretical mechanics and thermodynamics. The third year will include statistical mechanics, electrodynamics, methods of mathematical physics, and some modern physics, specifically including nuclear physics. The fourth year will involve quantum mechanics, solid-state physics, and a number of elective courses, depending upon the student's aptitude, interests, and career directions.

Foreign experts—of whom T. D. Lee of Columbia University is perhaps the most striking example—were in China at the time of our visit delivering extended lecture series that will subsequently form the basis for textbooks. Lee had been lecturing in Beijing for 3 hours each day to about 600 very carefully selected students and faculty, and planned to cover much of theoretical physics. Notes on his lectures will be widely disseminated and used; he himself will edit a second generation of these notes before they are published as texts.

In addition, faculty are being sent abroad for specialized training. During 1978-79, for example, from Beijing University alone, 13 went to the

United States, 22 to France, and a significant number to Canada, Australia, and Western Europe. Beijing University has a special sister relationship already established with the University of California at Berkeley, for instance, involving an agreement to exchange both faculty and teaching materials directly. This is part of a national exchange program under the aegis of the Ministry of Education; however, the sister relationship permits exchanges outside of the Ministry program as such.

But a much more serious question concerns some of the teaching staff itself. While no appointments to associate or full professorships were made during the Cultural Revolution, many individuals were added to university teaching staffs for reasons other than professional standards of ability and some of these remain. A slow and difficult weeding process is in progress wherein the least capable have already been moved back to the factories or the farms to work better matched to their abilities. A more able segment is being utilized whenever possible to assist in lectures and laboratory work, and the most able group is being given additional education and opportunities to bring them to a professionally competitive level.

Whenever we asked about this latter program, we were told that these individuals were being given time off from normal responsibilities so that they could do more "research." We question whether, given their backgrounds, such research will be of the character or quality to substantially advance their qualifications. Possibly a language problem exists here, and "research" may simply mean additional study. Clearly, however, this is recognized as a serious problem.

In general, it was our impression that the faculty members at Beijing (and Qinghua) universities suffered less during the Cutural Revolution than did the researchers at the Academy of Sciences' institutions; 6 months of manual labor in the country as opposed to 2 years was a not uncommon report. During the Cultural Revolution all research was deemed bourgeois and capitalistic, and theoretical research was the most capitalistic of all.

Following graduation from undergraduate school, students are "assigned" to jobs, although we were told that the students had some choice. The People's Liberation Army (PLA) is one of the most highly sought-after placements, but only very few of those chosen are given the opportunity to remain in the Army for more than 3 years.

Beijing University currently has 22 departments,* 12 of which are in the natural sciences; it also has 11 research institutes, 3 in social sciences

---

*The 12 science departments are Biology, Chemistry, Computer Science and Technology, Geology, Geography, Geophysics, Mathematics, Mechanics, Physics, Psychology, Radio Electronics, and Technical Physics. The 10 liberal arts departments are Chinese Language and Literature, Economics, History, International Politics, Law, Library Science, Oriental Languages and Literature, Philosophy, Russian Language and Literature, and Western Languages and Literature.

(Asian and African studies, South Asian studies, and history of philosophy of foreign countries) and 8 in the natural sciences (mathematics, solid state, theory, heavy ion physics, physical chemistry, molecular biology, computer sciences, and geological remote-sensing techniques).

Currently about 130 foreign students are in residence, as well as 24 foreign "experts" who are teaching their respective languages. Of the 460 graduate students, about 50 are in physics (15 in theory, others in low-temperature physics, solid-state, magnetism, etc.). We were told that programs are in place, but apparently as yet little utilized, whereby students can retain their affiliation with Beijing University while doing research work utilizing the facilities of an appropriate institute—either within or outside of the University's own structure.

The University has essentially no nuclear research instrumentation beyond access to the 2.5-MV Van de Graaff dating from before the Cultural Revolution and installed in the Institute of High-Energy Physics of the CAS. The buildup of research has a second priority after the rebuilding of the teaching activities of the University. It is this priority that also appears to

The central processing unit of the DJS-18 computer, constructed and installed in the Computer Center of Beijing University.

work, as yet, against establishment of much in the way of cooperation between the Chinese universities and the research institutes, e.g., with the Institute of Atomic Energy. We would anticipate marked increase in such cooperation once the first group of 4-year students in the new pipeline graduates 2 years from now. The necessary formal structures are all in place.

Following the genral introduction and briefing, the delegation divided into two groups, one visiting the computer center and the library and the other the undergraduate teaching laboratories of the Physics Department. During the course of these visits, we learned (rather by accident) of the plan for a substantial new nuclear accelerator system in the Technical Physics Department and so made arrangements for Tombrello to pay a separate visit to that Department.

The Computer Center houses a DJS-18 unit that we saw in operation.

Peripheral equipment for the DJS-18 computer at Beijing.

Visits to Educational Institutions

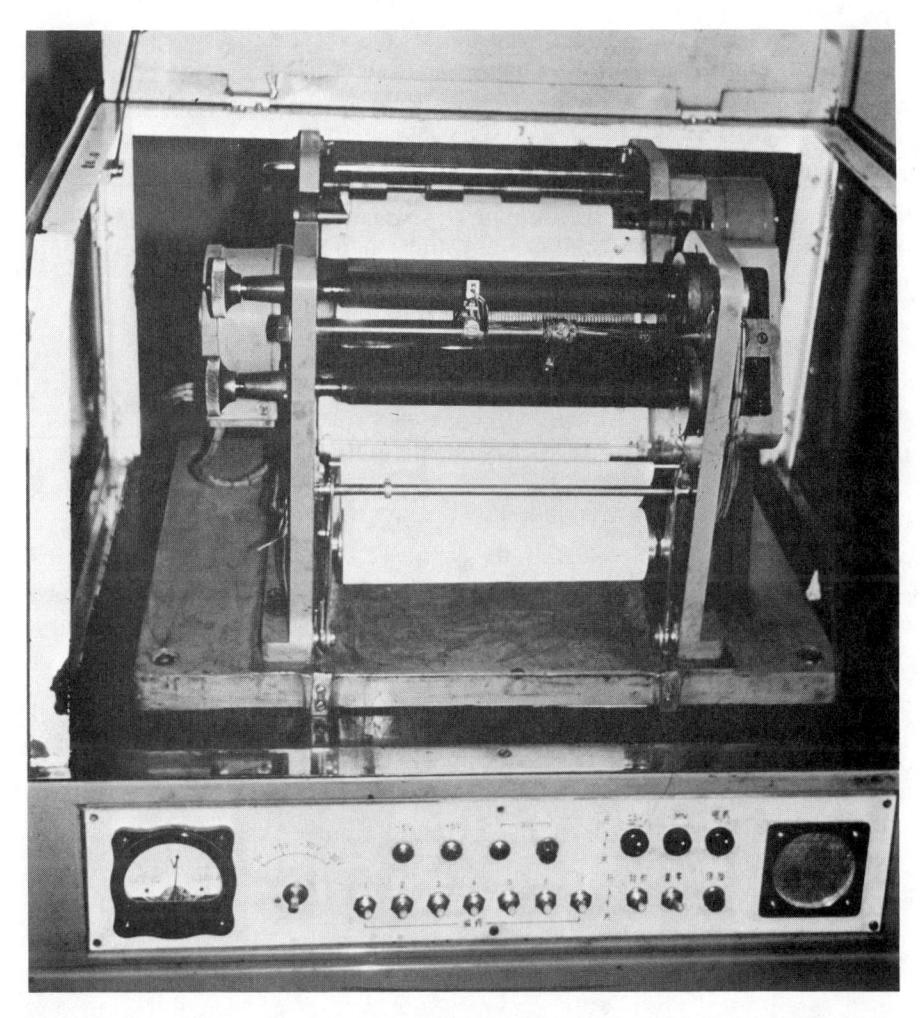

The line printer of the DJS-18 computer at Beijing University with its cover removed. The printing paper is some 10 inches in width and, as indicated, is fed from the roll below the type bar. This and all the other peripheral equipment shown in the above figures appear to have been constructed in the Computer Center itself.

It was built during the Cultural Revolution, has 64 K of 48-bit words, 16-track magnetic tapes, and 500 bpi paper tape input via a photoelectric reader. Output was via an 11-inch paper printer that appeared to have paper handling problems and what appeared to be a modified mechanical typewriter. A 1 × 1 meter plotter was also in evidence. Temperature and humidity controls were relatively simple by U.S. standards involving simple on-off relays driven by the sensing elements. Strangely, we were told that the radical elements "didn't bother with that sort of thing" when we asked how it had been possible to obtain the computer during the Cultural Revolution. On the other hand, we were told that much of the teaching instrumentation had been removed entirely from the campus and used, often ineffectively or in ignorance, in factories old and new as aids to production. In any event, much was destroyed; this has created a distinct advantage, albeit the hard way, for all the universities we visited. Because they have found it necessary to start from scratch in outfitting their undergraduate laboratories, much of what we saw was on the average much more up-to-date and modern in use of electronic techniques, lasers, airtracks, etc., than is the case in comparable laboratories in even the best U.S. universities!

The library is a heroic structure boasting an enormous statue of Chairman Mao in its courtyard. It currently contains 2,500,000 volumes, of which about 600,000, mostly of foreign origin, are distributed among the teaching departments. It has generous space for expansion and has a pleasant, workmanlike atmosphere. Huge student reading rooms, each housing several hundred students, were jammed during our visit. We were told that this is typical and that indeed very few of the students leave the University during vacations or lecture breaks, but instead work full time in the library. These students are clearly dedicated to making the most of the opportunity given them by University admission.

The Physics Department building was occupied in 1959, and we were shown undergraduate laboratories for electronics, optics, and electricity to which all the above comments apply. Most of the equipment, including lasers, had been constructed by the technicians and teaching staff assigned to the laboratories. Since many students rotate through the laboratories, they are generally occupied mornings, afternoons, and evenings, 6 days per week.

For the faculty actually engaged in research, the normal 12-hour teaching load is reduced to 6-8 hours. We were shown some of the equipment that is being assembled to begin research. A laser system is currently being used in a study of atmospheric pollution, with emphasis currently on carbon dioxide; a system incorporating an old 8 litre/hour compression-type helium liquifier and a new partially constructed 20 litre/hour liquifier will be housed in a new laboratory established for research on superconductivity.

Theoretical activity has made somewhat more rapid progress. Work in nuclear theory involves study of collective motion, pair correlations, nuclear field theory, and nuclear charge distributions. At a discussion session, Henley heard from Zeng Jinyan about phenomenological work on nuclear charge distributions and pair correlation work. Zhang Qiren discussed early stages of work on abnormal nuclear matter, which came out of T. D. Lee's visit and a semiclassical relative theory of pion condensation, also in its early stages.

Visits to Educational Institutions

The digital plotter associated with the DJS-18 computer at Beijing University. The plotting surface is roughly 1 m² in area.

The discussion session included presentation of theoretical work by a group of 11 theorists drawn in part from the Institute of High-Energy Physics (IHEP) and in part from Beijing University. There are six particle physics and two nuclear physics students currently studying at IHEP. Some work presented by Zhang Zongye of IHEP involved giant $\bar{p}$ resonances in nuclei, hypernuclear physics with SU(3) including pair correlations, and pion condensation. Other work, presented by Zeng Jinyan of Beijing University, involved pairing (BCS-type) correlations, nuclear field theory, and nuclear charge distributions. Zhang Qiren of Beijing University discussed work on pion condensation with which the IHEP group working on the same subject appeared to be unfamiliar!

The Technical Physics Department at Beijing University has a staff of over 100, including 20 theorists; their primary concern has been, and is, neutron physics. Zhang Qiren, mentioned above, however, is a member of this Department and is branching out into medium- and high-energy work together with some of his colleagues. The Chairman of the Technical Physics Department, an entirely separate entity with its own faculty, students, and courses (similar to, but still different from, those in the Physics Department), is a theoretical nuclear physicist, Hu Jimin.

Although there was no mention of a new accelerator during our discussions with the staff of the Physics Department at Beijing University, in a special discussion period arranged with Tombrello, Professor Hu described his intention to set up a 4.5-MV Van de Graaff accelerator and his subsequent plans for building (in stages) a HILAC that would be injected by the Van de Graaff. The electrostatic accelerator has already been ordered and is being built in the Vanguard factory in Shanghai. It is expected to be operational in 4 years; it will have a PIG ion source and terminal bunching. In its stand-alone mode, it is intended for a research program that includes the study of proton and alpha particle induced X-rays for materials analysis, charged particle backscattering analyses, and neutron production (used in connection with their teaching program). The accelerator is intended to produce modest (50-100 μA) beams of light ions.

This Van de Graaff will also be expected to produce pulsed heavy ion beams (up to argon initially and eventually up to xenon) for injection into a low-phase velocity HILAC. The intention is to build a 27-MHz, β_{min} = 0.03 helical cavity linear accelerator. This machine will have a duty factor of about 20 percent; the initial sections will produce beams with energies in the range of 1.0-1.4 MeV/nucleon.

Ten years ago (before the political disruptions of the mid-1970's), the Technical Physics Department staff had initiated experimental studies related to this project. They had produced a 34-cm-long cavity (β = 0.031, f = 27 MHz, 20 percent duty factor—200 to 500 Hz modulation) that had a shunt impedance of 22 MΩ/m and an energy gain of 1 MV/m. They had made electric field maps of the central region of the resonator and had studied its properties under beam loading by injecting a beam (1 kW) from the Cockcroft-Walton accelerator at Beijing Normal University. They had measured the energy spectrum of the accelerated beam and confirmed that phase bunching was occurring as predicted.

This prototype resonator had an outer can of aluminum alloy (inner diameter, 25 cm) and a silver-plated stainless steel helical central conductor (mean diameter, 10 cm). To improve the maximum field, they had flattened the helical coils: radial axis, 7 mm; longitudinal direction, 4 mm; spacing between coil centers, 6 mm. This group (headed by Professor Chen Jiaer) is obviously aware of all published work on helical resonators and had even taken advantage of some esoteric tricks of their own devising to improve cavity performance.

The choice of a helical resonator (which has many intrinsic disadvantages) was probably unavoidable because of the low operating frequency, 27 MHz. Apparently, for high-power RF only two frequencies are commercially available in China: S-band, because of radar applications; and 27 MHz, which is the standard broadcast frequency. Within the limitations inherent in the forced choice of this frequency, this group has done as well as they possibly could thus far. They should be able to design an adequate feedback stabilization system for the resonator at modest power levels (0.8-1.0 MV/m) and seem quite capable of carrying out the design and fabrication stages of the project. (In fact, their process to flatten and wind the helical coils in a single operation is excellent.)

The proposed HILAC will be quite expensive to operate because of its power requirements, and the Beijing University group members see no way to go beyond a final energy of about 4 MeV/nucleon. They expect to use the machine in a program focussed on radiation damage and on nuclear chemistry research.

During the discussion with Tombrello, the members of the group (about 20 present) asked excellent questions and showed considerable enthusiasm in their approach to the many design problems of HILAC. There was an atmosphere of excitement and an aggressive behavior that augurs well for the future of this group and that was not present in some of the other laboratories that we had an opportunity to visit while in China.

At Beijing University, as indeed throughout China, it would be fair to conclude that nuclear research is relatively low in the priority listing. The Chinese clearly see no need for nuclear energy in the near future given their hydroelectric and fossil resources, although they do want to have the technology in hand; the original emphasis in nuclear energy was clearly spurred by military considerations. At present, solid-state and related areas of physics have high priority because of obvious commercial applications and the Chinese desire to establish a competitive, indigenous computer and electronics industry; particle physics has high priority because it has been selected for showcase treatment as the major Chinese entry into large-scale international science. This latter is clearly a decision that is less than obviously correct in the view of a great many scientists with whom we had discussions in China; but all recognize it as firmly established and not subject to change, although the time scale for construction of the 50-GeV machine at IHEP will almost certainly be extended substantially beyond current goals as various economic and high technology manufacturing realities are addressed.

QINGHUA UNIVERSITY*

Qinghua is a solidly built university located on spacious grounds away from the center of Beijing, but in the same general area as Beijing University. The University was founded early in the twentieth century (1911), but most of the buildings in its present location seem to date from the late 1950's, and the architectural style is reminiscent of Moscow. It is a university of science and technology consisting of 11 departments in the natural sciences and engineering.† Since we are told that there are plans to add a Department of Industrial Economics, it would not be imprecise to make a rough comparison of Qinghua with MIT (or perhaps a much larger version of Caltech would be even closer). Virtually all the faculty, staff, and students live on the university grounds, which gives it something of the atmosphere of a small, self-contained town. Within China, Qinghua clearly has an outstanding reputation as a science and engineering school, and its graduates hold a disproportionate number of senior posts in scientific and technological areas.

We were told that it currently has an enrollment of 4,000 students after graduating 2,000 in April 1979. After the 1979 summer vacation, 2,000 more will enter, bringing the total to 6,000 (approximately 20 percent of whom are female) for the three classes now enrolled. The stated goal over the next few years is to increase this enrollment perhaps to an ultimate total of 12,000. (We would note that in our casual inspection of the campus we might have guessed that it would easily accommodate many more—perhaps as many as 40,000. We were told that they had 500,000 m^2 of building space already available.) We visited only the main campus; there are two other campus sites (5,000 students at each) somewhere in downtown Beijing. The students at these latter branches are not provided with dormitory space and presumably live at home or independently in the city. We gained the impression that many of them may be part-time, studying in addition to their normal employment. Qinghua is responsible for the course content at these branch campuses, but their administration is the formal responsibility of the Municipality of Beijing.

*The entire delegation visited Qinghua University in the afternoon of May 23. Bromley and Middleton returned 2 days later to give lectures and hold discussions with faculty members. The delegation was greeted initially by Vice President Zhang Wei and by Professor Zhang Li, Deputy Chairman of the Engineering Physics Department.
†The 11 departments are Engineering Physics, Engineering Chemistry, Mechanical Manufacturing, Precision Instruments, Civil Engineering, Hydraulic Engineering, Electrical Engineering, Radio Engineering, Automation, Engineering Mechanics, and Electronics.

We were told that the graduate program at Qinghua was stopped completely by the Cultural Revolution; indeed, we were told elsewhere that Qinghua had suffered perhaps more than any other university in China during this period. The programs are now being rebuilt systematically; there now are 350 graduate students in residence and 300 to 400 more will be added in June 1979. These students take basic courses full time for 2 years. After some weeding out, it is anticipated that most will then engage in research projects for an additional 2 years (a variant of the Oberlin system?). As in other Chinese universities, no advanced degrees are given at present, but both doctoral and associate doctoral (equivalent to master's) degrees are planned. Before 1949 Qinghua was closely associated with a number of universities in the United States and had basically an American course structure. At that time it had departments in the social sciences, liberal arts, law, and agriculture. When the school was reorganized in 1952 to become a more specialized school of science and technology, these non-natural science departments (with associated faculty, libraries, etc.) were transferred directly to Beijing University. We were told that Qinghua University played a substantial role in the development of Chinese nuclear weaponry; the Engineering Chemistry Department is almost entirely devoted to nuclear chemistry, and the Engineering Physics Department is similarly devoted to nuclear engineering.

There is currently a faculty of 2,800, of which only 180 are associate or full professors (although we were told that a number of promotions were pending). Some of them are engaged purely in research, while the remainder combine activities in teaching and research. We were told that the faculty in the various departments suggest their research programs to the University administration, which in turn, and within its understanding of its mandate from the Ministry of Education, decides on whether or not these programs will be carried out. University funding comes via a regular annual budget from the Ministry of Education and from more specific research funding from the State Scientific and Technological Commission. We subsequently learned of direct funding by different ministries of research directly pertinent to their missions, and individual factories under Ministry purview can negotiate research contracts directly with university departments, presumably with the approval of university administrations.

The State Scientific and Technological Commission, we were told again, is responsible for an overall plan for research and development for all of the PRC, which is made after discussions with scientists, engineers, and administrators in all parts of China. The plan segment evolved for a given university is not compulsory, but is taken as a general guide together with the specific needs of various industries and ministries and the ideas and goals of the university faculty itself. The division of effort between research and teaching is based on general policy produced by the Ministry of Education, but again the university appears to have some latitude within the promulgated guidelines.

In discussions related to the effect of the Cultural Revolution, it was stated that Qinghua and Beijing universities—apart from the faculty members themselves—were affected more than any other educational institutions in China, since the hard core of the Red Guard activists was primarily recruited from students in these two universities. We were also told that a "henchman of the Gang of Four" was put in charge of Qinghua University during the decade of the Revolution; from this position he also managed to control events at Beijing University. The situation was said to be less severe at institutions outside Beijing, and our own observations bear out this assertion.

We noted the presence of occupied army barracks and a major construction and equipment yard within the campus area. It was explained that Vice Premier Deng Xiaoping had sent approximately 1,000 soldiers to help build new buildings at Qinghua; they are reputed to be excellent workers. Similar

The prototype electron linear accelerator developed at Qinghua University with support from the Beijing Municipality. The stacked electrodes are here contained within a glass vacuum system.

Visits to Educational Institutions

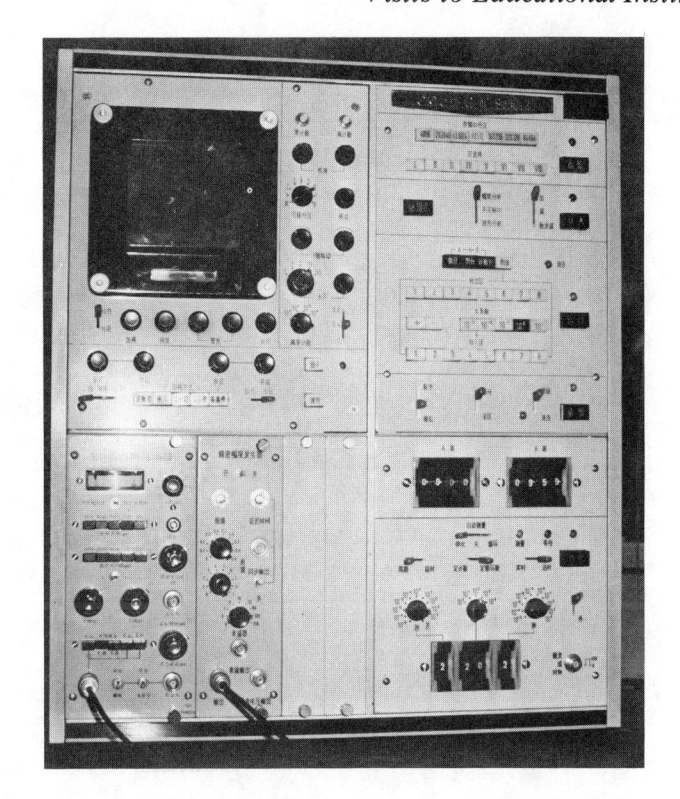

A 400-channel pulse-height analyzer constructed at Qinghua University for use within the University and for sale throughout China. This particular unit features memory switching so that two-dimensional spectra may also be accumulated.

groups from the People's Liberation Army (PLA) have been sent to other universities and institutions of the Chinese Academy of Sciences to do such construction work.

The physical condition of the main building (built late in the 1950's) and reminiscent of MIT and of the library (ca. 1920 vintage) were excellent. The reading rooms in the library were filled with students and teachers, who were busy with their studies. We saw many Chinese-language technical books from Taiwan in the science library; there was a small, eclectic collection of new scientific books in English. The Architecture Department (includes civil engineering as well) has its classrooms and laboratories in the main building. It is responsible for the design and supervision of building construction on campus: We saw designs (student projects!) for a new physics building containing extensive classrooms and lecture halls and for an ultraclean laboratory for the fabrication of very large-scale integrated circuits. We were told that the latter is one of a series of prototype designs for industry. We were much impressed by the professionalism and enthusiasm displayed by this group and by the very effective integration of education and productive real-world experience.

Returning to projects initiated by industry, we saw several examples. We were told of, and shown, the development of a 10-MeV electron linac (3,000-MHz, magnetron powered) for clinical X-ray therapy. The builders proudly displayed a certificate of excellence that had been awarded to them by the Beijing Municipality for their work on this device. This work was initiated in 1972 and finished in 1976, spanning the Cultural Revolution. Funding for the linac development came from the Municipality; this project has been accepted for effective mass production. The second industrial project inspired the development of a 4,096-channel pulse height analyzer. This was based on an Italian design (not French as elsewhere!), uses small-scale integrated circuits, is switch-selectable for two dimensions, and is now in general production. We were told that it had been developed initially as part of the

Typical electronic instrumentation used at Qinghua University in the development of electron linear accelerators for medical purposes. All the instrumentation shown was constructed in China. The 220-V power distribution system shown on the rear wall was typical of that in almost all the laboratories visited by the delegation.

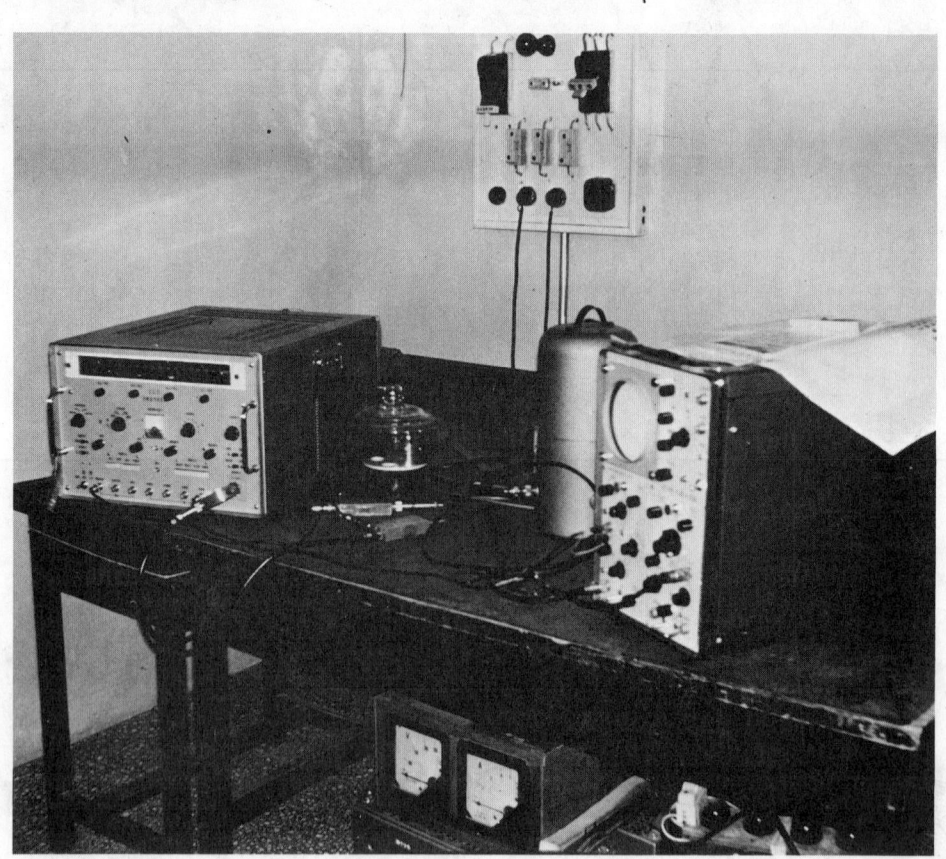

Visits to Educational Institutions

Stanley Hanna viewing the control console of the Soviet-made betatron installed at Qinghua.

military nuclear energy program and had subsequently been used in radiometric prospecting for oil and in uranium mining applications. It would be noted that, although the Qinghua group copied an Italian design, they incorporated many improvements of their own, not least of which was a CAMAC system.

The contrast between the multichannel analyzers—three of which were operational in a single laboratory room—and the electrical wiring in that room was striking. Room lights were suspended from their power cords; knife switches, fuses, and controls were attached more or less at random to wooden boards hung on the walls, and exposed 220-V wiring and switch elements were frequent, and hazardous!

It seems clear that a significant fraction of the departmental funding has come from such projects; it is also quite possible that these industrial tasks were particularly important in maintaining some University validity during the Cultural Revolution.

We were also taken on a tour of the Department of Engineering Physics

NUCLEAR SCIENCE IN CHINA

Bernard Harvey with the Qinghua University betatron. Mounted on the stand in the foreground is an ionization chamber for beam intensity measurement.

by its Chairman, Professor Zhang Li. Conditions there were significantly different from those in the other sections of the University that we visited—the buildings were dirty and cluttered, there was little sign of activity, and many of the offices seemed to be either unoccupied or only very recently reoccupied. We were told that most of the equipment had been removed for use in factories during the Cultural Revolution and that some of the laboratories had been converted for horse-breeding experimentation! We were shown a 25-MeV Soviet-built betatron that was used for photonuclear research until 1958; at present it is used only to take X-ray inspection pictures of industrial castings and other components, which is a very reasonable way to exploit its rather limited capabilities. We also saw a disassembled 900-KV Cockcroft-Walton accelerator; though we were told that it was under repair, the disassembled parts were dust-covered and activity appeared to be at a very low level.

A group representing the nuclear science activities at Qinghua recently toured the United States while gathering information on commercially available electrostatic accelerators. On their return in February 1979 they submitted a proposal for a tandem accelerator (super FN or 8-10 UD). This proposal has not been approved, and the Qinghua physicists estimate that it will take at least 2 to 5 years before the foreign exchange situation might permit the purchase of such an accelerator. During this interim period they

The Cockcroft-Walton accelerator at Qinghua was disassembled at the time of the delgation's visit and is being reconstructed with a variety of changes and improvements. It was constructed initially by the Vanguard factory in Shanghai.

plan to devote their efforts to improving and exploiting the 2.5-MV Van de Graaff accelerator at the Institute of High-Energy Physics. After the HVEC tandem is operating at the Institute of Atomic Energy (IAE), they say that they will use that facility. However, the distance involved (about 50 km), the problems of commuting, and the fact that they have thus far had absolutely no input into the IAE tandem or its laboratory will probably mean that their involvement will be rather minimal and may consist mainly of sending some of their students to the Institute on a relatively permanent basis.

From our visit it it clear that Qinghua University has every intention of rebuilding to its former status as one of China's—and the world's—major science and engineering universities. A start has been made, but much remains to be accomplished.

LANZHOU UNIVERSITY*

On our visit to Lanzhou University we were greeted by the Vice President, Nie Dajiang; the Dean, Lu Runlin; the Head of the Physics Department, Duan Yishi; the Deputy Head of the Modern Physics Department, Zheng Chihao; and a selection of senior academic and administrative staff. During the formal introductory period, Vice President Nie Dajiang provided us with general information concerning the University prior to our visits to teaching laboratories and research activities.

The University is located near the Institute of Modern Physics (IMP). It was founded about 40 years ago, and is one of China's "key" universities. At the moment it has roughly 3,000 students and 2,000 teachers and staff in 17 departments.† Of these 2,000, 960 are members of the teaching staff, and of these 62 are professors or associate professors, 405 are lecturers, and the remainder are teaching assistants. Although the two organizations are in close proximity, the IMP and Lanzhou University have no direct relationship. We were told that while the University can send graduate students to work at the IMP, they have none as yet that are adequately qualified; some members of the teaching faculty have apparently initiated some minor research collaboration with the IMP staff. We were given no examples of such collaboration in response to a direct request, however. Students graduating from Lanzhou University can expect to be assigned to the IMP only through Ministry of Education channels, although in other discussions with

---

*Parts of the delegation visited Lanzhou University on the afternoon of May 30. Earlier that day Henley gave a talk at the University.

†The science departments are Mathematical Mechanics, Physics, Modern Physics, Chemistry, Biology, and Earthquake Geology. The liberal arts departments are Chinese Language and Literature, History, Economics, Philosophy, and Foreign Languages.

Director Yang Chengzhong at IMP we gained the impression that really outstanding Lanzhou students come to his attention, and we believe that he has sufficient influence locally that he is able to recruit the students he wants into the IMP.

We were told that some faculty promotions have taken place in the past year, the first since before the Cultural Revolution. Such promotions are based on accomplishments in research and teaching. Teaching achievements are measured by some subjective evaluation of the candidate's attitude toward teaching and by comments given by other teachers; student comments are given very secondary importance as a holdover from the bitter antagonism that developed during the Cultural Revolution, when students were expected to—and did—critize their teachers. A typical teaching assignment is for six 50-minute lectures per week.

Student numbers were reduced during the Cultural Revolution; prior to 1966, 3,600 students had been enrolled. An estimate was also given that approximately 80 percent of the faculty spent some time at rural labor during this period, but we gathered that the average time so spent was significantly less than was the case for faculty of the universities in Beijing and Shanghai, and very much less than for the Academy institutions located in Beijing. By 1985, Lanzhou University expects to have an undergraduate enrollment of 10,000, with an additional 1,500-2,000 graduate students.

Currently there are 680 graduate students in the university; 180 of these are in the Physics Department and 30 are in the Modern Physics Department. These two departments are quite separate: Physics specializes in high-energy theory, classical and applied physics; Modern Physics primarily works in nuclear and particle theory physics and radiochemistry. There appears to be little communication between the two departments or their members; our meetings with personnel from each of them were completely separate.

In response to a direct question, we learned that what was generally considered the most difficult problem yet to be solved concerns the quality of the teaching staff. Many of them were added during the Cultural Revolution with less-than-normal qualifications; many of the older faculty suffered very serious hardships and deprivation during this period resulting in a major loss of contact with their professional life; and there is a substantial residue of resentment left between those who did and those who did not support the "Gang of Four." The University recognizes that it must provide many of its faculty with remedial opportunities. Some of the least-qualified persons have been removed to other occupations. Several remedial approaches are being tried. Professors and associate professors are given a larger fraction of their time for reseach, together with the best-available personnel and equipment with which to work. Members of other ranks, if they are deemed promising, are also given more research time. The younger teachers are asked to raise the level of their professional knowledge. Some departments hold seminars for them, some teachers take refresher courses, and some are sent to other universities. The youngest associate professor is now 41 years old, reflecting the fact that promotions were eliminated during the Cultural Revolution.

We remain unconvinced that these mechanisms are adequate to the task, although they will undoubtedly help. Research done without adequate background will not, in itself, improve professional qualifications.

Department of Physics

All physics undergraduates take the same basic courses in classical physics, quantum mechanics, mathematics, solid-state physics, and electronics, covering at least 2 years. These 2 years of the program are now in place, and this year 1,132 students took the general physics sequence. They will then spend at least 1 more year in relatively standard second-level physics courses, and in their final fourth year have several options or specialized courses selected from among seven areas. These areas involve both formal teaching and reseach laboratories and involve the following specialties:

1. Theoretical physics, with emphasis on particle physics theory. Courses include quantum statistics, quantum theory, and elementary particle physics.

2. Metal physics: microscopic study of the physical properties of metal and phase transitions in metal. Main courses include metal physics, strength of metals, and methods of metal physics studies. We would probably call this area metallurgy.

3. Magnetism: basic theory of magnetic properties of matter and the production and application of new magnetic materials. Special courses include ferromagnetism, magnetic materials, magnetic measurements, and experiments.

4. Semiconductor physics: semiconductor device physics and research on integrated circuits. Courses include semiconductor physics, semiconductor device physics, integrated circuit theory, and corresponding experiments.

5. Radiophysics: microwave technology and electronic circuit theory.

The Modern Physics Department offers two additional options as follows:

1. Nuclear physics: students in this specialty take basic courses in mathematics, physics and chemistry, nuclear physics, detector techniques, and nuclear electronics. Graduates are expected to have the basic knowledge

to carry out research in nuclear physics and have technical competence in work related to nuclear physics.

2. Radiochemistry: students in this specialty study preparation, separation of isotopes, and applications of radiochemistry. Main courses include inorganic chemistry, analytic chemistry, and nuclear physics. Graduates are expected to do research work in radiochemistry and nuclear engineering and be equipped to teach in schools of higher education.

During the first 3 years the students also take formal courses in political theory, mathematical physics, physical education, and at least one foreign language. We were shown examples of teaching and research laboratories. As elsewhere we were much impressed by the elementary physics laboratory and by the enthusiasm and dedication of the post-Cultural Revolution students.

A description of the Physics Department was given by its Head, Duan Yishi. There are now 140 faculty members, including professors, associate professors, lecturers, and assistants. There are more than 40 assistant teaching personnel; some are graduates from polytechnic schools, some are middle school graduates. Graduate students themselves may teach after they have passed certain exams. In the future, assistants may be research students, since their quality has improved very much since 1977.

There are more than 500 students in the Department and about 140 graduate students (they expect an equilibrium number of 180 graduate students in a few years). There are 30 postgraduate research students and about 20 "refreshers." Most students specialize in theoretical physics; some (we think 6) are studying theoretical biology and quantum chemistry, because they believe that the future looks more promising in these fields than it does in high-energy physics. Duan Yishi and some external experts have lectured in these fields. As elsewhere in Chinese universities, very little research instrumentation survived the Cultural Revolution, if indeed it existed prior to then. And the emphasis currently is definitely on rebuilding the teaching program, with the buildup of research instrumentation having a very much lower priority.

The Laboratory of Metallurgy is used for both teaching and research, mainly in microscopic metallurgy. It is used primarily by third-year students. We saw an array of Chinese microscopes of apparent excellent quality and a microhardness (Brunnel) instrument. The Laboratory is also used for the experimental and theoretical study of corrosion fatigue, as well as metal fracture, and there is also some theoretical work in progress. Some of the research is done in cooperation with local industry and research institutes. Studies on amorphous solids are in progress, and we saw a wide variety of locally prepared calchogenide glasses. The microstructure of alloys is also studied.

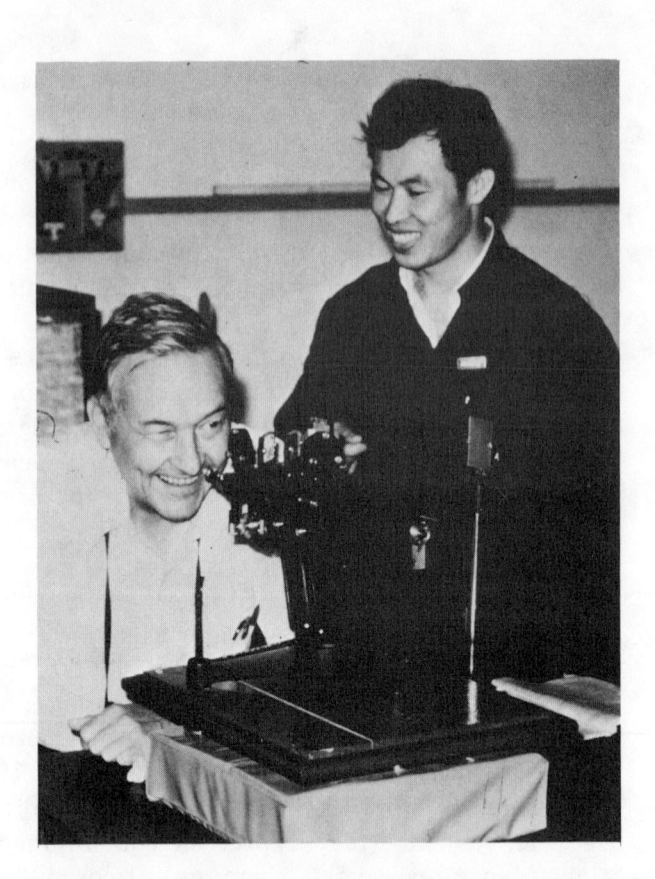

A staff member demonstrates a metallurgical microscope to Stanley Hanna in the Metallurgical Laboratory of Lanzhou University.

The Laboratory of Magnetism is primarily for teaching. There are currently five experiments in place for senior students: power loss in silicon steel sheet, a bridge to measure magnetic properties from 200 to 20 KHz, a high-frequency Q-meter to measure permeability and the tangent of the loss angle, a microwave system to measure wavelength and the standing wave ratio, and a system for measurement of the switching time of a computer memory element. About 60 students per year do these five experiments. There is, in addition to the teaching laboratories, a research laboratory where studies are carried out on microstructure of ferromagnets, permeability of materials, and ferrites under pressure and at high temperatures. Properties of magnetic materials used in magnetic tape and disc recordings are also studied.

The Laboratory for Semiconductors also has five experiments in place that are done by about 30 third-year students per year. They are: magnetic field measurement via the Hall effect, use of a 4-point probe in delineation of sample resistivity, measurement of the lifetime of minority carriers in semiconductors, measurement of the resistivity of an epitaxial layer on silicon with a 3-point probe, and electrical properties of amorphous semiconductors, such as calchogenide compounds, and the effect of impurities and defects in amorphous silicon.

The Applied Microwave Laboratory does applied research for the oil industry to find out whether microwave absorption can be used to measure the water and oil content of a porous rock formation and, in particular, whether the oil-water interface can be located in this fashion. The scanning electron microscope pictures of oil-bearing rock that we were shown were of outstanding quality, but we were told that they had been made in Beijing at an oil research institute. This group also studies small microwave devices.

In the Electronics Section of the Physics Department, emphasis is on automatic controls. In the Theoretical Physics Section they have recently concentrated on gauge field theory, relativity, conservation of topological currents, and magnetic monopoles. Some of this work was stimulated by C. N. Yang's visit in 1977.

Department of Modern Physics

We received a second rather formal introduction to this Department from Wang Yungchang, who is one of its associate professors.

This Department was established in 1958 and has a faculty of 62. Of this number, 12 are in nuclear or particle theory, 16 are in experimental nuclear physics, 10 in electronics, 13 in accelerator building, and 13 in radiochemistry. They have more than 100 undergraduates, most of whom are studying nuclear physics.

It became very clear during our visit that there is almost no connection between this Department and the Physics Department; however, some faculty in both departments specialize in elementary particle theory, and the first-year physics courses are taught jointly. Beyond this the departments

The 300-kV Cockcroft-Walton neutron generator in the Physics Department of Lanzhou University. The high-voltage terminal is here shown opened to give access to the radiofrequency ion source and other terminal components. The voltage distribution system for the accelerating tube is shown to the left of the open terminal and to the right of the closed cabinet, which contains pumping systems and power supplies. The beam tube passes out of this figure to the left.

NUCLEAR SCIENCE IN CHINA

Liu Zhaoyuan and his colleagues in the Physics Department of Lanzhou University describe the target assembly of the 300-kV neutron generator to Bernard Harvey and Allan Bromley.

appear to have no interaction and are located on adjoining but different campuses of the University.

The theoretical group in this Department, headed by Gong Xuehui (Associate Professor), teaches and does research in hadron structure, internal symmetries, inclusive reactions, collective motion in nuclei, heavy ion reactions, and preequilibrium processes in nuclear reactions.

The groups in experimental nuclear physics, headed by Liu Zhaoyuan (Lecturer), and those in accelerator design and electronics have recently completed a 300-KV neutron generator. It appears to be a highly professional piece of work that was built for their own use, not as an industrial prototype. It was unique among all the Chinese instrumentation that we saw in having benefited from modern industrial-level packaging with attractive colors, external sheet metal housing of components, etc. It could easily have been produced by any contemporary U.S. instrumentation industry as far as external appearance was conceived. It uses an RF source, is in a testing stage, and has, during the past year, only accelerated a proton beam. It is to produce $1-2 \times 10^{11}$ neutrons/s using a 1.5-3.0 mA swept deuteron beam on a tritiated titanium target. It has just been moved to its present location in a new building where it was expected to start operation about a week following our visit. We were baffled, however, by the fact that this excellent instrument, designed for work with 14-MeV neutrons, had been installed in a very small room with enormously thick concrete walls. Unless the beam can be taken out of this vault for use in a much more lightly constructed target area, it will be almost impossible to do experimental work because of the neutrons backscattered from the walls.

Before the Cultural Revolution, we were told, the Experimental Nuclear Physics Department had measured angular distributions for neutron elastic scattering as well as cross sections for (n,p) reactions, both at 14 MeV. During the Cultural Revolution, however, we were told that only applied work such as using neutrons to measure the moisture content of soil

Visits to Educational Institutions

was permitted. The group is now planning to study the spectra and angular distribution from (n,α) reactions on a variety of targets.

The Modern Physics Department also teaches nuclear physics via student experiments on radiation detection and electronics. The electronics group has built four 400-channel pulse height analyzers partially of their own design but bearing substantial resemblance to the French Intertechnique units.

The Radiochemistry Department, headed by Qiu Ling (Associate Professor), showed us a system that is designed for separation of rare earth elements. It uses a high-pressure ion exchange column technique; the one we saw cannot, lacking any shielding, handle radioactive material. We were told that their methods are similar to those in use at our Savannah River Plant. We were told that the techniques developed here would be used in Beijing and elsewhere; we suspect that this activity was stimulated by—and remains

Lanzhou, the eastern terminus of the ancient silk route, is in a very heavily eroded section of the Chinese Northwest. This photograph is taken from the road leading from the airport to the city, a distance of some 30 miles required inasmuch as no adequate flat area is found closer to the city. This photograph is representative of many features of the topography of the area. The hills in the background are typical of the eroded landscape of the area, and it is noteworthy that there is no forest cover at all.

NUCLEAR SCIENCE IN CHINA

A photograph taken from the CAAC airliner en route from Lanzhou to Shanghai showing the heavily eroded terrain and the remarkable extent to which the Chinese have converted the valleys to agricultural cultivation. A small tributary of the Yellow River flows from the middle left to the lower right providing irrigation water for the agriculture in this valley, and a small settlement appears in the lower foreground.

part of—the Chinese nuclear weapons program and is designed for use on the waste remaining after reprocessing of spent nuclear fuel elements.

In another laboratory in this Department, we were shown glass columns (1-cm dia.) capable of withstanding a pressure of 30 kg/cm^2. They were filled with a Chinese-made Dowex-50 resin (40-60 μ particle size). They are used for visual studies of the rate of band motion and general experiments in separation science.

Unfortunately, because of lack of time the delegation had to cut short its visit with more than a dozen laboratories remaining on our visit schedule.

FUDAN UNIVERSITY*

The delegation was greeted by Vice President Xie Xide, who received her Ph.D. from MIT (working with Philip Morse at the same time as did

A park scene in Lanzhou showing two members of one of the far-western minority groups together with Lanzhou children.

Kerman). She also is Director of the University's Institute of Modern Physics. She indicated that she had suffered substantial hardships—physical as well as personal—during the Cultural Revolution but clearly had retained her enthusiasm, drive, and leadership abilities despite this.

Fudan is a comprehensive university founded in 1905, which has departments in both liberal arts and sciences.[†] In addition, the University has research institutes in mathematics, genetics, modern physics, electric light sources, and world economics.

At the present time there are 3,800 undergraduates in three classes of a 4-year program; by this fall a new class will have been admitted, giving a total of about 6,000. It is expected that this number will rise to 12,000 by the mid-1980's, but more dormitory space will be needed since all students live on the campus. (The campus is far from the center of Shanghai.) The 200 graduate students are divided equally between liberal arts and science.

---

*The entire delegation visited Fudan University on the afternoon of June 4.
†The seven departments of humanities and social sciences are Chinese Language, Foreign Languages, Philosophy, History, International Politics, and Political Economics. In the sciences there are departments of Mathematics, Biology, Physics, Chemistry, Computer Science, and Nuclear Physics.

The teaching staff totals more than 2,000, but only about 200 are professors or associate professors. Although there were no promotions during the Cultural Revolution, some 30 have been made recently and more are planned. There is no definite ratio of professorships to associate professorships; however, a promotion to the rank of professor must be approved by the Ministry of Education. (One should note, however, that all teaching positions are permanent.)

There was an inescapable discussion of the Cultural Revolution and its impact on the program of the University. At Fudan it was clearly stated that during this period practical (applied) work was stressed at the expense of both basic research and teaching. The projects initiated, however, were definitely worthwhile, but the exclusion of research and the teaching of fundamentals caused a generation of students to be very ill-prepared for advanced work. We were told that there was no way that these students could be recovered and that apart from rare exceptions they would end up in other occupations. Many of the persons of worker or peasant background added to the University staff during the Cultural Revolution have now been transferred to other occupations more suited to their backgrounds and capabilities; for those with potential, however, a very real salvage and training program is under way.

The University plans to create eight new research institutes for low-temperature physics, optical properties of solids, surface physics, superconductivity, semiconductors, lasers, and theory. The support for both new and existing programs comes primarily from the Ministry of Education, but some funding also comes from local government agencies.

Department of Physics and Institute of Modern Physics

The Department has six specialties: physics, semiconductors, radioelectronics, laser physics, electron physics, and gas discharge physics. It also has five identified teaching and research groups: basic physics, theoretical physics, radio physics, general physics laboratory, and intermediate physics laboratory.

The size of faculty in this area is 400 and includes 5 full professors, 11 associate professors, and 144 instructors. A listing of the professors appears in Appendix D.

Teaching In their first 3 years students of all specialities follow the same basic curriculum: politics, physical education, foreign languages, advanced mathematics, mathematical physics, general physics (mechanics, thermodynamics and molecular physics, electromagnetism, light and atomic physics), theoretical mechanics, electrodynamics, statistical mechanics, quantum mechanics, solid-state physics, electronic circuit fundamentals, etc.

In their fourth year students take elective courses depending on specialties. Examples of these are: radioelectronics specialty: networks and systems, signal detection, microwave network, microcircuit, etc.; semiconductor specialty: semiconductor physics, principles of transistors; semiconducting materials and their applications, semiconductor experiments, principles of computers, fundamentals of integrated circuits, etc.; and physics specialty: fundamental particles physics, statistical physics, superconductivity, surface physics, etc.

Scientific Research The University's Institute of Modern Physics has eight research groups: surface physics, semiconductor physics, theoretical physics, low temperature and superconductivity, laser physics, vacuum technology, solid-state optics, low-energy nuclear physics.

The Department of Physics has three research groups: large-scale integrated circuits, biomedical engineering, and microwaves. Areas of research include: superconductivity theory, fundamental particle theory, surface physics, the relation between semiconductor material and components, semiconductor integrated circuits, integrated circuits in designing of computer peripherals, circuit and system engineering, microwave integrated circuits and biometrical engineering, nonlinear laser spectroscopy, holography and light signal processes, laser physics, ultra-high vacuum, electron optics, and electron beam components.

In recent years we were told that they have obtained good results in the following areas of research: impurities and defects in silicon, bipolar large-scale intergrated circuits, high-speed analog-to-digital and digital-to-analog converters, multihead ultrasonic imaging, and multifunction heart pacemakers.

*Department of Nuclear Science (Atomic Energy)**

The Department has two specialties: nuclear physics and radiochemistry. The total size of the staff is 115, which includes 1 full professor, 3 associate professors, and 49 instructors. The names of the professors are included in Appendix D.

Teaching The curriculum for the nuclear physics specialty includes courses in politics, foreign languages, physical education, advanced mathematics, mechanics, molecular physics, electromagnetics, optics, atomic physics, mathematical physics, quantum mechanics, radio physics and experiments, general physics and intermediate physics experiments, nuclear physics, ex-

---

*The literal translation of the departmental name is "atomic energy" (he-neng), but the English speaking staff prefer to use "nuclear science"—a more apt description.

perimental methods of nuclear physics, nuclear electronics, nuclear physics experiments, nuclear electronics experiments. Elective courses include nuclear theory, nuclear physics experiments, selected topics, neutron physics, accelerator nuclear instrumentation, quantum field theory, programming language.

The curriculum in the radiochemistry specialty includes courses in politics, foreign languages, physical education, advanced mathematics, general chemistry, physical chemistry, analytic chemistry, organic chemistry, chemical engineering preparation, electronics, instrument analysis, nuclear electronics, introduction to nuclear theory, nuclear fuel chemistry, radiochemistry, radiochemistry experiments, radioactivity, and protection.

Scientific Research The Department has a low-energy nuclear physics group (which also belongs to the University's Institute of Modern Physics) and a laser chemistry group (being planned).

Topics of scientific research include neutron physics, calculation of interaction cross section for scattering protons or neutrons from deuterons, proton-induced fluorescence analysis and proton microprobe, beam-foil

Second-year undergraduate students in a Fudan University teaching laboratory on heat and thermodynamics.

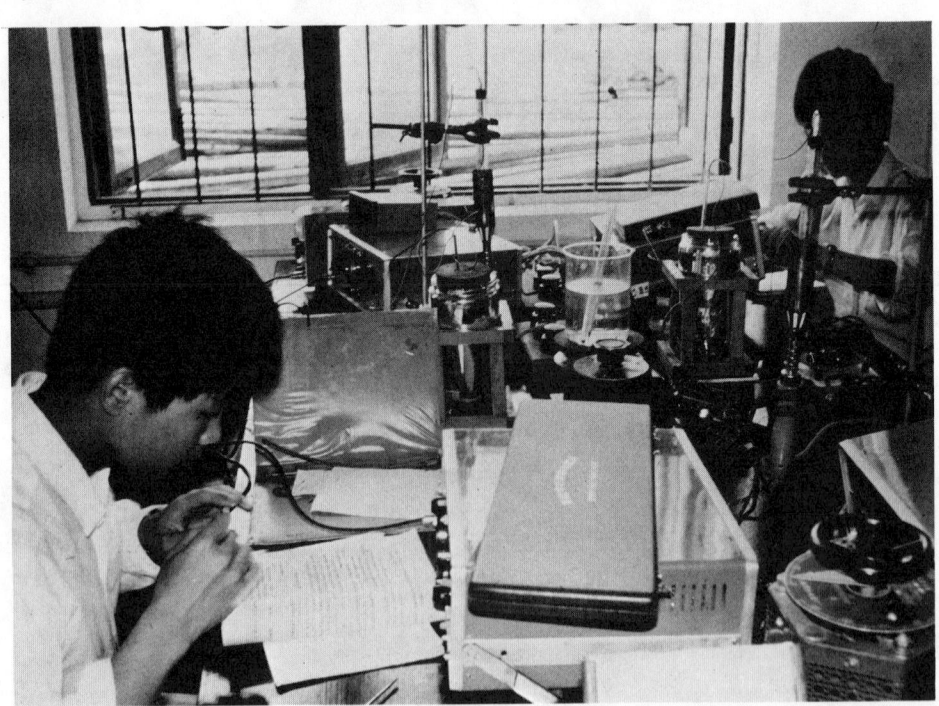

Visits to Educational Institutions

First-year undergraduate students at Fudan University making measurements on vibrating strings. Much of the instrumentation shown was constructed within Fudan University.

spectroscopy, backscattering and channeling, charged particle blocking, radioactive isotope separation, actinides and their laser chemistry and photo chemistry, industrial application of radioactive isotopes, medical radioactive isotopes, laser separation of isotopes.

Following this detailed introduction, we toured the facilities. We saw first-year physics laboratories in general physics that were quite well-equipped, even in comparison with some of the best universities in the United States. In one laboratory, the students were performing mechanics experiments: velocity of sound, resonances of a tuning fork, and moments of inertia. In another laboratory, we saw experiments on specific heats, thermal conductivity, and the thermocouple. Inasmuch as all laboratory equipment had been removed during the Cultural Revolution, Fudan had the opportunity—indeed the necessity—to start afresh, and the teaching instrumentation now assembled for the first 2 years clearly indicates that they have taken full advantage of this opportunity. We were told that funding for purchase of such equipment made in China was readily available, but that hard currency required for foreign purchases was not available at all. Much of the laboratory equipment had been produced in Fudan's own shops.

Until very recently Fudan had three departments in physics—Physics, Nuclear Physics, and Optics. There has been an obvious desire to merge these, and during the past year Physics and Optics have merged. The problem involved in merging Nuclear Physics into this combined department—not unknown in the U.S.!—is that the Chemistry Department does not recognize the nuclear chemists now in the Nuclear Physics Department as real chemists and is not prepared to accept them into its ranks, thus making it very difficult for the physicists to desert them and move into the new combined department. No obvious resolution of this impasse appears in view. Yang Fujia, an active, aggressive, young nuclear physicist, well known in the nuclear science community outside of China, remains as Head of the Nuclear Physics Department.

The next part of our tour took us to an exhibit of the research institute, which produces prototypes of new gas discharge light sources. We were told that this institute had evolved from the observation, in the early 1950's, that it was impossible to import specialized projector and other lamps into China, and one of the Fudan faculty took up the challenge of developing an indigenous production. China's lighting industry, we were told, had been a spin-off from this activity. Rather outstanding progress has been made. We were shown a variety of interesting products: miners' lamps, a 5-MHz RF-powered lamp that is intended as a simple replacement for screw-in incandescents and boasts an output of 40 lumens per watt, large Xe arc lamps (200 kW!), fluorescent tubes, high-power lamps for projectors and monochromators, and a variety of other types.

Our last stop at Fudan University was in the Department of Nuclear Physics. They have a 2.5-MV Van de Graaff accelerator that they designed and constructed together with the Vanguard factory in Shanghai during the 1959-1965 period. They have begun a project to upgrade this machine to 4.5 MV, which is estimated to cost 300,000 (~ $200,000 U.S.) yuan and which is supposed to be finished by the end of this year. Here again Vanguard will play a central role. (They expect that the period between the end of 2.5-MV operation and the completion of this project is to be 4 months, which seems optimistic.)

The present machine has a magnetic analyzer that allows the beam to be sent into two target rooms. The first is used for a student-oriented program in neutron physics. The students do three experiments: a neutron-alpha particle coincidence in $t\,(d,n)\,\alpha$; the excitation curve for protons incident on a LiF target; and the total cross section for neutrons on silicon. This target area is also used for experiments in materials analysis using proton-induced X-rays (PIXE).

In the other target room are three beam lines for beam-foil spectroscopy, backscattering or channeling, and pulsed beam (microsecond resolution) experiments on solids.

The quality of the equipment is reasonable, though they are limited to a single 400-channel Intertechnique pulse height analyzer. We were told, however, that $80,000 worth of Canberra modules and a PDP 11/34 computer had been ordered and would arrive in the fall of 1979.

Research presentations (using an overhead projector brought to Fudan by Professor Georges Temmer of Rutgers University a few years ago) were limited to projects in backscattering and channeling. The backscattering technique is being applied to measuring: film thicknesses, the compositions of semiconductor materials such as Si(As) or magnetic bubble materials, chlorine in SiO_2, and archaeological relics (an ancient Chinese sword has gained them substantial publicity in this respect). Channeling has been used to observe the effects of laser annealing and the annealing properties as As implanted into Si crystals.

Proton-induced X-ray analysis is being used for problems in Chinese archaeology and medicine. There is also a program in atomic polarization using beam-foil techniques. The present program is one-half to two-thirds in solid-state research, and it is expected that this fraction will increase. There are no plans for specifically nuclear physics research except as part of the teaching program.

Plans for future development include: a proton microbeam, proton-induced Auger analysis, an ultra-high vacuum chamber (10^{-12} Torr) for surface analysis, and a beam line for molecular ion experiments. (The local grasp of ultra-high vacuum techniques is, as yet, primitive.)

Our overall impression of this group is that they have chosen a research program that is well matched to their facility and to the interests of local industry. They seem to be making good progress on their projects and have established solid contact with groups outside the PRC who are engaged in similar work.

At the conclusion of our tour, we were given an attractive booklet that shows color pictures of the campus, facilities, and faculty. It is quite well done; since it is written in both Chinese and English, one might guess that it was aimed at foreign students as well as those in China. At the time of our visit, 28 such foreign students, including one from the United States sponsored by the CSCPRC, were in residence at Fudan University.

ZHEJIANG UNIVERSITY*

Before 1949 Zhejiang University, which was founded in 1897, was a comprehensive one with schools of liberal arts, sciences, engineering, agriculture,

*The entire delegation visited Zhejiang University on the afternoon of June 6.

medicine, law, and teacher training. In the reorganization that followed the 1949 Revolution, the campus was moved to its present site (with a branch campus near the Liu Ho Pagoda on the Zhejiang River) and was transformed into a school of science and engineering. At present it has 5 departments in the natural sciences (Mathematics, Physics, Chemistry, Mechanics, and Geology) and 10 in engineering (Mechanical, Electrical, Chemical, Civil, Radio, Thermal, Optical Instruments, Scientific Instruments, Materials Science, and Computer Science). In addition, it has four research institutes (Optical Instruments, Chemical Engineering, Electrical Engineering, and Materials Science) and a special program in administration. The University also operates six shops that both provide practical experience for the engineering students and produce mechanical and optical devices for sale and internal use.

Until 1978 Zhejiang University was administered jointly by the Ministry of Education (MOE) and the Hangzhou municipal government. Now, however, the Chinese Academy of Sciences (CAS) has taken over the administration of the University (the CAS administers only four universities all together), and Qian Sanqiang, one of the vice presidents of the CAS, is also President of Zhejiang University. In discussions with Professor Qian, we learned, however, that in this area the Chinese system resembles the British in that the presidency is largely honorary and the senior Vice President, Yang Shilin, actually runs the University. The current program involves collaboration with other institutes and industries, as well as in national defense.

There are 1,819 teaching and research faculty (including 121 professors and associate professors and 700 lecturers), 438 technicians, and 942 skilled workers (the latter primarily in the shops) at Zhejiang University. As a result of the Cultural Revolution, the younger faculty members are substantially less well-trained than are their older colleagues. There were, however, a few promotions last year. Promotion to the rank of associate professor is based on accomplishments in research and teaching skill and requires the approval of the CAS. Proposals for promotion are put forward by the departments and discussed by a University-wide academic appointment committee. (The committee is appointed on the basis of suggestions by the various departments and approved by the Vice President of the University. This was the only example of such a committee that we encountered in China.)

There are currently four visiting scholars from Zhejiang University in Germany and one in the United States; four more are preparing to go to the University of Wisconsin in the near future. Most of these are drawn from the faculty, but a few graduate students are included. The University's current plan is to send abroad 25 faculty and 5 graduate students who work in mathematics, mechanical engineering, and optical instrument design. (The

Visits to Educational Institutions

Buildings One and Two of Zhejiang University.

Zhejiang University faculty already has 20 members with advanced degrees from MIT and Caltech, and there are now about 500 Zhejiang graduates in the United States—more than from any other Chinese university.)

Before the Cultural Revolution, Zhejiang University had 7,000 students in a 5-year program. This number decreased significantly in the early 1970's, but has now been brought up to 4,996 (including 167 graduate students) and is expected to reach 7,000 by the fall of 1979. As at all other Chinese universities, students are currently present in only the first 2 years of the 4-year undergraduate program. In the fall of 1979, those completing the second year of their 4-year curriculum in June will move into their third-year program. By 1985 Zhejiang University plans to reach an enrollment of 10,000. (The rate of growth may be controlled by the need for more dormitories—virtually all students and faculty live on the campus.)

The minimum grade on the national college entrance examination that was accepted for admission during the past year at Zhejiang University was 340. However, we learned that there is a quota for each province of the PRC that is based on exam performance in past years; thus, if the students of a given province have a performance that is especially good, the grade needed to gain admission from that province may be raised; e.g., Fujian Province students last year did well, so a minimum grade of 400 was required of them this year. Although the University charges no tuition, living expense support is based on student need. Students who have already worked for 5 years elsewhere are allowed to retain their salaries; students with less prior work experience get a basic living expense subsidy from the government; students whose parents have sufficiently high salaries (not specified) are expected to be supported entirely by their parents. The relative populations of male and female students are said to be about equal.

The academic year is divided into two semesters: the first is February to July, and the second is September to January. This calendar varies slightly throughout the PRC because of variations in climate. For example, in Hangzhou the summers are very hot, so the summer vacation is lengthened at the expense of the winter one. The opposite is true in Beijing or Haerbin. Because of the excessive summer heat, most students prefer to go home or to the countryside to work, rather than stay in the Hangzhou area.

The first 3 years of the undergraduate curriculum consist of a basic program that includes general physics, chemistry, theoretical mechanics, quantum mechanics, electrodynamics, and statistical mechanics. During the senior year the courses are elective and depend on the specialty chosen by the student. (These specialized courses are somewhat vague so far, because only the first two classes are under way, and the junior and senior year programs are still being evolved.)

We saw several undergraduate physics laboratories where the students were doing experiments in mechanics (air troughs), electricity and magnetism (inductance of a coil and the potentiometer), and optics (Newton's rings). The equipment was a combination of old but serviceable and very new; in general, the laboratories were comparable to those in some of the best universities in the United States. (The laboratory courses are common to all students at Zhejiang University, so they teach about 2,000 students per year.)

We saw no research labs on our tour and were told that recovery in the research program is slow except where there is collaboration with other institutes or industry. In this regard, their plans for future development stress interdisciplinary work (e.g., energy research and computer aided design) that will involve people from several departments working on a general problem. Here again the emphasis has been on rebuilding the teaching program at the expense of any such rebuilding of the University's research programs.

The campus looks somewhat like that at UCLA. There were a number of buildings under construction, including a new library. Late in the afternoon we saw many students engaged in sports (basketball, volleyball, track); there is apparently a University requirement that the students spend several hours a day in athletic activity. One afternoon a week the students must take part in political studies—this was also true for the faculty and workers and is apparently a countrywide and rigid requirement, except that in special cases one evening per week can be substituted for the half-day.

On our tour we saw two of the University's production shops. The first was for the construction of lenses, mirrors, and other optical components. There were extensive facilities for grinding and polishing, but it did not seem that a large fraction of the intrinsic capacity for production was being used—on mentioning this we were told that our visit coincided with the political-discussion afternoon for all the workers in this shop. We were told that all the grinding and polishing machines were built on campus. The vacuum coating equipment for making antireflection dichroic and other mirror coatings was in good condition and was being used actively. There were three evaporator systems that were diffusion-pumped—no LN_2 traps or even chilled baffles were in evidence. (The optical products made thus far were used in the laboratory teaching program; it was not clear what fraction had been—or would be—produced for outside orders. Clearly Zhejiang teaching laboratories had first priority.

We then were taken to a large machine shop. The shop contained about 50 geared lathes ($\sim 12''$-diameter capacity), about half a dozen large lathes, perhaps a dozen light vertical mills, and a half dozen planers of various sizes. There were about a dozen large-gear cutting machines. We saw about half the total work force, i.e., about 70 of 130. On the floor in various stages of assembly were 20 more of the geared lathes, about 10 watch-gear cutting machines, and perhaps 15 small ordinary-gear cutting machines. In all, we were told, about 100 machines are completed every year; some are used for improving shop facilities, while the remainder are "sold" and the income is used by the University to purchase other equipment. (The watch-gear cutters are priced at 50,000 [$\sim$\$33,000 U.S.] yuan; the small-gear grinding machines cost 4,000 [$\sim$\$2,600 U.S.] yuan.) They have campus facilities for casting; sheet metal parts seem to be made by welding—not forming. The machines produced appear to be of international commercial quality; we did not see any in operation other than the lathes. Work is only now beginning at Zhejiang on the development of automatic, computer-controlled machine tools, although we were told that some were in production in various machine tool factories elsewhere in China. Safety precautions were almost nonexistent; no workers wore safety glasses, and many operators of large machine tools were wearing standard canvas sandals.

The purposes served by the shops shown to us, we were told, were student exposure to practical problems and the generation of extra money through product sales. We do not know what fraction of the shop workers were students, but it is not 100 percent. In response to our questions, we were told that student and nonstudent machine operators work harmoniously together.

Many of the new designs are produced by a collaboration of faculty and shop personnel, and there is obviously excellent "market" analysis. The Zhejiang faculty seem very much aware of the priorities and needs of their external "customers"; apparently they have substantial autonomy in deciding what products to build and how to build them.

From our exposure to its teaching laboratories and shops wherein its students gain hands-on experience, we can only conclude that on graduation, 2 years hence, the Zhejiang student would provide formidable competition for the graduates of even the best U.S. universities.

At the conclusion of our tour, we were given copies of a handsomely produced booklet—in color and with both Chinese and English captions for the illustrations, as well as a parallel text describing Zhejiang University. We were told that it had been prepared as part of the program to attract the best students from throughout China to Zhejiang.

6
Visits to Research Institutes

INSTITUTE OF PHYSICS (BEIJING)*

The Institute of Physics (IOP) of the Chinese Academy of Sciences was established in 1950 at the time of the amalgamation of the Beijing Academy and the former Academia Sinica. It was originally called the Institute of Applied Physics, but the name was changed to the present more general one in 1958 at the same time that the then Institute of Modern Physics was renamed the Institute of Atomic Energy. The Institute of Acoustics was incorporated into the Institute of Physics in 1967, while former departments of the Institute have been spun off into institutes in their own right in such fields as semiconductors and plasma physics.

The Director, Shih Ruwei, received an M.S. degree from the University of Illinois in 1931 and a Ph.D. from Yale in 1934; the Deputy Director, Lu Xueshan, received his Ph.D. from the University of Manchester.

Its departments include: Crystallography, High-Temperature and High-Pressure Physics, Low-Temperature Physics, Acoustics, Magnetic Resonance, Magnetism, and Statistical Theory. It maintains laboratories in the fields of lasers, chemical analysis, crystallography, electronics, high-pressure physics, low-temperature physics, magnetism, optics, physics of metals, ultrasonics, solid-state physics, theoretical physics, and spectroscopy.

The total staff numbers roughly 1,000, of whom 307 are female; of this total staff there are 300 scientists, 300 "graduate students," and 400 support personnel. The annual budget is approximately 6 million yuan.

*Half the delegation (Bromley, Kuo, Middleton, Tombrello, and Zucker) visited the Institute during the afternoon of May 22. Hanna and Zucker each spent half a day subsequently lecturing and holding discussions at the Institute.

Major instrumentation at the Institute includes: a Tokamak device completed in July 1974; three small-scale tabletop plasma devices designed and built in the Institute; a theta pinch device; a plasma focus device; and a laser focus device, as well as diagnostic equipment designed in the Institute. Laboratories were well-equipped with Chinese-made glass Dewars, evaporators, X-ray recorders, oscilloscopes, and East German microscopes. A French ion microprobe will be used for more detailed study of magnetic films. Other equipment included a 20 l/h helium liquifier, a three-dimensional dynamic spectrograph built in cooperation with the Tianjin "Red Lantern" Radio Factory, a vibrating magnetometer, a superconducting gravity meter for earthquake detection, and a laser interferometer built since the Cultural Revolution.

In our discussion with the Vice Director, we learned that the Institute hopes to add programs in the following topics: surface studies, superconducting materials, energy spectra of condensed matter, laser research, plasma physics, gravitational radiation (Weber bar), Mössbauer effect, neutron diffraction studies (to be carried out at the Institute of Atomic Energy), implanation studies (to be carried out at Beijing Normal University), channeling measurements, positron annihilation studies, and further Mössbauer studies (the latter three are already being carried out at the High-Energy Institute). It was clear from discussion and touring the Institute that many of these programs have not been started as yet, some are just beginning, and in a few cases some research is actually in progress. While a significant amount of equipment and instrumentation was ordered and obtained during the Cultural Revolution, it appears clear that no serious research started until after 1977.

In 1975 the NMR group ordered a standard Bruker 100-MHz NMR apparatus from West Germany, but research with this equipment is only now beginning 4 years later; it appears to be equipped with a standard readout system. At present the NMR of ^{23}Na is being used as a probe in the study of NaCl, which has cubic structure. Members of the Institute staff are carrying out relaxation studies with various orientations of the applied magnetic field (about 2.1 Tesla) relative to the crystal field axis. As yet no measurements at various temperatures have been made, although the researchers have the capability of making measurements between 150 and 450 K. A doublet structure has been found in the basic NMR response, which they were interested in studying further.

Altogether, there are six people in the group. One is now at Nottingham, one at Stanford, and one will go to Germany (this person is interested chiefly in electronics). The group has no students as yet (and has not had any for the past 10 years), but it would like to have some in the future. For future work it has a He Dewar, also obtained from Bruker, which can go down to 3.8 K but it cannot be adapted for use with the NMR apparatus.

There are no present plans to go to lower temperatures. The group would very much like to obtain a superconducting magnet and has been in touch with Bruker (apparently the supplier of such magnets through Oxford Instruments) concerning possible purchase. Currently the group is assembling as much information as possible on competing suppliers of superconducting magnets before it decides on which one to buy. It bears noting that when we came into the NMR laboratory the group leader himself was taking data, and we were shown an accumulation of data on the NaCl problem.

Mössbauer Group

The Mössbauer group consists of three people and is led by Guang Meizhen. A Mössbauer drive had been assembled, but it was lying on a table and obviously was not in operation. On inspection, it seemed to have a good suspension and looked like a copy of a standard Kankaleit drive. A complete El scint system has been ordered and should arrive in a month; we were told that everything was ordered except a superconducting magnet that they seem to feel to be an important part of a Mössbauer program. There was no discussion of plans for future research; in fact, it seemed clear that the group would welcome whatever help it could get in planning such a program. In discussions following Hanna's lecture, it was brought out that Mössbauer data have been obtained at the High-Energy Institute, but lack of a suitable computer precludes proven analysis of these data. The group was aware of the standard analysis techniques but apparently had not reached the point of programming even the most simple analysis for a computer. In consequence, it had no appreciation of the rather large computer capability required for even routine analysis of Mössbauer spectra.

Plasma Group

The plasma group was started in 1973 with five staff members, two of them holding advanced degrees from institutions in the Soviet Union. There are currently three programs: a Tokamak project, a laser target program, and a linear theta pinch program.

The Tokamak program was begun in 1973, and construction was completed in 1974; since 1974 more than 2,000 discharges have been studied. The Tokamak design parameters are: major radius, 45 cm; minor radius, 10 cm; maximum toroidal field, 2 TG; maximum current, 30 kA; flux, ~ 0.3 V-s; vertical field, ~ 100 G. The Tokamak has copper bars bent in toroidal direction, brazed together at various points; its vacuum chamber is made of sections of bellows welded together, having a total resistance of $10 > m\Omega$. Pre-ionization is induced by a 50-kV, 3-μF pulse transformer at filling pressure of $\sim 10^{-4}$ mTorr. Without water cooling, the toroidal field pulse can be repeated every 30 s at 0.8 T or every 5 min at 1.7 T.

There are two port sections, diametrically opposite to each other in the toroidal direction. One section is used for pumping to maintain vacuum; the effective pumping rate is 100 liter/s. Background pressure is 10^{-7} Torr. In addition, there are three ports used for pre-ionization, magnetic-probe measurements, and photo-diode measurement of general discharge characteristics, respectively. Particle confinement time is estimated to be ~ 30 ms, and the discharge $q \cong 3$ to 4. After 1,000 initial cleaning-up pulses, it was found that the discharge current duration lengthened. Plasma resistance is measured to be about 0.5 mΩ. Negative voltage spikes have been observed. Most of the instrumentation, including 200-MHz oscilloscopes and cameras using conventional film, is made in China.

Experimental work on the laser target program was begun in 1973 with a staff of 10; construction of the laser system was completed in 1974. The glass laser system can deliver 36 J of light energy in a 6-ns pulse. The storage bank capacity is 10^6 J, and the system uses six glass rod amplifiers, two Faraday isolators with lead-flint glass, and piles of glass plates at the Brewster angle for polarizers. The beam diameter at the final amplifier stages of 60-cm length is 5 cm. Polishing of all optical elements is done in the Institute. No attempt is made to achieve either spatial or temporal mode control. The system output is focused onto LiD or CH_2 targets of 1-mm diameter. Production of X-rays from plasmas with temperatures or about 300 eV has been observed. Safety precautions are minimal by United States standards.

Construction of the 100-kJ linear theta pinch device was initiated during the Cultural Revolution and was completed in 1969. Measurements include those on neutron emission, streak photography, magnetic probing, soft X-rays, and use of a ruby laser end-on interferometer. The streak photographs have been obtained with a rotating mirror camera, capable of 10^3 rev/s. Magnetic probe coils are wound from 0.07-mm wire and typically have 20 to 50 turns and an outside diameter of 2 mm; they are then inserted in glass or quartz tubes of 3 mm diameter. The neutron count, averaging 10^5/ pulse, is obtained with plastic scintillators and the electron temperature is estimated to be 300 eV. A ruby-laser, 90°-scattering experiment is in the planning stage.

A ruby-laser illuminated interferometer used in the theta pinch experiment reportedly gives good end-on interferograms; the laser pulse duration (~40 ns) determines the temporal resolution, which appears to be sufficient to resolve the entire pinch motion except during the peak implosion phase when velocities reach ~10^7 cm/s. Spatial resolution is estimated to be about 100 μm.

The major theta pinch experiment conclusions are that with bias field the plasma is stable, and both peak density and peak neutron emission occur prior to maximum compression.

The Associate Director, Liu Jiarui, who has visited both Frascati and Munich, seemed to be quite aware of the limitations of the program and indicated that its goal was that of making basic measurements on plasmas, rather than competing in further developments directed toward fusion power generation. The Tokamak now operates at 20 kG in the toroidal ring; the plasma current has recently reached 50 kA out of an expected maximum of 100 kA. Electron temperatures up to 300 eV have been achieved, but no plasma density measurements have yet been made. A microwave interferometer is being constructed but is not yet ready.

The present emphasis is on measuring the output of neutral atoms escaping from the Tokamak. A system providing charge exchange in a gas cell, followed by energy analysis, is being built up and was being worked on when we visited the laboratory. The hope is to measure the plasma temperature by optical spectroscopy; it appears unlikely that a UV spectrometer will be available for this purpose. A quadrupole mass spectrometer has been built to aid in the analysis of particles escaping from the plasma.

The magnetic system of the Tokamak was built at the Institute of Electrical Engineering in Beijing and all other parts of the facility at the Institute of Physics. Since completion in 1974, only simple experiments have been carried out: vacuum tests, the effects of strong fields on the plasmas, etc.; at present diagnostics for studying the plasma are being established to permit further measurement of plasma properties. We were shown a high β belt apparatus with a pinch toroid operating with a 15-kG field at a level of 2.5 MJ. It is hoped that this system will be operational by the end of 1979. The goal here also is that of making measurements in basic plasma physics. Altogether, there are now 100 people in the Institute's plasma physics group.

The Institute has a small theory group with 10 physicists and theoretical workers from other departments. The major areas of activity are relativity, quantum theory, Josephson function theory, spin wave modes in solids, relativistic moving medium electrodynamics, gauge theories of gravitation, optical information processing, crystal growth, increase of neutron scattering under applied static electric fields, and scaling laws for magnetic phase transitions. We heard no details concerning any of these activities, but we suspect that the available theorists must be very thinly spread over this broad list of topics.

INSTITUTE OF THEORETICAL PHYSICS (BEIJING)*

The Institute of Theoretical Physics (ITP) was founded in May 1978 as an interdisciplinary theoretical effort to complement the more specialized

---

*The Institute was visited by Hanna, Harvey, Henley, and Kerman on May 22.

theory groups of the other CAS institutes and to promote contact between disciplines. At present the Institute is housed in six small rooms on the top floor of the Zoology Institute, with one of the rooms functioning as a small library. The Director, Peng Huanwu, could not be present during our visit, but the Deputy Director, He Zuoxiu, told us that they hope to obtain a new building in the not too distant future.

Altogether there are 27 members of the Institute, many or most of whom have some other professional affiliation, such as with Beijing University or with the Institute of High-Energy Physics. They work in 10 different areas as follows: theoretical physics, particles and fields, gravitation, astrophysics, mechanics, mathematics, numerical mathematics, statistical physics, computational physics, and nuclear theory.

The nuclear theory group does not include anyone working on intermediate energy problems, because there is a relatively large group in this area at the Institute of High-Energy Physics. As pointed out above, the basic function of the Institute is the promotion of contact and collaboration among theorists. The members publish their work in *Acta Physica Sinica* and in a new journal entitled *Chinese High Energy and Nuclear Physics*, of which Yang Chengzhong, Director of the Institute of Modern Physics in Lanzhou, is the coeditor responsible for the nuclear physics content. Most of the work is published in Chinese, although there is an English edition of *Scientia Sinica*. Almost all Chinese papers, however, are accompanied by an English abstract. Here, as in most other institutes visited, younger scientists are learning English and are now listening to the Voice of America, especially for its English lessons, which are conducted twice daily.

Many of the theorists now in the Institute have had no formal graduate school training, but did have what was the usual 5 or 6 years of undergraduate work more than 10 years ago, prior to the Cultural Revolution. Most of them had not been involved in theoretical work during the entire decade of the Cultural Revolution, and, although they apparently continued to receive preprints from CERN, SLAC, Fermilab, etc., had to a considerable degree lost touch with all international activity in the field. Nevertheless, they have a few good graduate students at the Institute now enrolled in the formal graduate school program of the Chinese Academy of Sciences. It is expected that after 1 or 2 years such students will go on to work in one of the institutes of the Academy.

Leading personnel of the Institute of Theoretical Physics told us that they would like to send more people abroad for postdoctoral work, and they are also thinking of sending some of their younger students out of the country for predoctoral training. We were told, for example, that T. D. Lee had just selected two students, after interviewing many from different institutions, who will enter the standard graduate school program in physics at Columbia University in September 1979. We were assured that of the 600 physicists who attended Lee's remarkable series of lectures this spring, fully 80 percent were able to benefit fully from the lectures. Presumably most of them are self-taught and suffering from what was described as a 10-year thirst for knowledge and contact with other physicists! This year three members of the Institute were abroad, one at the Institute for Advanced Study in Bures, France; another worked with Trautmann in Poland, and a third somewhere in Australia. In addition they have had some contact with the new NSF Theory Institute in Santa Barbara, through Raymond Sawyer, and are hoping to increase such contacts.

As to receiving foreign visitors, the Institute now has its first such in the person of Sam Wong, a nuclear theorist from the University of Toronto. The interest within the Institute in statistical and collective theories of nuclear reactions will make his visit very appropriate. The hope is that when the new building is completed it will be possible to attract more such foreign visitors.

It appears that the Institute of Theoretical Physics will start a graduate teaching program; it was not clear during our visit whether courses have been given as yet, but we were told that a nuclear theory course will be given next year. The Institute has accepted 19 graduate students out of the 1,000 (about 300 in Peking) who passed the national graduate school examination (10,000 took this exam—to be distinguished from the national college entrance examination) for the roughly 120 institutes of the Academy. It should be borne in mind, however, that this represents a harvest of 10 years, so that in the next few years, until the present group of undergraduates who have only completed their sophomore year of education finish the 4-year program laid out for them, it may be difficult to find this number of adequately qualified graduate students.

We did have some discussion concerning the areas of nuclear physics now under active investigation within the Institute. These included two topics in which Institute members were particularly interested—the generalization of the Glauber multiple-scattering method to relativistic systems and the application of cluster methods to low-energy nuclear reactions. Our general impression was that those involved are quite sophisticated in their theoretical approach. It was more difficult to gauge the level of their physical intuition, perhaps because of the language barrier.

Chinese physicists now generally have access to all the international literature (even though it may reach them only after substantial delays). The problem of the theorists is that there are no parallel Chinese experimental activities as yet; in consequence, many of the theorists appear to lack a sense of what problems are interesting. This lack of intimate communication, not only with the international scientific community but also with local experimentalists, currently hampers them in doing much topical or contemporary research.

INSTITUTE OF HIGH-ENERGY PHYSICS (BEIJING)*

The Institute of High-Energy Physics (IHEP) was formally transferred from the Institute of Atomic Energy to separate status as an Institute in 1975 and is under the sole jurisdiction of the CAS.

Currently it has a staff of about 500, 80 percent of whom are scientific and technical personnel and 20 percent of whom are administrative and support personnel; 25 percent of the total are female. The Institute has five Divisions: Experimental High-Energy Physics, High-Energy Accelerators, Chemistry and Chemical Theory, Applied Research, and Theory. Primary activity in this Institute now centers about the design and construction of the 50-GeV proton accelerator, highlighted as one of China's eight major projects under the "four modernizations."

The delegation's primary contact with the Institute was in the area of theory, which includes some nuclear work. About 20 persons work in intermediate- and low-energy nuclear theory, and some of them have formal ties to ITP. We heard repeatedly of a 2.5-MV positive ion Van de Graaff—the only one in the city of Beijing—located in the Institute but did not see it.

The Head of the theory group is Zhu Hongyuan, who holds a 1948 Ph.D. from the University of Manchester, was at Dubna during 1959-1961, and was Deputy Leader of the Chinese High-Energy Physics Delegation to the United States in May 1973. Zhu served as Kerman's host during his visit to the Institute and to its theory group.

Before discussing theoretical matters, Kerman was shown some of the development work associated with the planned 50-GeV accelerator. Several linac model sections have been built for study, as well as a small (2-ft^2) streamer chamber, including its associated Marx generator and Blumlein, and a 10-ft-long Cerenkov counter. When asked how these detectors would be tested, it was implied that cosmic rays would be the best-available source. In addition, he was shown a building that was said to be for construction of a hybrid bubble chamber; apparently, however, this project has been abandoned as not suitable for their purposes. No reason for this was given.

In subsequent discussions, it appeared that the high-energy theory included classical solutions for gauge theories, including the fashionable theta vacuum problem, along with Soliton models for composite particles and investigation of Drell-Yan mechanisms for lepton pair production. In addi-

---

*Harvey lectured and lead a discussion with members of the Institute who were hosting an all-China physics conference at a Beijing hotel during the entire day, May 25, while Kerman toured the Institute itself and held discussions with other members not attending the conference.

tion, some purely formal field theory work is in progress.

The intermediate-energy group is probably the largest in China and is working on a wide variety of current problems. However, once again we have the sense that those involved are essentially trying to keep up with current literature by doing practice problems. They are working on a variety of high-energy reaction problems, including proton nucleus scattering, the $(p,\pi^\pm)$ reaction, the (π,D) reaction, and pion charge exchange. In addition, they have an interest in the problems of Baryonium, hypernuclei, and pion condensation; they also seem to be interested in relativistic heavy ion reactions.

There has been a major transition within the Institute from nuclear to intermediate- and high-energy theory; currently of the eight graduate students enrolled in the Institute, there are six in particle and two in nuclear theory.

In parallel with Kerman's visit to the Institute, Henley had discussions while at Beijing University with Zhang Zongye, who is also associated with the IHEP, and learned of additional theoretical studies in progress at IHEP on proton-antiproton bound states, giant resonances for antiprotons in nuclei, and hypernuclear physics, including level structure calculations exploiting symmetry group concepts and pair correlations, as well as pion condensation.

Throughout all our contact with Chinese theoretical physicists, we have detected clear familiarity with the most current literature but some evident reluctance to strike out in new directions and a rather marked lack of self-confidence.

INSTITUTE OF ATOMIC ENERGY (BEIJING)*

Originally known as the Institute of Modern Physics, the Institute of Atomic Energy (IAE) was established in 1950. It is under the joint administration of the Chinese Academy of Sciences and of the Second Ministry of Machine-Building (in charge of nuclear energy and nuclear weapons development). The original Director was Qian Sanqiang, now Vice Director of the CAS and our formal host in China. He received his B.S. degree from Qinghua University in 1936 and his Ph.D. from the French National University of Paris in 1943, during World War II. The original Deputy Director, and later Director, was Zhao Zhongyao, who received his Ph.D. under Milliken at Caltech in 1930. In 1976, Wang Ganchang, who had been a Deputy Director since 1954, assumed the leadership of the Institute. He received his Ph.D. in 1934 from the University of Berlin, was a Deputy Director of the Joint Institute

*On Thursday, May 24, the whole delegation spent half a day at the IAE; on the 25th, Bromley, Middleton, Tombrello, and Zucker spent the entire day, and on the 26th Hanna and Harvey visited for the entire day.

ADMINISTRATION of the INSTITUTE of ATOMIC ENERGY (BEIJING)
(Under the Dual Administration for the Chinese Academy of Sciences and the Ministry of Machine Building)

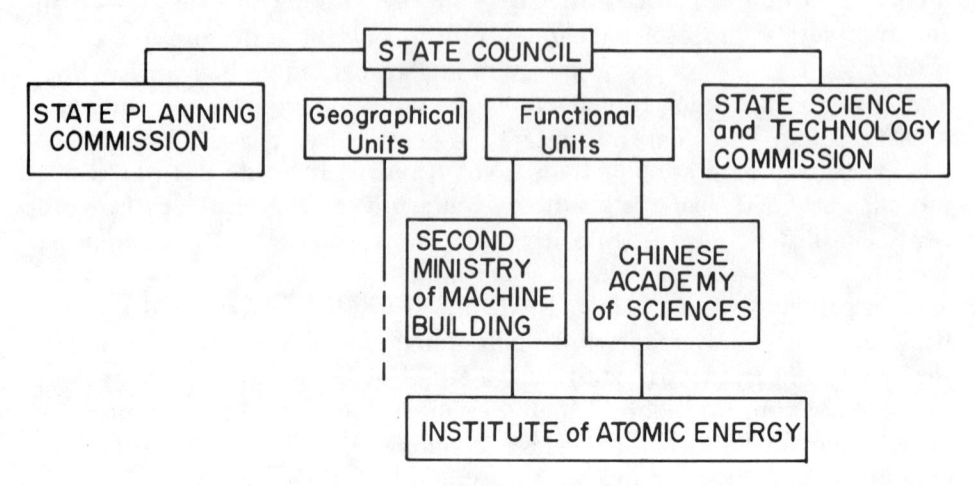

```
                        STATE COUNCIL
       ┌──────────┬──────────┬──────────┬──────────┐
  STATE PLANNING  Geographical  Functional   STATE SCIENCE
   COMMISSION       Units        Units    and TECHNOLOGY
                                            COMMISSION
                       │            │
                   SECOND        CHINESE
                  MINISTRY       ACADEMY
                  of MACHINE    of SCIENCES
                  BUILDING
                       │            │
                  INSTITUTE of ATOMIC ENERGY
```

Administration of the Institute of Atomic Energy (Beijing).

of Nuclear Research at Dubna for several years, and is concurrently Vice Minister of the Second Ministry of Machine-Building, President of the Chinese Nuclear Energy Society, and Vice President of the Chinese Physical Society, in addition to his IAE responsibilities.

The Institute is in Tuoli, 50 km southwest of Beijing proper, and consists of a number of widely dispersed brick buildings, each apparently with its own function. Besides the main administration building, we were shown but did not visit the reactor chemistry building. We visited a number of other buildings, as will be described below, and they were all very much alike in construction: sturdy, serviceable, crowded with equipment, and without any embellishment. We were struck by the lack of traffic, on foot or bicycle, between the buildings. On the whole, the Institute looked rather uninhabited until one got into a particular laboratory.

Programs of the Institute

We were greeted upon arrival by the Director, Wang Ganchang, a forceful person, whose agile mind and body belie his 72 years. In his introductory remarks at the customary introductory session to such visits, Wang asked particularly for two things from our delegation. First, he would like to see a number of IAE people visiting the United States and he asked for help

Visits to Research Institutes

Members of the delegation and of the Institute of Atomic Energy on their arrival at the Institute. From the left, those present are Ding Dazhao, Arthur Kerman, Yang Minzhang, P. K. Kuo (back), Dai Chuanzeng (front), Chen Yongshou, Ernest Henley, Bernard Harvey, Yang Zhen, Pierre Perrolle, Wang Ganchang, Roy Middleton, Zhuo Yizhong, Allan Bromley, Tom Tombrello, Alex Zucker, Weng Peikun, Wang Dexi, Wang Chuanying, Ding Shengyao, Stanley Hanna, and Li Shounan.

from us in making the necessary arrangements. We agreed that this was a good idea, and a feasible one, and agreed that we would be prepared to respond to any specific requests. The second request was a plea for honest comments and criticism of the programs and equipment at the Institute. Bromley declined, saying that, while we would make some general comments, we did not yet know enough about conditions in China to be able to evaluate the scientific progress at the Institute properly or constructively.

Wang Chuanying, Deputy Director of the IAE, then proceeded to describe the Institute. It was founded in 1950, and currently has three principal programs: physics, chemistry, and technology. The areas of physics being studied are nuclear physics and solid-state physics (the latter is a recent addition). In nuclear physics there are theoretical studies on the cluster model, high-spin states, nuclear field theory, coupled channel optical models (although no adequate computer appears to be available within the Institute), statistical models, and three-body reactions. Fundamental experimental nuclear physics has been based on the three accelerators (a cyclotron, a Van de Graaff, and a Cockcroft-Walton, described below) and deals with low-energy charged particle reactions, studies of clustering in lithium, three-body reactions, a search for intermediate structure by way of deuteron reactions on carbon, and preequilibrium emission. The applied nuclear physics program includes activation analysis, compilation and evaluation of nuclear data, and a wide variety of neutron cross-section measurements related to reactors (more detail follows below).

The technology program, we were told (but did not visit), deals with nuclear materials, reactor fuel and pressure vessel steel irradiations, thermal hydraulics, and reactor chemistry. When we inquired why they felt they had to measure radiation damage in steel when so much data already exist in the open literature, the reply was that radiation effects are so strongly dependent on small amount of impurities, and vary so much from melt to melt, that they had to get data specifically for steel manufactured in China.

There are currently two reactors at IAE. The larger one is a 10-MW D_2 cooled and moderated reactor, originally purchased from the Soviet Union in 1958, upgraded to 10 MW in 1976, and now undergoing reconstruction. The operating central flux is $\sim 10^{14}$ neutrons/cm^2/s, and the reactor has been used to study materials via neutron diffraction and materials for "future design of power reactors." We were told that the enrichment of the reactor fuel is 3.2 percent, although 1.2 percent has been reported elsewhere. Apparently a reasonably sophisticated lattice design involving transfer of rods from the outer edges to the central core provides improved burnup and a flatter flux distribution. We did not see this reactor, although we requested such a visit; our hosts indicated that the reactor was under reconstruction.

The smaller reactor is of the 7-m deep swimming pool type with a design power of 3.5 MW and a flux of 3.5×10^{13} neutrons/cm^2/s. The fuel is 10 percent enriched and is a mixture of UO_2 and Mg (or MgO) in aluminum cladding. Both beryllium and carbon reflectors are used. The total ^{235}U inventory is about 5 kg. It is used for materials testing, particularly for pressure vessel steel for which there is a small test loop; fuel is also tested in this loop. There are five horizontal holes, but the only use of which we were told was activation analysis and production of radioisotopes for medical purposes.

The small reactor operates 180 days/yr to 42-45 percent burnup; it has never had a fuel failure, but during our visit we were cautioned not to touch anything because some ^{32}P had gotten loose. The reactor was not operating during our visit. Its construction started in 1960 and it went critical in 1964.

The technology program also operates hot cells for materials examination. We saw five hot cells with a radioactivity capacity of 10^4 curies in one room and four others at 10^3 curies. Aside from the usual manipulators, the hot cells contained almost no equipment; they were very clean and looked unused, but they were lined in stainless steel and the windows were of high-quality lead glass. The only piece of actual research equipment we saw in this hot cell area was a remote metallographic camera, but unhappily it did not spring to life as various people tried to activate it by vigorously pushing a few buttons. The visitor effect on research equipment appears to be a longitude invariant!

We learned very little about the chemistry program. The principal lines of research, we were told, deal with reprocessing technology; study of U, Pu, and Np chemistry; and production of radioisotopes and stable isotopes by means of two electromagnetic separators. We believe that the waste management research program is also part of the chemistry effort. They now store high- and medium-level radioactive waste, but low-level waste is treated and "disposed." The waste research program is quite broad in scope. They find bitumen a good material for medium-level waste and look to glass or concrete for high-level disposal. They made a brief foray into pyrometallurgy for reprocessing, but discarded this idea, as have all others, in favor of aqueous reprocessing.

Nuclear Physics—Experimental Facilities

We were shown a table loaded with various nuclear detectors arranged as an exhibit. These included gas-filled counters and ionization chambers, thin-window counters, NaI and CsI scintillation counters, an array of 2-inch photomultiplier tubes, a variety of semiconductor detectors ranging from surface barrier detectors to GeLi detectors (largest is 50 cc, and best resolution is 3 KeV for cobalt), and a large intrinsic germanium detector. All of these were made in China; the Ge is refined elsewhere and bought by the IAE. They displayed two two-dimensional multiwire detectors, the larger about 15 cm on a side, and they report that they are building a 35-cm × 35-cm multiwire detector with 0.9-mm spatial resolution. We were told that the multiwire counters were for medical X-ray utilization.

The largest piece of research equipment in the Institute is a 1.2-m cyclotron originally purchased from the Soviet Union, which was removed from service in the spring of 1979 and is currently being reworked into an AVF 3-sector machine. This cyclotron, incidentally, has all the characteristics of being Russian-made, including the gigantic scale of its power supply and control console. It has now been designed to accelerate protons from 3 to 20 MeV and will produce 40-MeV α-particles. We saw the new dees, beautifully made and ready to be placed in the gap that is now occupied by a Hall probe field measuring rig. The rebuilt cyclotron is expected to operate by the end of 1979. There are no plans at present to accelerate heavy ions. The rebuilt machine will have three beam lines, and a single experimental room measuring roughly 30 × 50 ft.

There is also a 2.5-MV Van de Graaff accelerator at the IAE originally

NUCLEAR SCIENCE IN CHINA

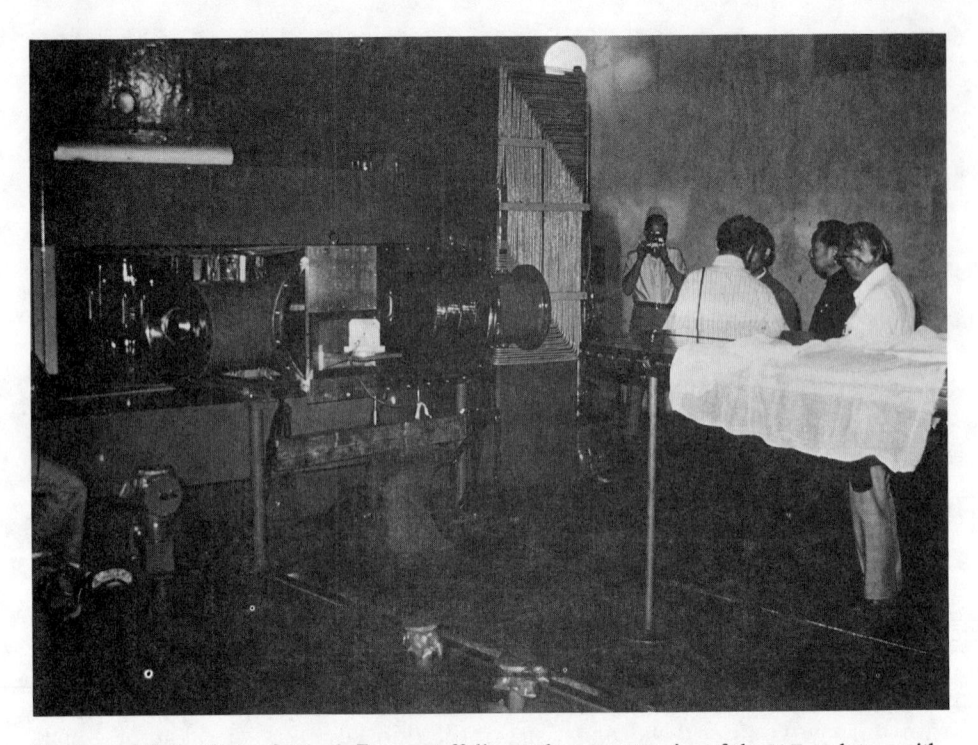

Members of the Institute of Atomic Energy staff discuss the reconstruction of the IAE cyclotron with members of the delegation. On the right, and covered with cheesecloth, is the new set of dees that has been fabricated as part of the reconstruction program. The entire dee and oscillator assembly can be rolled forward on the tracks shown in the floor into the vacuum chamber, here shown within the poles of the magnet itself.

purchased in Russia in 1959, but, since it was not completely installed when the Soviet technicians were withdrawn from China in 1960, it was subsequently completed by the Chinese themselves. We suspect that this time period marked the beginning of accelerator construction at the Vanguard factory in Shanghai and that its subsequent 2.5-MV Van de Graaffs draw heavily on the Soviet design. At the IAE, the Van de Graaff is used mainly for the study of charged particle-induced reactions. We did not spend much time with this machine, but data obtained with it were presented to us. For reasons unspecified, it was not functioning during our visit.

A 600-KeV Cockcroft-Walton high-tension set, also manufactured in the Vanguard factory in Shanghai, appeared to be a heavily utilized device. Its construction was started in 1975 and completed in 1977; it features a 2.2-mA deuteron beam from an RF source. With a Ti T, or Ti D target it produces 2×10^{11} n/s. We were told that the machine operated for 4,000 hours during the past year. Neutron spectroscopy is accomplished by time of

Mrs. Zho Yizhong in the experimental data-taking area associated with the IAE cyclotron.

flight using associated particle triggering. Fourteen MeV neutrons are also used here for activation analysis of O, F, Fe, Si, Al, and Mg. The 43-cc GeLi detector system used here, built at IAE, is of the plug-in type, and appears roughly equivalent to devices made 10 years ago in the United States.

The Institute has two electromagnetic isotope separators, the smaller one, that one of us saw in operation, has a dispersion of 10 mm for 1 percent ΔM, a 35-cm gap, and a 1 m-radius. The larger machine has apparently never worked satisfactorily and is currently being reshimmed. Both were originally obtained from the Soviet Union, except for the source and receiver assemblies that were made in China. The source we saw was beautifully made of stainless steel with a 20-cm-long arc chamber. The cathode is indirectly heated tungsten, and the anode a small graphite button. The sources are normally run at 1-2 A and 100-200 V, and produce 200-400 mA, of which 100-200 appear at the receiver. The source floats at 30 KV, and there is a 5-10-KV accel-decel slit voltage. About 20 elements—among them Pb, Sm, Ti, In—have been separated, but there seems to be little demand as yet for the product. The rationale for building the larger machine under these conditions was not clear.

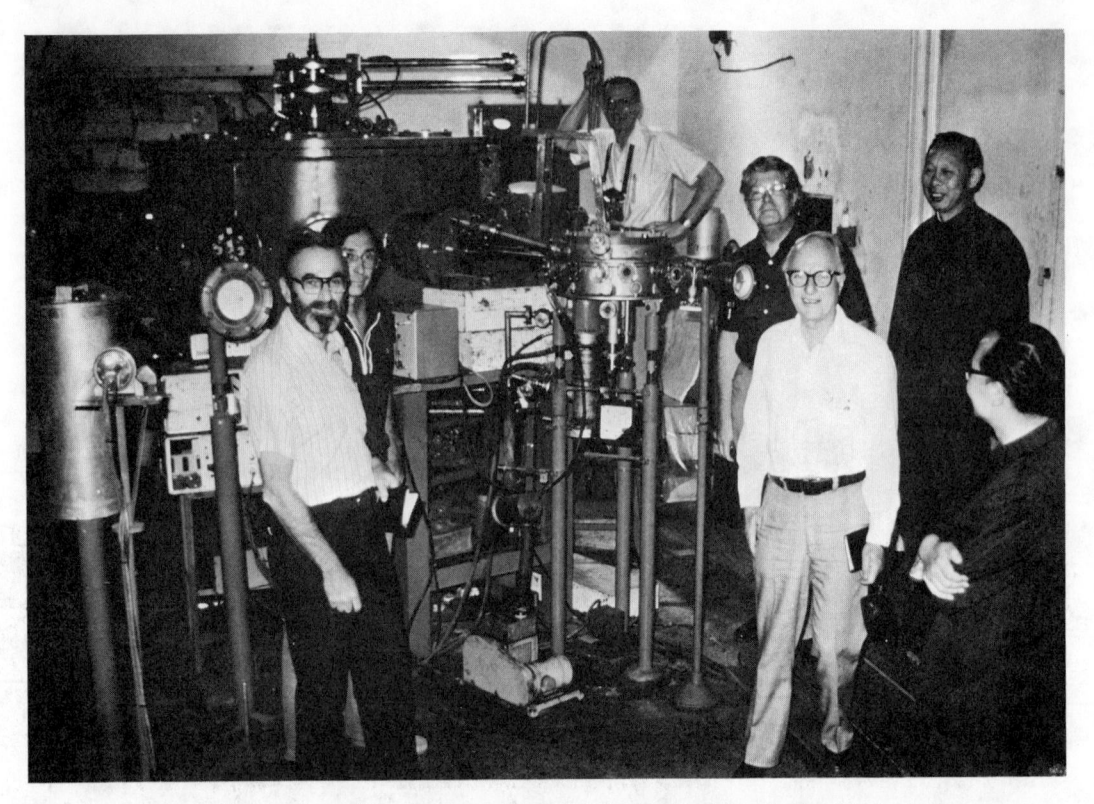

An overall view of one of the target rooms associated with the IAE cyclotron. The large scattering chamber was fabricated in the Institute and is mounted in series with a smaller one.

Two additional accelerators are being acquired by IAE. First, they have bought a 13-MV tandem from HVEC and plan to use it for a wide range of nuclear science research. These plans will be discussed in detail below.

Second, the IAE is in the early stages of developing a 100-MeV electron linac to be used for neutron time-of-flight work and mainly for cross-section measurements. They are working on a 20-MW klystron, which we saw, but which has so far achieved only 10 MW. They plan for an initial repetition rate of 50 pps, going subsequently to 300 and then 1,000 pps. The pulse width of their proposed design is to be 5-10 ns. All this is very ambitious, and is estimated to cost about 30 million yuan, (~U.S. $20 million).

The 13-MV HVEC Tandem Accelerator

Bromley spent half a day in detailed discussions with about 25 staff members from the Institute who will be involved in the development and use of research instrumentation to be associated with the HVEC tandem accelerator, for which an order has already been placed and for which delivery is

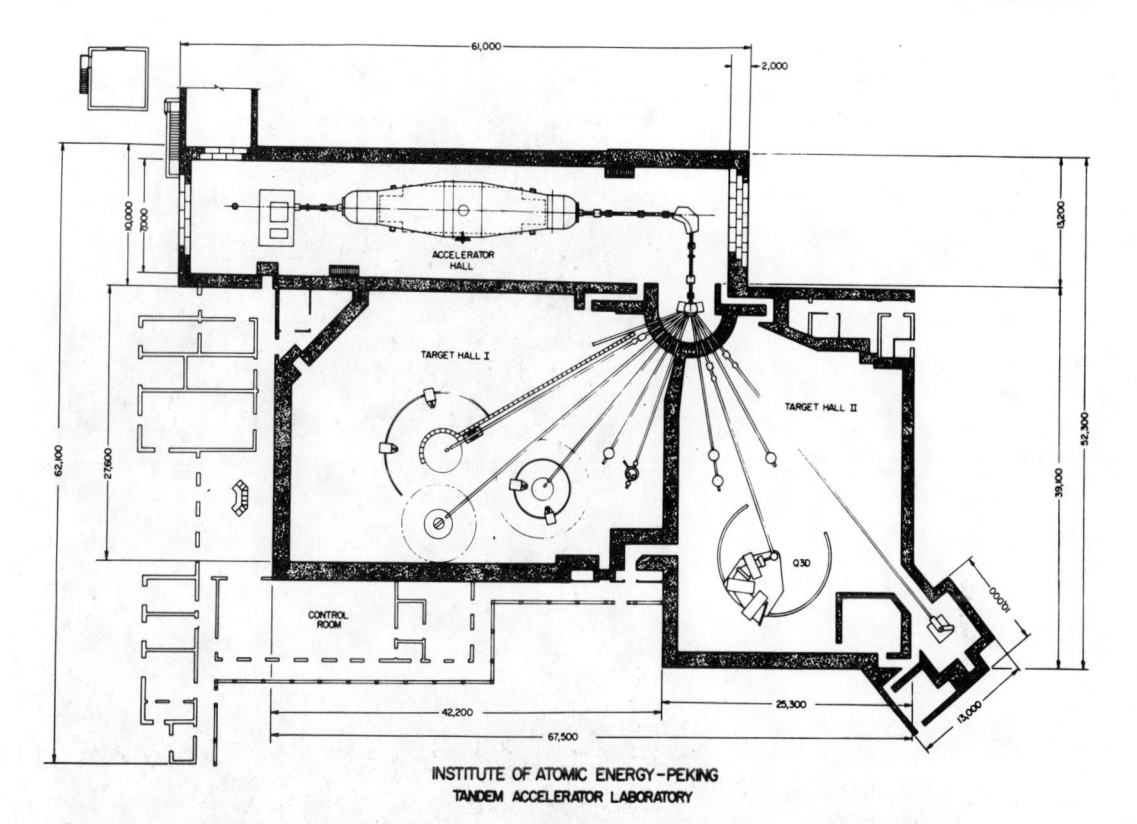

Visits to Research Institutes

INSTITUTE OF ATOMIC ENERGY – PEKING
TANDEM ACCELERATOR LABORATORY

The planned laboratory to house the 13-MV HVEC tandem Van de Graaff accelerator that has been purchased in the United States. All dimensions are given in millimeters, and a few of the major pieces of experimental equipment are shown in place. Target Hall I will be used primarily for neutron studies, while Target Hall II, which includes the Q3D spectrometer systems, will be devoted to charge-particle research. At the lower left is a gamma cave with a large goniometer, which will be used in the study of angular distributions and correlations with both charged particles and gamma radiation. The control room for the accelerator is shown below Target Hall I, while the experimental data acquisition and computation facilities are shown to the left of Target Hall I.

anticipated in 1981. Apart from a change in the tank shape to eliminate the troublesome corners in the original design (the tank will be fabricated in China), the accelerator will be almost identical to that installed in the Wright Laboratory at Yale.

Wang Chuanying and eight of his senior associates spent several days at Yale in July 1978 and have subsequently read all available material concerning the laboratory and publications from it. A similarly detailed study appears to have been made for all the other MP laboratories.

As ordered, the accelerator is guaranteed to operate at terminal potentials from 3 to 13 MV, with proton currents of 5, 10, and 5 μA, respectively,

Dr. Ding Dazhao and Mrs. Zho Yizhong discuss the construction of the 100-MeV electron linac at the Institute of Atomic Energy with Tom Tombrello, Allan Bromley, Roy Middleton, and Bernard Harvey.

at terminal potentials of 3.0, 7.5, and 13.0 MV. Three ion sources have been ordered with the accelerator: a sputter source, a direct extraction duoplasmatron, and a lithium charge exchange source for helium ions. Although nine beam lines are planned for the original installation, only three are included in the initial order. Apparently the decision has just been made to order the remaining six from HVEC.

An order has also been placed with Scanditronix for delivery of a Q3D spectrograph at about the same time as the accelerator; a price of $1.6 M was quoted for this instrument.

Two major target areas, together with a cave for gamma radiation work, are included in the present design, and the nine beam lines span the ±60° ports in the switch magnet. The −60° line is specifically reserved for neutron time-of-flight work. Although the exact dimensions were not available, they can be scaled from the dimensions of the tandem tank (80 ft in length) in the figure included herewith. The general impression is that the laboratory has been designed after much thought and study of alternative designs and with generous space provided for research and for possible expansion of the tandem itself (e.g., an ESTU tank) and for ultimate addition of a postaccelerator system. Construction will begin shortly. Substantial discussion was devoted to such questions as elimination of ground loops in signal cables, provision of electrical power to adequate stability, provision of additional vacuum pumping on the accelerator and beam lines, possible advantages of insulating gas mixtures, design of goniometers and scattering chambers, need for special low background shielding, and possible advantages and disadvantages of possible beam layouts. Quite obviously all present had done their homework well.

Ding Dazhao, who will apparently be in charge of the direct research program with the facility, noted that the original program would have eight components.

1. High-resolution spectrometry with both neutrons and charged particles.
2. Nuclear scattering and reactions involving light heavy ions.
3. In-beam gamma radiation spectrometry.
4. Capture reactions, including both light and heavy projectiles.
5. Fast neutron interactions with nuclei.
6. Nuclear fission induced by charged particles.
7. Studies involving use of polarized beams (it is not clear whether the intent is to buy the polarized source or develop it locally).
8. Nuclear science applications, including the interfaces with atomic physics, solid-state physics, and materials science.

Individual staff members have been assigned specific responsibility for arranging for the necessary instrumentation in each of these areas, and both design and procurement are well under way. In response to direct questioning, it was agreed that it would be desirable to consider instituting cooperation with universities and other institutes now so that the outside users could participate in the planning and construction phases. But although it seemed clearly agreed that such users would be welcomed, the general discussion suggested that the local staff really considered it their function to prepare the facility without outside help. The discussion may have stimulated more active consideration of user participation.

In general, the planning for this new facility itself seems to be proceeding smoothly and in highly professional fashion. It would appear that the planning for the actual research program, however, would benefit considerably from much greater interaction between experimentalists and theorists—and it was emphasized by members of the delegation how important it would be for members of the research team to be sent abroad to gain actual experience with existing similar accelerator facilities before the Chinese one became operational. Members of the delegation volunteered to help both in terms of their own laboratories and in terms of identifying other appropriate institutions and locations. Although no concrete arrangements were developed during our visit, Wang Ganchang indicated that he will be in touch with us after appropriate internal discussions on this matter within the Institute. It is probable that our hosts did not anticipate that delegation members were prepared to make on the spot commitments to accept appropriate visitors and thus had not prepared such plans in advance. Everyone with whom we talked, however, agreed emphatically with the desirability, and even necessity, of exposing the Chinese researchers to hands-on activity in foreign laboratories.

Negative Ion Source Development

Although, as noted above, the Institute plans to take delivery of an HVEC Super MP tandem accelerator during 1981, very little has been done as yet in the way of negative ion source development. Interest is high in this area, however, both at the Institute and at Qinghua University. Our general impression is that a fairly large development program, possibly a joint one, will be implemented shortly.

To date, work at the Institute has been confined to the type of source developed by Moak and McKibben in the late 1950's and early 1960's. The test facility does not even have an analyzing magnet and consequently all measurements, some of them fairly detailed, have been made with hydrogen. In spite of rather crude design and engineering, it was surprising to learn that the source contained an indirectly heated LaB_6 cathode.

The source yields about 100-130 μA of H^- together with 1 or 2 mA of electrons. The largest problem appeared to be source lifetime, which was limited to about 100 hours because of severe erosion of the tungsten extraction aperture. Although the extracted beam was accelerated only to about 20 KeV, it was also surprising to see that the entire test facility was contained in a removable 6-ft^3 fabricated from sheet lead.

A seminar given by Middleton at Qinghua University on negative ion source development was heavily attended by personnel from the IAE, as well as from the University, and was followed by 2 hours of discussion. Plans were shown for a sophisticated ion source test facility that included a 45-cm double focusing 90° magnet, emittance measuring devices, and a large vacuum chamber designed to accommodate sources other than the direct extraction duoplasmatron, probably of the sputter type. It was not clear whether this facility will eventually be located at the Atomic Energy Institute or at Qinghua University. This collaboration provides an excellent illustration, however, of what the future may hold in the way of University-Institute interaction.

Nuclear Physics—Research

We were told that neutron research includes work on the following problems:

1. $\bar{\nu}$ measurement for ^{239}Pu from 0.5 to 1.5 MeV.
2. $\bar{\nu}$ and the distribution of neutrons from the spontaneous fission of ^{252}Cf.
3. $\bar{\nu}$ for ternary fission of ^{252}Cf.
4. Angular distributions for elastic and inelastic scattering of 14.7 MeV neutrons from C by time of flight.
5. Elastic scattering of 14.7 MeV neutrons from deuterium and measurement of neutron spectra from the breakup reaction $d(n,p)2n$.
6. Elastic scattering differential cross sections for neutrons from Be.
7. Measurements of σ_f for ^{233}U, ^{235}U, ^{239}Pu from 0.02 to 0.3 eV.
8. Fission cross section for ^{233}U, ^{235}U, ^{239}Pu as a function of neutron energies. The energies covered are 0.03 MeV, 0.12-1.5 MeV, 2.5-3.0 MeV, 3.5-5.6 MeV, and 14 MeV. All this work utilizes the 2.5-MV Van de Graaff.

Charged particle research that was described to us includes:

1. D + ^{6}Li, α + ^{6}Li, and α + ^{7}Li three-body breakup reactions, to study cluster states, using 9 MeV deuterons and 18 MeV α-particles.
2. Quasi-free scattering in the ^{6}Li$(d,2d)$ and ^{6}Li$(\alpha,\alpha d)$, ^{7}Li$(\alpha,2q)$ systems, and the quasi-free reaction ^{6}Li(α,tp) were studied at the same energies as above. Agreement with a distorted wave impulse approximation calculation was good, but we received no detailed information about the results or about the calculations.
3. (α,p) reaction studies from ^{59}Co at 18 MeV show a departure from statistical behavior that is ascribed to preequilibrium emission. Agreement was obtained with a Griffith-model calculation. No equivalent preequilibrium emission was observed for an Al target in agreement with expectations based on such a model.
4. The reaction ^{12}C$(d,p)^{13}$C was investigated at deuteron energies between 1.726 and 1.860 MeV to search for intermediate structure. Four 2$^-$ resonances were observed and the tentative conclusion is that this may indeed be a fragmented doorway state centered at 11.46 MeV in ^{14}N. Similar studies were reported on the ^{28}Si$(d,p)^{29}$Si reaction in the same general energy range.

NUCLEAR SCIENCE IN CHINA

Because the delegation members were interested in seeing a Chinese typewriter, Wang Ganchang arranged for one to be demonstrated to us. The large carriage carrying the type slugs is free to move in two dimensions and is controlled by foot pedals. The actual typing mechanism is controlled by the cluster of keys under the typist's right hand, while the left hand controls the paper-carrying platen. We were astonished to find that none of these motions have detents, so that the spacing is under the full control of the typist. Using such a typewriter, an experienced typist, after perhaps 6 months of training and practice, might be expected to type one standard page per hour. As a peripheral note, this typist was one of the few Chinese women whom we saw who had taken advantage of the brief availability of permanent hair curling that had been made available in Beijing by a group from Hong Kong. This was available, however, only for a period of at most a few weeks and was then terminated by the Chinese authorities as being undesirable.

INSTITUTE OF GEOLOGY OF THE STATE BUREAU OF SEISMOLOGY (BEIJING)*

The State Bureau of Seismology was established with the strong backing of the late Premier Zhou Enlai, in 1966, as part of government initiatives to minimize earthquake danger to the Chinese population. (The Bureau

*Because of his interest in earthquake prediction, Tombrello was invited by the Institute of Geology of the State Bureau of Seismology to give a talk on radon monitoring. The information presented here was obtained from Liu Pengxin, a seismologist from the foreign affairs section of the Seismology Bureau, who accompanied Tombrello and translated for him, and from Lucille Jones, a doctoral candidate in geophysics at MIT, who was the first American to carry out long-term research in China. She began 5 months of research in March 1979, under the sponsorship of the CSCPRC-administered National Educational Exchange Program. Neither Liu nor Jones spoke in an official capacity, of

operated under his direct aegis until his death.) Virtually every region of the PRC is an area of high seismic risk. Since construction standards have, in the past, not taken this into account, an unpredicted earthquake invariably involves an appreciable loss of life. The Bureau now has more than 10,000 employees, 60 percent of whom are scientists; it has an annual budget of 70 million yuan (~$45 million U.S.), and this does not include either capital equipment or construction. About 60 percent of the budget is related to earthquake prediction. There are regional bureaus in each province and an active, enthusiastic, and organized contingent of well over 100,000 amateurs who do much of the fieldwork, sample collection, and the like.

The Bureau has its own training programs and actively "advertises" among graduating high school students at the time of the national examination for college entrance. Since it has an excellent reputation, it apparently gets the young people it wants, and new projects appear to be given additional funding without substantial question. The Bureau predictions are not expected to be completely accurate (it is still recognized as an "infant" science), but its members are expected to pay attention to their duty in order to do the best job possible. We were told that earthquake prediction is viewed as a very attractive career choice by young people, because it combines a new and expanding scientific field with the opportunity to provide positive and obvious help to society. There appears to be a much larger fraction of women in this field than in the more established disciplines—a situation not unlike that in lunar science in the United States.

In Tombrello's meeting at the Seismology Bureau's Institute of Geology, contrary to our experience during all other visits, there was no mention of the effects of the Cultural Revolution. It appears that no one in this Institute was required to stop research work during the period. In fact, the Seismology Bureau's members were all considered heroes after their successful prediction of the Haicheng earthquake (early 1975). The official position is that the failure to predict the Tangshan earthquake (early 1976) did reflect the influence of the Cultural Revolution. It is clear that well-defined precursors were, indeed, observed prior to the latter earthquake; however, the sequence of subsequent events is not well-defined, and even

---

course, but Tombrello noted great consistency in their description of Chinese research activities in seismology.

The CSCPRC has been particularly active in promoting exchanges in the field of earthquake research. Reports of CSCPRC-sponsored groups include:

Earthquake Research in China. EOS (Transactions, American Geophysical Union), v. 56, no. 11, 1975: pp. 838-881.
Prediction of the Haicheng Earthquake. Prepared by the Haicheng Study Delegation. *EOS* (Transactions, American Geophysical Union), v. 58, no. 5, 1977: pp. 236-272.
Earthquake Engineering and Hazards Reduction in China. Earthquake Engineering Delegation (August, 1978). Washington, D.C.: National Academy of Sciences. Forthcoming.

Bureau members note that there were scientific problems in addition to the political ones. It was reported to us that the period of influence of the Cultural Revolution in the Bureau was short-lived, but that there was a struggle for control and some Bureau members were sent to the country for 6 months to 2 years. It has been suggested that had such persons been actively interpreting the data coming in from field observers prior to the Tangshan earthquake the enormous death toll (estimates range between 600,000 and 750,000 persons) might have been substantially reduced. We were told that alleged followers of the "Gang of Four" have now been sent to local brigades, if they are scientifically competent. Those whose skills were exclusively political have been sent to perform physical labor on farms or in factories. This was the most explicit description we received anywhere concerning the fate of Cultural Revolution activists.

The physical facilities of the Seismology Bureau's Institute of Geology were as cluttered as any we visited in the PRC. No time was devoted to any formal introduction, but there was an obvious and active research atmosphere. The questions that followed Tombrello's talk were very much to the point and involved a large amount of detailed information on the part of the audience. One woman suggested, politely, that the Caltech data might be of relatively low sensitivity because the bore holes were so shallow. She then proceeded (through the interpreter) to develop her argument in detail. The audience was an interested and aggressive group, working on a wide variety of techniques involving hydrological and geochemical precursors for earthquakes. In most respects we, in the United States, can learn more from the Chinese research workers in this area than they can learn from us; we can, however, provide them with considerable help in advanced instrumentation, and for this reason they want very much to have closer ties with colleagues in the United States.

Tombrello's overall impression of the Seismology Bureau was that it is quite well-funded and enjoys a favored position among applied science activities in the PRC. It attracts extremely able people and continues to be in an expansion phase. Its members publish their work in both Chinese and foreign journals, attend international conferences, and are actively sought out by experts in the field from outside the PRC. In earthquake prediction (only one of the Bureau's activities), the PRC probably has the world's best program.

INSTITUTE OF MODERN PHYSICS (LANZHOU)*

The Institute of Modern Physics in Lanzhou is one of the most active centers for nuclear science in China. Only very recently has the Institute, or indeed the entire city of Lanzhou, been opened to visits by foreigners. And for

The delegation is officially welcomed to the Institute of Modern Physics in Lanzhou. From the left, Xie Bowang (Secretary of the Communist Party for the Institute), P. K. Kuo, Arthur Kerman, Bernard Harvey, Stanley Hanna, Roy Middleton, Ernest Henley, Allan Bromley, Pierre Perrolle, Yang Chengzhong (Director of the Institute), Alex Zucker, and Tom Tombrello.

many years even Chinese citizens were not free to travel to the area. This clearly reflects a parallelism with the history of Los Alamos and the influence of the Chinese nuclear weapons program on R&D in the area.

The Director of the Institute, Yang Chengzhong, received his doctorate at the University of Liverpool some 30 years ago and while there was responsible for some of the original deuteron stripping reaction studies first subjected to Butler analysis for the extraction of nuclear spectroscopic data. As Director of the Institute and Vice Director of the Lanzhou Branch of the Chinese Academy of Sciences, he and Xie Bowang, the Secretary of the Institute's Communist Party Committee, were our co-hosts during our stay in Lanzhou.

The current construction program for major nuclear facilities at the Institute is a very ambitious one—and one that would strain the capabilities of even the largest U.S. national laboratories. Specifically, an existing Russian-built fixed-field cyclotron is being converted to a sector-focused cyclotron that will serve as an injector for a large separated-sector post-accelerator, and, in parallel, a 20-MV terminal tandem accelerator is planned for construction as an alternate injector capable of yielding higher energies and

---

*The entire delegation visited the Institute for a full day on May 29. Hanna, Kerman, Middleton, Tombrello, and Zucker returned for lectures and discussions at various times on May 30 and June 1. Details are given in Appendix A.

heavier species than will be available with the cyclotron injector alone. Yang's candidly stated philosophy is that unless he takes some risks, China will never catch up to the world frontiers in nuclear science.

Our initial visit to the Institute began as usual with formal introductions and welcome followed by a brief presentation by the senior person in each of the five major divisions of the Institute. The organization of the major research activities in these divisions is as follows:

I NUCLEAR PHYSICS DIVISION

Vice Directors: Dai Guangxi, Lu Jianye

Staff: Includes 17 experimental physicists, 8 theorists, 5 nuclear chemists, and 25 laboratory assistants. The research groups, which focus primarily on heavy ion interactions, are:

Group 1 Fusion and Fission—synthesis of transuranium elements, mechanism of fusion reactions, lifetime measurement for compound nuclei, etc.

Group 2 Quasi-Elastic Scattering and DIC—transfer reactions, elastic and inelastic scattering, deep inelastic collisions.

Group 3 Nuclei Far from the β Stability Line—decay properties of neutron deficient isotopes produced by heavy ion reactions.

Group 4 High-Spin States—γ-ray multiplicity, α-α angular correlation, etc. (experimental equipment in preparation).

Group 5 Nuclear Theory—macroscopic mechanism of heavy-ion reactions, high-spin states, etc.

II THE CYCLOTRON DIVISION

Vice Directors: Xi Shiyuan, Li Xuekun, and Jiang Weimo

Staff: Includes 5 accelerator physicists and engineers, 15 technicians, 10 skilled craftsmen, and 20 accelerator operators.

The parameters of the 1.5-M classical cyclotron are:

Magnet

Pole face diameter	1.5 M
Extraction radius	0.660 M
Gap	210 M
Max field	18 KG
Power of the main coil	300 kW
Weight: Fe	225 T
Cu	8 T

RF System

Frequency range	8.6-16 MHz
Max RF voltage	250 kV
Energy constant	46.7 MeV

Characteristic beams	E(MeV)	$I_{ext}(\mu A)$
p	20	
d	24	30 μA
α	48	

The cyclotron was converted to accelerate heavy ions in 1973 with K = 61 MeV:

Characteristic beams	E(MeV)	$I_{ext}(\mu A)$
C^{4+}	76	4
N^{5+}	102	0.4
O^{5+}	89	0.5
$(DH)^+$	18.15	2

Plans are for the cyclotron to be converted to a 1.7-M sector-focusing cyclotron (K = 69 MeV) and plans call for first beam in 1982. The design parameters of this converted machine will be listed in detail below.

III ACCELERATOR DEVELOPMENT DIVISION

Section I The Separate-Sector Cyclotron

Director: Zhang Shouchin
Vice Directors: Wei Baowen, Zhang Mingling, Chiao Chingwen
Staff: Eight groups have been organized for study and design work on the SSC:

Group 1 Theoretical study. *Staff*: 5 accelerator physicists. *Research topics*: beam dynamics, accelerator parameters, stability and tolerance, etc.

Group 2 Magnet. *Staff*: 4 accelerator physicists, 6 accelerator engineers, 5 assistants and technicians. *Study and design*: magnetic circuit, isochronous field trimming, model test, magnetic-field mapping, etc.

Group 3 RF system. *Staff*: 6 RF engineers, 3 physicists, 4 technicians. *Study and design*: model test RF cavity, RF power supplies, and allied stabilization circuitry, etc.

Group 4 Beam transport. *Staff*: 3 physicists, 3 engineers, 4 technicians. *Study and design*: beam injection and extraction, transport and focusing system, etc.

Group 5 Vacuum. *Staff*: 4 engineers, 5 technicians. *Study and design*: vacuum chamber, pumping system, vacuum sealing, vacuum mesurement, leak hunting, etc.

Group 6 Beam diagnosis. *Staff*: 3 physicists. *Study and design*: beam diagnostic system.

Group 7 Control. *Staff*: 3 electronic and computer engineers, 3 technicians. *Study and design*: design principle, CAMAC modules, control software, etc.

Group 8 Electronics. *Staff*: 2 engineers, 6 technicians. *Study and design*: current stabilizing circuitries for magnets, etc.

Section II The Tandem Accelerator

Vice Director: Guo Qidi
(Cooperates with the similar division in the Shanghai Institute for Nuclear Research)
Staff: 10 physicists and engineers, 5 technicians.
Study and Research:

1. Pelletron and laddertron—full-scale model test, mechanical design, etc.

2. Accelerating tube—to study the technique of metal to ceramic seal; voltage gradient, vacuum, and thermal shock test for the tube, etc.

3. Negative ion source—duoplasmatron type.

Section III Mechanical Design

Staff: 6 mechanical engineers, 10 technicians, 4 assistants (machine drawing).
Study and Design:

1. The overall mechanical structure of the separated-sector cyclotron.

2. The mechanical properties of the magnets, RF cavities, and the vacuum chamber—stress and deformation, and dynamical properties (vibrations of dee-system, etc.).

3. The mechanical structures of the beam injection systems, etc.

IV ELECTRONICS AND DETECTOR DIVISION

Director: Chen Yiai
Vice Director: Yan Zhongli
Staff: 21 physicists and engineers, 14 technicians, 16 assistants.

Group 1 Detector development: semiconducting detectors, gas counters, multiwire counters, etc.

Group 2 Electronic devices: NIM, CAMAC, etc.
Group 3 Computers: operation, keeping, etc.
Group 4 On-line data acquisition.
Group 5 Isotope separator.

V APPLIED NUCLEAR PHYSICS DIVISION

Director: Wang Shufen (f)
Staff: 23 physicists, chemists, and engineers; 20 laboratory assistants.

Group 1 Development of 14-MeV neutron source. Accelerator: 600-kV Cockcroft-Walton set. Neutron intensity achieved (3-4) 10^{11} neutron/s. Neutron intensity achieved (3-4) 10^{11} neutron/s.

Group 2 Application and measurement of fast neutrons—fast neutron activation analysis, etc.

Group 3 Application of Mössbauer effect—analysis of the composition of ore samples.

Group 4 Production of radioactive isotopes and their applications.

Group 5 Application of heavy ion physics and techniques.

The 600-kV Cockcroft-Walton accelerator at IMP in Lanzhou. This machine was fabricated by the Vanguard factory in Shanghai and is used extensively at IMP in studies on neutron-induced interactions.

Following these presentations, the delegation members separated into two groups that toured the individual laboratories. These tours occupied the remainder of the morning and much of the afternoon of our first day in Lanzhou. Late in the afternoon we received formal presentations, in English, from Zhang Mingling, Director of the Accelerator Development Division, and Dai Guangxi, Vice Director of the Nuclear Physics Division. Unfortunately, time did not permit our receiving corresponding presentations from the other divisions, particularly inasmuch as we appreciated the effort that had been devoted to preparing them for delivery in English for our benefit. On the second day of our visit, as indicated in our itinerary (Appendix A), several members of the delegation returned to IMP for lectures and more detailed discussions, while the remainder visited Lanzhou University; and on the fourth day several delegation members again lectured at IMP.

The Cyclotron Laboratory

When the Russians withdrew from China in 1960, the 1.5-M classical cyclotron was far from completed; the Russians, we were told, even took some of the cyclotron and related equipment away with them. The IMP staff completed the construction in 2½ years, and the first beams were produced in 1963. Between 1963 and 1973, the machine was used in support of the "atomic energy" program for the measurement of fast neutron cross sections and the study of light ion reactions. In 1973, the field was reshimmed to allow acceleration of heavy ions, such as C, N, and O obtained from a PIG source. A limited amount of basic research was undertaken, but interruptions during the Cultural Revolution prevented much progress from being made. We were, for example, shown experimental results for ^{12}C elastic and inelastic scattering from ^{12}C and ^{208}Pb, with corresponding optical model fits; we were told that the fits had been calculated using a "large" computer in Shanghai (which was not specifically identified). We suspect that the applied nuclear science laboratories engaged in classified work in the Lanzhou area may also have "larger" computers and that some collaborative use of them was probable.

The cyclotron has been shut down for about a year for conversion to a sector-focused design (SFC) that will serve as one of the injectors for the larger separated-sector cyclotron (SSC) that is being designed. The SFC will have spiral sectors, a single dee (voltage 120 kV), 10 trim coils, and 3 harmonic coils in each valley. There will be three probes and a three-section electrostatic deflector.

The cyclotron energy constant K will be 69, giving beams of $(^{12}C)^{4+}$ from 0.5 to 6.85 MeV/A. For beam species up to ^{20}Ne, intensities are expected to be in the range of 10^{12}-10^{13} pps; from ^{20}Ne to ^{40}Ar, in the range of 10^{11}-10^{12} in a phase width of 6-10° and with an emittance of 20-25

A large $n = \frac{1}{2}$ spectrometer magnet constructed for use with the IMP cyclotron.

mm mrad in each plane. The energy resolution of the extracted beam is expected to be $\Delta E/E = 4 \times 10^{-3}$. The design work seems to be completed and the pole pieces are being fabricated. A 1/3-scale model magnet and a prototype ion source have been constructed and are being tested.

In the experimental area, there are two beam lines that use Chinese-built quadrupole doublets of rather crude construction. We saw a partly built new stainless steel scattering chamber of about 1 m in diameter. The standard of machining looked reasonably good, although the tapped holes were very rough.

The operation of the cyclotron requires 20 people, 3 at any given time, perhaps reflecting in part the enormous length of the Russian-built control desk. An additional 30 people are currently working on the cyclotron conversion project. We did not see any great signs of activity in the building—

NUCLEAR SCIENCE IN CHINA

FIRST FLOOR

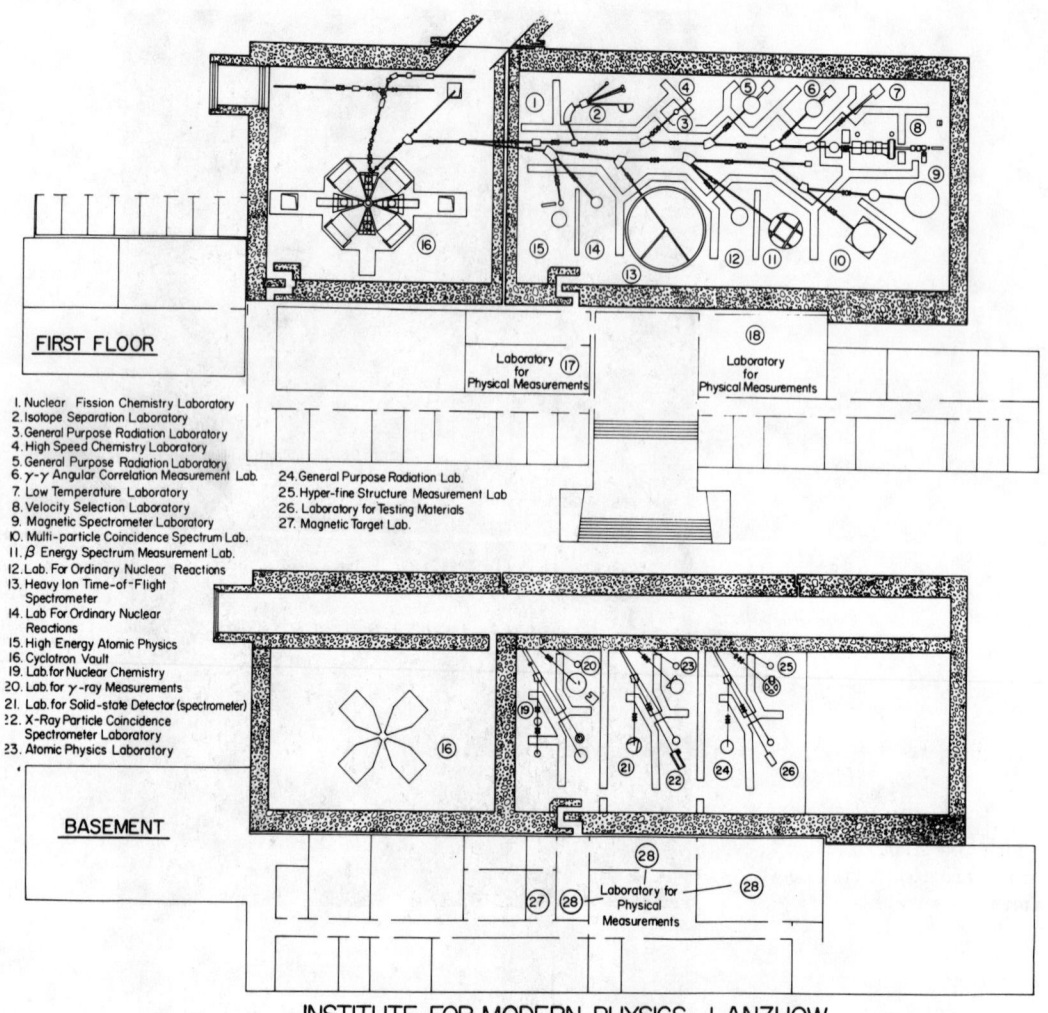

1. Nuclear Fission Chemistry Laboratory
2. Isotope Separation Laboratory
3. General Purpose Radiation Laboratory
4. High Speed Chemistry Laboratory
5. General Purpose Radiation Laboratory
6. γ-γ Angular Correlation Measurement Lab.
7. Low Temperature Laboratory
8. Velocity Selection Laboratory
9. Magnetic Spectrometer Laboratory
10. Multi-particle Coincidence Spectrum Lab.
11. β Energy Spectrum Measurement Lab.
12. Lab. For Ordinary Nuclear Reactions
13. Heavy Ion Time-of-Flight Spectrometer
14. Lab For Ordinary Nuclear Reactions
15. High Energy Atomic Physics
16. Cyclotron Vault
19. Lab. for Nuclear Chemistry
20. Lab. for γ-ray Measurements
21. Lab. for Solid-state Detector (spectrometer)
22. X-Ray Particle Coincidence Spectrometer Laboratory
23. Atomic Physics Laboratory
24. General Purpose Radiation Lab.
25. Hyper-fine Structure Measurement Lab
26. Laboratory for Testing Materials
27. Magnetic Target Lab.

BASEMENT

INSTITUTE FOR MODERN PHYSICS – LANZHOW
CYCLOTRON LABORATORY PLAN – APRIL 1978

Schematic plans for the basement and first floor of the new cyclotron laboratory at the IMP as of April 1978. A second floor of the planned building contains offices and laboratories associated with the cyclotron activity but is not shown here. In addition, there are a number of laboratories and offices available both in the basement and on the first floor, as shown here outside the heavy machines shielding.

certainly nothing resembling a total staff of 50—but, as we subsequently learned in Hangzhou, all such staff must spend at least one half-day per week in political discussions, and our visit may have accidentally coincided with such a schedule at the IMP.

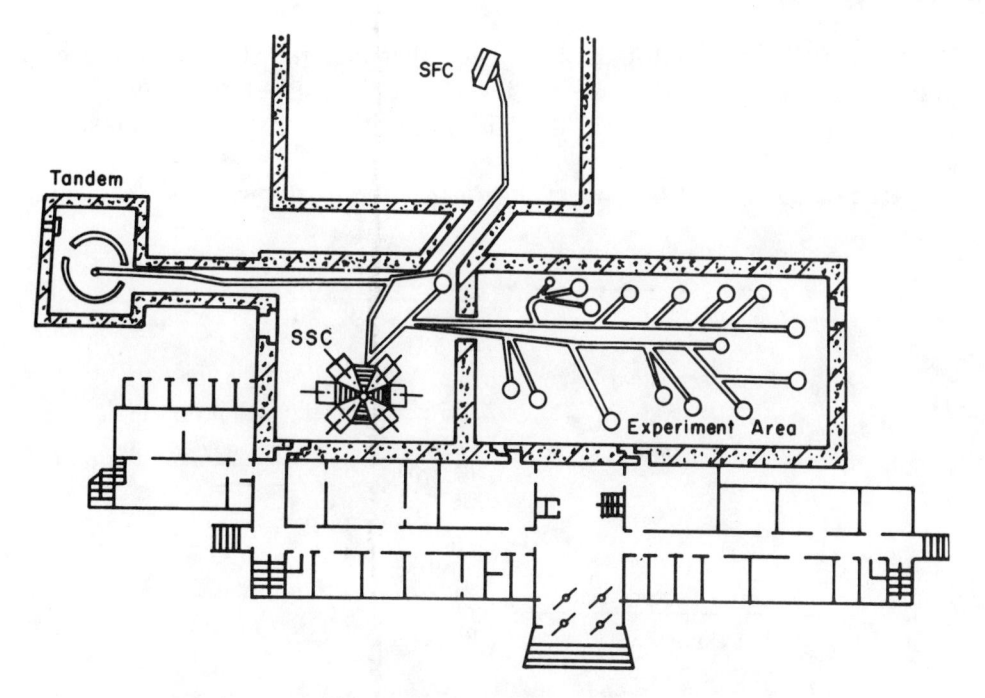

THE LAYOUT of the HEAVY-ION ACCELERATOR SYSTEM

A very schematic layout drawing of the proposed accelerator complex at the IMP showing the beam transport layout, as of April 1978, for connecting the planned 20-MV tandem and the existing cyclotron (after its modification to SFC characteristics) to the large SSC post-accelerator.

We saw several PLA guards with rifles and fixed bayonets, but we were unable to discern any logic to their stationing at some laboratories and not at others. Director Yang explained that they were holdovers from the Cultural Revolution.

During the afternoon we were further briefed by Zhang Mingling on the cyclotron project. The separated-sector cyclotron (SSC) with K = 450 will be injected by the upgraded SFC (Phase I) and later by a 20-MV tandem accelerator (Phase II). Phase I will be completed in 1985; work on Phase II has already begun in terms of tandem development, to which we shall return below.

The Phase I facility will produce light heavy ions up to 50 MeV/A and Xe at 6 MeV/A. With the tandem injector, Phase II will provide light heavy ions to 100 MeV/A and ^{238}U to 10 MeV/A. The new laboratory will have 18,000 m² of floor area, not including a future addition for the tandem. The experimental floor space, built on two levels, will be 2,500 m² with 2.6-m shielding. Excavation has already begun for this laboratory, and IMP has structural steel, reinforcing bars, and other material stockpiled in every available corner of the IMP site for the planned construction. We were told that without such foresight in material acquisition construction can suffer very serious delays.

The parameters of the two cyclotrons will be as follows:

Sector-Focused Cyclotron

Sectors	3
Frequency	7-18 MHz
Energy constant	69
Emittance	20-25 π mm mrad in each plane
$\Delta E/E$	4×10^{-3}
Intensity	10^{13}-10^{12} pps, H-Ne
	10^{12}-10^{11} pps, Ne-Ar
Phase width	6-10°

Separated-Sector Cyclotron

Injection radius	0.9 m or 1 m
Extraction radius	3.2 m
ν_z	0.732-0.864
Energy ratio	12.7 or 10.3
Magnet sectors	52°
Magnet gap	10 cm
B_{max}	10 K gauss
Magnet power	660 kW
Magnet current (max)	1,500 A
Magnet iron (per sector)	800 tons
Coil weight (per coil)	3.7 tons
Current stability	10^{-5}
Trim coils	40
Trim coil power	168 kW
Dees	$2 \times 26°$
Dee voltage	100 kV (lowest frequency)
	250 kV (highest frequency)
Dee power	120 kW per dee
Frequency	6.5-14 MHz
Harmonic ratios	2-7
Phase stability	0.5-1°
Frequency stability	10^{-6}
Gap inside dee	5 cm
Total weight	2,500 tons
Vacuum	7×10^{-8} Torr

The magnet coils will be fabricated from 21 × 21-mm square copper with a 10-mm hole for water cooling. The magnets will be constructed of 50-cm-thick steel plates, none weighing more than 50 tons. The coils and pole tips will be inside the 1-cm-thick stainless steel (316 L) vacuum tank. There was some discussion of the coil insulation. Zhang Enhou said that it would be mineral (Al_2O_3), but Director Yang said it would be fiberglass and that the trim coil insulation might be Al_2O_3 like that at Indiana. The dees are supported on carriages so that they can be pulled out of the monolithic vacuum box; their general design draws heavily on that developed for the GANIL project in France.

Field measurements have been made with two 1/4-scale sectors, both excited, and with 10 trim coils (copper plate); the field can be made isochronous up to 100 MeV/A.

Several RF cavities have been considered, and a full-scale $\lambda/2$ resonator

A typical PIG cyclotron ion source developed for use in the IMP cyclotron.

NUCLEAR SCIENCE IN CHINA

The IMP test fixture for PIG positive ion sources.

was built. However, it was found to be mechanically too long, so they are now planning to copy the GANIL inclined (35°) resonator. (A GANIL delegation visited Lanzhou in December 1978.) There will be a variable capacity for coarse tuning; at the lowest frequency the capacitor gap is 2 cm, so the dee voltage must be limited to 100 kV.

The planned vacuum system involves a combination of oil diffusion pumps and 20°K cryopanels. The volume is 10 m^3, and the outgassing area is 1,000 m^2. The pressure required is 7×10^{-8} Torr; since the coils and poletips are inside the vacuum chamber, this poses a nontrivial challenge.

We were told that the cyclotron would cost roughly 70 million yuan (~$45 million U.S.), the building about 5.7 million yuan ($3.7 million U.S.), and experimental equipment about half as much as the cyclotron. During our visit, in addition to the large stockpiles of reinforcing steel and other building supplies, we noted a very large bridge crane that, we were told, was for the new SSC cyclotron laboratory.

Although we had little time to spend on the building and experimental area, we noted that the transport lines from the SFC and tandem as planned would be very long (60 m for the latter) and complex. Moreover, there was

Visits to Research Institutes

no provision for independent use of either of the injectors. We asked about the status of injection and extraction design, but were told that another group was responsible for it; we suggested that it might pose greater difficulties than the presentation appeared to suggest. The group took the point of view that inasmuch as these problems had already been solved in other world laboratories they could obviously be handled in China.

Tandem Accelerator Development Program

Phase II of the Institute accelerator facility planning involves using a 20-MV tandem as an alternate injector into the SSC cyclotron. Not only will it increase the energy of light ions (e.g., 50 to 100 MeV/nucleon ^{12}C), but will also extend the range of masses that can be accelerated from about Xe to U_i. Table 1 lists the design characteristics of both phases I and II, as well as of the stand-alone characteristics. The target date for completing Phase II is unclear, but a small division including 10 physicists and engineers, supported by 5 technicians, under the directorship of Guo Qidi, has already been formed. Guo spent the past year at the MP tandem installation in Munich. This division was formed about a year ago, is cooperating with a similar division at the Institute of Nuclear Studies in Shanghai, and appears to be systematically tackling the problems associated with building a 20-MV tandem. Although we heard that the possibility of purchasing such a machine, presumably from the United States, has not been excluded entirely as yet, it appears highly probable that the Chinese will build their own, pre-

Test modules fabricated within the Institute use techniques similar to those used by National Electrostatics Corporation in the United States. These prototype tube sections were produced using ultra-pure argon atomsphere brazing with aluminum to bond titanium electrodes to aluminum oxide ceramic insulating sections. The section on the left has been fitted with end flanges for vacuum and mechanical tests, that on the right was placed in boiling water and then immediately in liquid nitrogen to test for stability against thermal stresses, while that in the center is a prototype section of a possible corona voltage control column.

TABLE 1   Main Parameters

	Multi-Stage Operation		Phase II		Single-Stage Operation	
	Phase I					
	SFC	SFC + SCC	UR	UR + SCC	SFC	UR
Energy constant, K		450 (SSC)			69	20 MV
Ions	C　4.6	C—Xe	C　6.85	C—U	C—Cl	C—Ca
Maximum energy,	Xe　0.47	C　50	U　0.78	C　100	C　7.7	C　11.7
MeV/A		Xe　6		U　10	Cl　5	Ca　5
Maximum flux,	<Ne 10^{12}-10^{13}	<Ne 10^{11}-10^{12}	C—U	C—U	C—Cl	C—Co
pps	>Ne 10^{11}-10^{12}	>Ne 10^{10}-10^{11}	5×10^{-10}-2×10^{13}	10^{-9}-10^{12}	10^{11}-10^{13}	10^{11}-10^{13}
Energy resolution	$(2-4) \times 10^{-3}$	$(2-5) \times 10^{-3}$	1×10^{-3}-5×10^{-4}	$(2-4) \times 10^{-3}$	1×10^{-3}-2×10^{-3}	1×10^{-3}-1×10^{-4}
Emittance H	20-25	10-15	3-5	3-5	20-25	3-5
V	20-25	10-15	5-8	5-8	20-25	5-8
Duty factor	$6°$-$10°$	$6°$-$15°$	$6°$-$10°$	$6°$-$10°$	$6°$-$10°$	100%
micro		1-2^{ns}		1-2^{ns}		

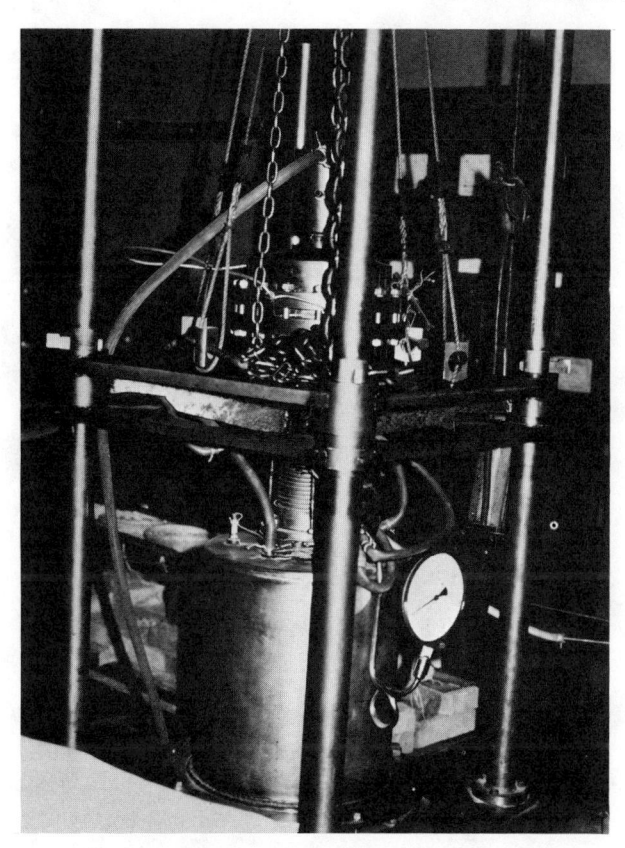

The argon-brazing furnace used at IMP in the fabrication of test accelerator and corona tube sections.

sumably drawing on the resources of the Vanguard factory in Shanghai as well as those of the IMP and INR.

Accelerator Tube Fabrication

About a year ago a small group was formed, headed by a new graduate hired by the Institute, to perfect the bonding of aluminum oxide insulators to titanium electrodes. The group appears to have been extremely successful, and we were shown one complete tube module—very similar to a standard U.S. National Electrostatic Corporation (NEC) product—that had undergone vacuum tests; the leak rate was reported to be about 10^{-9} Torr l/s. This module was complete with sturdy end flanges, but there was some indication that some difficulty was being experienced in joining these to the tube section. The module differed from an NEC one in that it had a smaller pitch, ~1.2 cm.

We were also shown a module, without end flanges, that had not been cleaned or pretreated in any way. The quality of the workmanship was remarkably good. There was almost zero visibility of any residual fillet from the 0.006-in.-thick aluminum foil used to bond the titanium to the ceramic; although they will still grit-clean, it hardly seemed necessary. The ceramic was ultra white and showed no discoloration, probably as a result of using ultra pure argon in their brazing furnace (we saw a large unit containing a molecular sieve that clearly was used for this purpose). The ceramic rings were about 10 cm in diameter and had a wall thickness of about 5 mm—the titanium electrodes appeared to be about 0.010-0.015" thick and projected in from the ceramic about 5 mm and out about 8 mm (no slots were evident for the bayonet fitting of internal baffles in the NEC fashion, but we learned that future units would have such slots).

We were also shown a short section of about a 5-cm diameter tube, presumably a prototype corona voltage distribution tube. This, we were told, had been heated to 500°C and then thrown into a bath of liquid nitrogen. Other than some discoloration of the titanium, it appeared entirely unscathed. Several tests had been made of the tensile strength of the bonds (a large tensile testing machine using hydraulic loading was installed in the laboratory), and, although we acquired no quantitative information, the strength appeared to be commensurate with that of the ceramic. Little has been done as yet in the way of voltage testing. We were simply told that 80 kV had been placed across a pair of adjacent electrodes without breakdown.

By any standard, we conclude this group has made remarkable progress in the short time since its founding. We asked about possible cooperation between IMP and other institutions, either at the Shanghai Institute for Nuclear Research, where we learned that a smaller tandem was to be constructed, or at the Vanguard factory in Shanghai. Apparently none of any consequence had yet occurred; we surmise that the IMP group wishes to work from a leadership position and will perfect its techniques before entering any such collaboration. In any event, it is clear that Director Yang himself will make this decision when he considers it appropriate.

Charging System Development

We were shown, tucked in the corner of a small laboratory, about a 5-ft section of a pelletron charging system. This appeared to be a direct copy of an NEC pelletron with the exception of the drive pulleys. These were of aluminum and bonded to the grooved edge was a conducting rubberlike seating material—we were told it was rubber heavily loaded with graphite (not graphite fibers); this instead of the steel contact plates of the NEC design. The pelletron chain had been run in air for about 400 hours, but not with the conducting rubber coated pulleys; a pressure vessel of just the right size to house this unit was adjacent to it, and some of us gained the impression that it had received pressure testing as well. In any case, the nylon

Visits to Research Institutes

Members of the delegation discuss the prototype development work on a laddertron-charging system with Yang Chengzhong and members of his staff in IMP. Contrary to U.S. practice, contact between the laddertron pulleys and the laddertron itself is made through rims of graphite-loaded conducting rubber, rather than via brushing contract with shim steel strips.

insulating bushings were blackened and appeared as though they had been carbonized as a result of extensive breakdown.

The highlight of this laboratory was a very recently completed laddertron section—about 6 ft long. To the best of our judgement this was identical in design and dimension with that developed at Daresbury, although the method of manufacture may be slightly different. The end "pellets" were cast from stainless steel and contained four internal bosses for the linkage pins. The "rungs" were essentially flattened stainless steel tubes brazed to the pellets. The entire assembly was highly polished and showed evidence of excellent workmanship. The linkage pins, we were informed, were made from cast nylon and contained metal bearing sleeves—the design closely resembled that of Daresbury. The linkage pins were comparatively crude, and we were told that they were only temporary—they had rather vicious screw

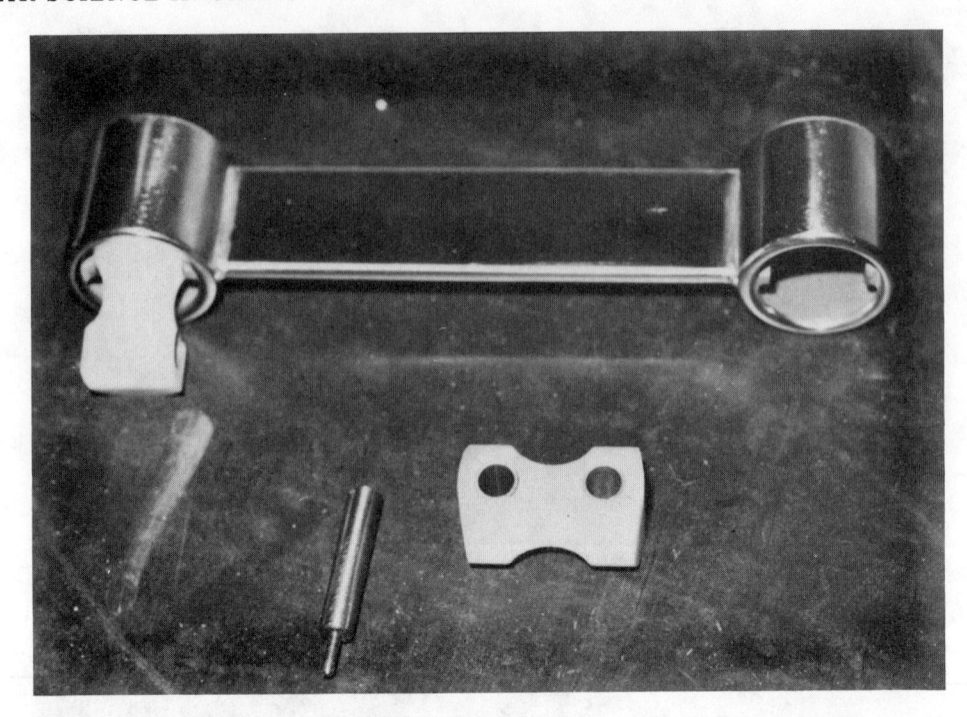

A typical element of the IMP laddertron test system showing one of the rungs, the nylon connecting links, and the pins used to secure those links.

drive slots that frequently protruded from the pellets. These will be replaced with Allan head pins, but apparently these are still very difficult to obtain in China and are made individually by machinists as needed. No charge induction system was shown to us, and it apparently is still under development.

The section was operated mechanically for us, and it ran very quietly and smoothly with very little lateral wobble; however, the linear speed was low—about 5.5 m/s—and the group plans to at least double this in the near future. At the present time no data are available about the lifetime of the conducting graphite-loaded rubber pulleys: Some of us have doubts concerning their longevity in actual use.

This charging system program was quite impressive, and there is little doubt that within a year IMP will have a successful operating laddertron charging system. Future plans include installing the system in a pressure vessel and making current measurements in a standard high-pressure environment of N_2 (80 percent) + CO_2 (20 percent)—not SF_6 (experience with the latter gas appears extremely limited in China, and we gather that production is extremely limited as yet).

Visits to Research Institutes

We later learned that the personnel of the Vanguard factory Accelerator Division and of the Institute for Nuclear Research (INR) in Shanghai are aware of the IMP work in this area and noted that they would "probably" make use of it in the 6-MV tandem now being planned for INR.

Negative Ion Source Development

We were shown a rather primitive negative ion source test facility that had very recently been relocated from a very small to a slightly larger room. As

The sputter ion source developed at IMP for ultimate use with the proposed 20-MV tandem accelerator injector to the separated sector cyclotron post-accelerator.

The negative ion source test assembly at IMP; the ion source is placed at the top of the ceramic insulating column, and the dipole magnet below is used to analyze its output.

in the Beijing IAE, tests had been made only with an offset direct extraction duoplasmatron. However, the test facility had a 90° analyzing magnet of about 20-cm radius that has permitted a few measurements to be made with ions other than hydrogen.

Negative hydrogen ion currents, after analysis, were typically about 80 μA, accompanied with about 7 mA electron beams—most measurements were made at an extraction voltage of about 27 kV. Unlike the situation at the IAE in Beijing, the most serious problem in Lanzhou was cathode lifetime—typically about 40 hours. They have tried a variety of cathodes and appear to have standardized on one formed from 1-mm diameter tungsten wire. When asked why they were not using indirectly heated LaB_6 cathodes (as in Beijing), they replied that LaB_6 was only available from foreign sources and that the IAE had somehow, presumably through personal contact, been fortunate to obtain some. Extraction aperture erosion that limited source lifetime at the IAE appeared to have been solved at the IMP in Lanzhou.

Test on ions other than H⁻ appear to be extremely limited in number and duration. 16 μA of ^{16}O⁻ has been observed while operating the source on oxygen gas—13.2 μA of ^{16}O has also been observed while operating on CO^2. When asked how long the source ran on CO_2 before the extraction aperture closed due to carbon deposition, they replied that the source was only run in this mode for a few hours, hence the problem was not encountered! A few measurements have also been made using chlorine as a feed gas; the observed Cl⁻ current (presumably both isotopes) was 7μA—and again no mention was made of source lifetime under these conditions.

Somewhat to our surprise, we were shown a close-to-completely fabricated Middleton-type sputter source. As in the case of many others who have started from scratch in this area, a number of design mistakes had been made and old problems encountered. For example, the electron beam welding of the porous tungsten frit into the molybdenum feed tube had been done incorrectly, resulting in a cracked frit. The surface ionization source had been designed with a cooled region located between the cesium reservoir and the ionizer that inevitably would have resulted in the condensation of cesium metal and ultimate plugging. The Cs⁺ beam extraction system was well engineered, but allowance had not been made to purposely allow this to run at an elevated temperature to prevent condensation of cesium vapor—the presence of which inevitably results in arcing. The cone wheel was extremely large—close to 1 ft in diameter—and was mounted in a large and extremely heavy steel chamber.

As a result of a well-attended and highly stimulating discussion group extending over several hours with Middleton, many of these problems were identified and remedied. Given the enthusiasm and drive of the group involved, we expect that rapid progress will be made at IMP in all ion source technology.

None of our remarks are intended as derogatory in any sense; it must be borne in mind that U.S. physicists have a tremendous background of technological development to draw on—much of which evolved from our space program—giving them an enormous advantage in developing such ion sources. If such information (which appears in the open literature) is available in China, it certainly does not appear to have been well-disseminated as yet. All senior Chinese scientists agree that technical information transfer is one of their very serious problems. Our impression is that it varies enormously from group to group, even within one institution.

We conclude that again the IMP group has, of all related Chinese institutions, made the most progress toward functional negative ion sources for tandems and that its program will provide a focus for Chinese activity in this area.

Heavy Ion Sources

We were shown a prototype heavy ion source similar to the one that is expected to be used in the SFC cyclotron injector mounted in a test stand inside a small magnet of about 50-cm diameter. The source apparently produces milliamperes of total current output; for example, the O^{5+} output is 2-3 mA. Only C, N, and O have so far been tested in the sources. The source itself is essentially a copy of the standard Soviet model. It has two molybdenum buttons indirectly heated by tungsten filaments; it is made entirely of copper, except for the extraction slit, which is made of an unspecified refractory metal. The arc chamber is about 15 cm high, but the body of the source is unusually wide, about 3 cm, and almost certainly will intercept some of the beams if it is used in the cyclotron in its present form. No work has been done as yet on producing ions from solids. With oxygen gas the source lifetime was reported to be 6-7 hours, similar to experience elsewhere. It is our impression that substantial work remains to be accomplished in this area, but the problems involved are being attacked in a professional manner, and we are optimistic concerning the success of this IMP program.

DJS-131 Computer

We were shown a DJS-131 computer that is made commercially in Shanghai. (DJS is simply the acronym for the Chinese words for "electronic computer" and 131 is the identification number for this relatively small model.) It appears an appropriate device for limited data acquisition and data analysis. It has a 32 k-bit fast memory and a speed of 2 μs/operation. It is a general-purpose computer, and intermediate-scale integrated circuits are used in its construction. There are 62 input/output channels available. We saw only punched paper tape input and a typewriter and plotter output. A magnetic tape drive is on order at IMP but not a disk, although we were told that disk memories are now being manufactured in China. Externally, the computer appeared attractive and professional; it is very substantially larger than U.S. computers of comparable power.

Electronics and Detector Division

We had only a brief exposure to the work of this Division beyond the initial display of detectors fabricated in it. We found, however, that standard NIM and CAMAC techniques are in use. The following modules were under test during one visit: constant fraction discriminations, fast discriminations, time-pick-off amplifiers, charge sensitive preamplifiers, time-to-amplitude converters—TAC's, delay line boxes, and power supplies (1 A at ±6, ±12, and ±24 V drift <0.1 percent per h ripple; <1 mV).

A single technician is responsible for the complete fabrication of each

Visits to Research Institutes

The canonical Chinese panda design available at all Chinese computer centers as a test pattern for the computer system.

unit from making the circuit board through wiring and assembly to final testing. We saw no evidence of assembly line or mass production techniques involving specialization by given technicians, but in view of the potential demand we believe that IMP will be forced in this direction. They also test and select switching transistors.

Integrated circuits are in widespread use but extremely limited supply. We were told that yields of a few percent were typical of the large-scale production of relatively complex circuits. Through ingenious design the Chinese have arranged to use rejects with respect to the complete design as entirely suitable IC's for less demanding applications so that a detailed sorting operation is performed on the newly manufactured IC's to assign them to categories in which they are functionally acceptable. The Chinese appear to have concluded (and we would agree) that their low yield reflects inadequate clean room characteristics. At Qinghua University we were shown the detailed architectural and mechanical design for an entirely contemporary clean room factory facility for IC production. Although produced as a student exercise, it was patently obvious that it had been commissioned and that, despite claims at Qinghua to the contrary, it would probably be implemented. The Chinese do not waste high-level student activity in architecture and engineering on hypothetical problems.

While the Chinese show every evidence of active progress toward self-sufficiency in modern electronics, it is very clear that the visit paid to the People's Republic by a group of French nuclear physicists some 4 years ago opened up a very substantial Chinese market for French nuclear and computer instrumentation. We saw, in almost all the nuclear installations we visited, examples of Intertechnique and other French multichannel analyzers, small computers, and the like. And it is clear that most current Chinese multichannel analyzers have been closely copied from the French units.

Nuclear Physics Division

At the end of the day, Dai Guangxi told us briefly about some nuclear science work. Much of it appeared to have been done about 5 years ago; it involved the production of isotopes of californium and fermium by heavy ion bombardment of ^{238}U. He noted that their results on ^{234}Cf and ^{247}Fm do not agree with those from Berkeley. They used a recoil catcher foil technique and prepared samples for α-counting by ion-exchange separation and electrodeposition; they also used a helium jet to transport recoils from target to detector.

They have had problems with Pb contamination of the ^{238}U target and evolving from this have used α-counting of products from ^{12}C bombardments to detect lead pollution in the atmosphere with a sensitivity to 10^{-8}-10^{-9} g/l.

Excitation functions for the (^{12}C, $4n$) and (^{12}C, $5n$) reactions on ^{238}U targets have been measured using a stacked foil-catcher-absorber technique; α-particles have been measured at 70° from 76 MeV ^{12}C bombardment of Pb. A large sharp peak at about 8 MeV, for which there is no explanation, was found in their data.

Some work has also been done on deep inelastic collisions of ^{12}C on ^{197}Au. Angular distributions were measured for ^{11}B and ^{9}Be products; cross sections are small because the energy is close to the Coulomb barrier.

High-Angular Momentum Group

This group is interested in measuring gamma-ray multiplicities. They have constructed a 5-detector planar array embedded in lead. Four detectors are 50 × 50-mm NaI crystals, and one is a Ge(Li) detector. We did not see any data taken with this system, however. The group has plans for a 15-detector spherical array: 13 NaI detectors and 2 Ge(Li) detectors. It was not clear whether they planned to use larger NaI detectors. In the detector group we learned that the largest Ge(Li) detectors generally available are 30 cc (limited by the availability of Ge crystals).

Search for Eka Platinum

We were shown briefly what can only be regarded as a low-key search for a superheavy eka platinum in nickel ores. A chemist had on the order of a kilogram or two of crudely refined nickel ore and was chemically extracting platinum. The extract was then placed in a counter and the energy of any emitted α-particles was then measured. There clearly must have been some misunderstanding, since she adamantly insisted that she was searching for 4.4-4.8 MeV α-particles (possibly an abosrber foil was used to filter out normal α-particles).

Nuclear Theory Group

Just as in all the other institutions that we visited, the theory group at IMP was founded only several years ago and is made up of people who graduated from a university before 1966. Most of them, moreover, had not officially done any work during the Cultural Revolution.

The head of the group is Shu Sicui, whom we did not meet because he was traveling. The group consists of nine staff members and two graduate students—one at Lanzhou University and the other at Nanjing University. Their work is primarily on nuclear reaction mechanisms, including heavy ion fusion and deep inelastic processes. They appeared to be familiar with all the current literature in the field, including quite recent work. In addition, they are engaged in work on nuclear structure, including mass formulas, high-spin states, the question of whether backbending reflects pairing collapse or rotational alignment, and pairing vibrations. However, it is probably fair to say that as yet they are only following these fields and have contributed little to them.

For their calculations (in collaboration with some of the IMP experimentalists) they usually use a DJS-6 (Chinese-made) computer, but also they apparently have access to a substantially larger Chinese computer installed somewhere near Shanghai not far from the Institute for Nuclear Research, and they use it for large distorted wave and similar calculations. They spoke,

An IMP chemist at work in her laboratory on the separation of eka platinum from nickel ores.

somewhat wistfully, of a hoped-for purchase of an IBM 370, but we were unable to obtain details of any actual negotiations.

Given the ambitious scope of the experimental facilities and programs planned for IMP, it would be our strong recommendation that the nuclear theory group be strengthened as soon as possible so that it can participate more effectively in the planning for future experimental research programs. We believe that it would also be particularly important for members of the present group to spend substantial periods of time as active collaborators at some of the major international nuclear theory centers. And we believe that it is essential that more extensive computer facilities be made available in IMP as soon as possible.

We are encouraged by the interaction that already exists between experimental and theoretical nuclear groups at IMP and would urge that such interaction be fostered.

Visits to Research Institutes

Mössbauer Group

The efforts of the IMP Mössbauer group, started in 1975, are devoted solely to qualitative and quantitative analysis of iron in various materials for industry, agriculture, and other such applications. They have a basic Mössbauer experimental system that they constructed themselves. It consists of a standard drive of the Kankaleit type that operates in the constant acceleration mode and is controlled by a triangular wave generator. The Mössbauer spectrum is accumulated in a locally constructed 800-channel analyzer, which should be satisfactory for most purposes. The ^{57}Co source material is produced using the IMP cyclotron and then transformed into a Mössbauer source in the IMP Chemistry Department. Apparently, the sources are of quite reasonable quality, since line widths of 0.3 mm/s (some 50 percent over natural line width) are obtained and this is a fairly routine international value. In the analyses they carry out, they obtain up to 12 overlapping Mössbauer lines whose relative intensities must be determined; for this purpose they appear to have an adequate Gaussian line-shape fitting program programmed for the IMP central computer. For quantitative work they use samples that are 5 mg/cm^2 thick, and it was not clear to what extent they are able to correct for exponential absorption in the Mössbauer lines; they

Mössbauer equipment used in studying the beneficiation of iron ores.

have calibrated their analyses against samples prepared in their laboratory. For qualitative work they use thicker samples.

They have plans for improving their Mössbauer apparatus, but the main function of the Mössbauer program is to provide analysis of iron in nickel ores. They obtain the residue from the commercial nickel extraction process and determine the presence of iron, its chemical form, and the phase of its compound. They subject the sample to various heat-treatment procedures, and these annealed samples are then analyzed. Apparently, they have built up a considerable empirical lore on the relationship of these analyses to the quality of the ore. They appear to be chiefly concerned with Fe_2O_4; the latter compound is the most important one in the analyses. They analyze about 10 samples a month.

It would be interesting to know of what actual benefit this work is to the refining and mining industries. The Mössbauer effect clearly can provide a relatively precise and efficient method for iron analysis. Although it has been used rather extensively in the United States in research in chemistry, biology, medicine, mineralogy, and archaeology, it has not been used extensively in industry. In this respect this rather small effort at IMP is a very interesting development.

Concluding Discussion

Prior to our departure from Lanzhou, the delegation met formally with Director Yang, Secretary Xie, and their senior colleagues in the Friendship Hotel for a wide-ranging concluding discussion; they were obviously very much interested in our candid comments and impressions of their activities. The delegation members responded with both general and detailed remarks. Among the most important suggestions made were the following:

1. That given the magnitude of the challenge that IMP had set itself in accelerator construction it would be essential for IMP to draw on all available world experience; and that brief visits could not substitute for extended periods of 1 to several years, during which IMP staff would be sent to world centers of accelerator expertise to gain firsthand experience.

2. That it was certainly not too early to develop a sharper focus on the precise research activity that the new facilities would support in order that design decisions that will affect the research capabilities might be made in the most informed manner possible; that the natural tendency to defer such considerations until later be resisted strongly; and that IMP researchers be sent to foreign centers to again gain firsthand experience at the current research frontiers. Both here and in item 1 above, the delegation members volunteered not only to welcome appropriate IMP staff to their own laboratories, but also to assist in identifying foreign laboratories and situations

that might be particularly suitable for the type of experience desired.

3. That given the magnitude and scope of the planned nuclear science facilities in IMP it was essential that potential users from universities and institutes throughout China be identified and associated with the various programs as soon as possible in order that they might assist in the design and construction efforts and in so doing evolve a sense of identification with the facility that would be of great importance in its subsequent research utilization.

4. That the layout of the proposed facility, including both injectors and the SSC, appeared rather strange in that (a) the beam transport lines from the injectors appeared much too long and complex and (b) there seemed to be no provision for using either of the two injectors— powerful accelerators in their own right—as stand-alone research facilities while the other was being used as an injector; that the layout would benefit from considerable additional thought in terms both of accelerator construction and research scope, flexibility, and convenience.

5. That given the magnitude of the overall planned construction program it was essential that priorities and resource allocations be monitored very carefully lest efforts become so diffused that no one of the project components would proceed expeditiously; in short, that they guard against spreading themselves too thinly.

Director Yang responded graciously to all our remarks, noting that they were not unexpected; he thanked us for our comments, lectures, and discussions and for our offer of continuing assistance; Secretary Xie and he then presented each member of the delegation with souvenirs of their Lanzhou visit that they will long treasure.

INSTITUTE FOR NUCLEAR RESEARCH (SHANGHAI)*

The Institute for Nuclear Research (INR) of the Chinese Academy of Sciences is located in the suburb of Jiading, about 30 km northwest of Shanghai, and was founded in 1959. The site, now recognized as generally inconvenient, was selected orginially by Soviet consultants who assisted in the early planning for, and construction of, the Institute. It has a staff of about 900, of whom about 500 are scientists and technicians, 150 are physicists, and 100 are chemists (of these, 17 are theorists). The Institute consists of five major laboratories in the fields of nuclear physics and techniques, isotope and radiation physics, radiation chemistry, accelerator

*The entire delegation visited the Institute on the morning of June 5.

Members of the Institute for Nuclear Research in Shanghai greet the delegation outside of the main building of the Institute. On the left, in the back row, we have Lai Weiquan, Lin Nianyung, Li Yongjian, Chang Hongjun, John Rasmussen (from the University of California at Berkeley, as a visitor at Fudan), Pierre Perrolle, Roy Middleton, Bernard Harvey, Jin Houchu, Allan Bromley, Zhang Jiahua, Arthur Kerman, Alexander Zucker, Cheng Xiaowu, Tom Tombrello, and Song Hongqiu. Kneeling in the foreground are, from the left, Cheng Yuandi, Yan Xiuying, Ding Dazhao, Mao Yu, Zhang Weizhong, Zhou Siyuan, P. K. Kuo, Ernest Henley, Fu Deji, Jin Hansheng, and Zhang Xiaoyang.

development, and nuclear electronics and detectors. Most of the Institute's work is in application of nuclear techniques, e.g., Mössbauer effects, solid-state physics, proton-induced X-ray emission (PIXE) using protons and light ions, channeling, and perturbed angular correlations. In nuclear physics some work is in progress on nuclear reaction mechanisms, nuclear structure, (α,p) reactions to investigate both preequilibrium and backward scattering, deuteron breakup reactions, and transport mechanisms in nuclear fission. Isotopes (e.g., In, Fe) are produced for medical purposes, and some compounds involving light isotopes (e.g., ^{14}C, ^{3}H) are sythesized. Chemists study radiation-induced polymerization work.

The Institute has a 1.2-M cyclotron, built locally between 1960 and 1964 and based on the Russian design of the IAE-Beijing machine. It was shimmed in early 1978 to increase its energy from 6.5 to 8 MeV protons;

it has a large internal current (~3 mA), and a very intense external proton beam is also available. The RF system was obtained as surplus from the Beijing Broadcasting Bureau in 1960. It can also be used to accelerate deuterons (16 MeV), α-particles and any light ions with e/m of 1/2 or 1/3. For example, it is used at present in the latter mode to produce 3.5-MeV protons by accelerating singly ionized molecular H_3. Indeed, it was one of the only accelerators we saw in China that was in actual operation. It is used about half time for physics and half time for activation analysis and isotope production. There are plans under way to convert the machine to a sector-focused cyclotron to accelerate protons from 10-35 MeV, and the intention is to use it primarily for protons. It differs in design from that planned in Lanzhou, because the latter accelerator will be used primarily for heavy ion work.

Other facilities at the Institute include ^{60}Co sources up to 120 kCu, a 200-KeV Cockcroft-Walton neutron generator, a 1.5-MV electron Van de Graaff, and a small zero-power pressurized light H^2O reactor for research

The cyclotron at the Institute for Nuclear Research in Shanghai. The cyclotron is here shown with its vacuum box opened.

(there is a PDP/11 computer available for use with this reactor—the only one we saw in China).

The Institute has a structure somewhat akin to universities, in that there are research fellows, associate resident fellows, assistant resident fellows, among the scientists and similar titles for engineers.

At the moment the Institute has 4 first-year graduate students in residence and expects to accept 12 next year. Graduate students at the Institute take formal courses at Fudan University for 1 year and then come to do their research using the facilities—and presumably under the guidance of staff—at the Institute. It is anticipated in each such case that the individual will remain as a staff member following his educational program unless he, the Institute management, or an appropriate central governmental group requests otherwise. In answer to the question as to how the Institute advertises its opportunities for prospective graduate students, we were told that an appropriate description appears in Chinese newspapers.

As everywhere else, the Director, Jin Houchu, felt that one of his most important problems was that of research lag reflecting the Cultural Revolution. He described the past decade as one of "open door policy" in that everyone could attend the University and those inside the University (faculty and students) were sent into the fields. (He himself spent 5 years there.)

Our group partitioned into subgroups that visited the cyclotron, the tandem planning section, the applications section, and the theory group.

Cyclotron Group

Operation of the cyclotron is apparently confined to two frequencies: 10 MHz for nuclear physics and 8 MHz for low-energy beams as required for PIXE experiments. This latter mode is run only during 1 month per year. The machine operates for three shifts per day, 5 days per week. The source uses a tungsten filament with a rather large slit and suppression shields on either side that require that the first-turn radius be about 40 mm. Main magnet power is from a motor-generator set. Our impression was very favorable: The cyclotron seemed to be well engineered, maintained, and operated.

The Institute is in the process of converting this cyclotron to a sector-focused design having three sectors: a spiral angle 45°, 9 valley coils, and 9 trim coils. There will be a single dee in the new design with two dee stems in parallel in order to reduce the inductance so that the frequency range can be raised to 8-21 MHz. The unusual shape of the dee will give a 7 percent variation in accelerating voltage across the length of the dee opening. The radius of the magnet will be increased from 1.2 to 1.44 m, giving proton energies from 10 to 35 MeV. A one-fifth scale model of the magnet has been constructed, and field measurements are completed. Orbit calculations with the measured field have been made at the same Shanghai computer

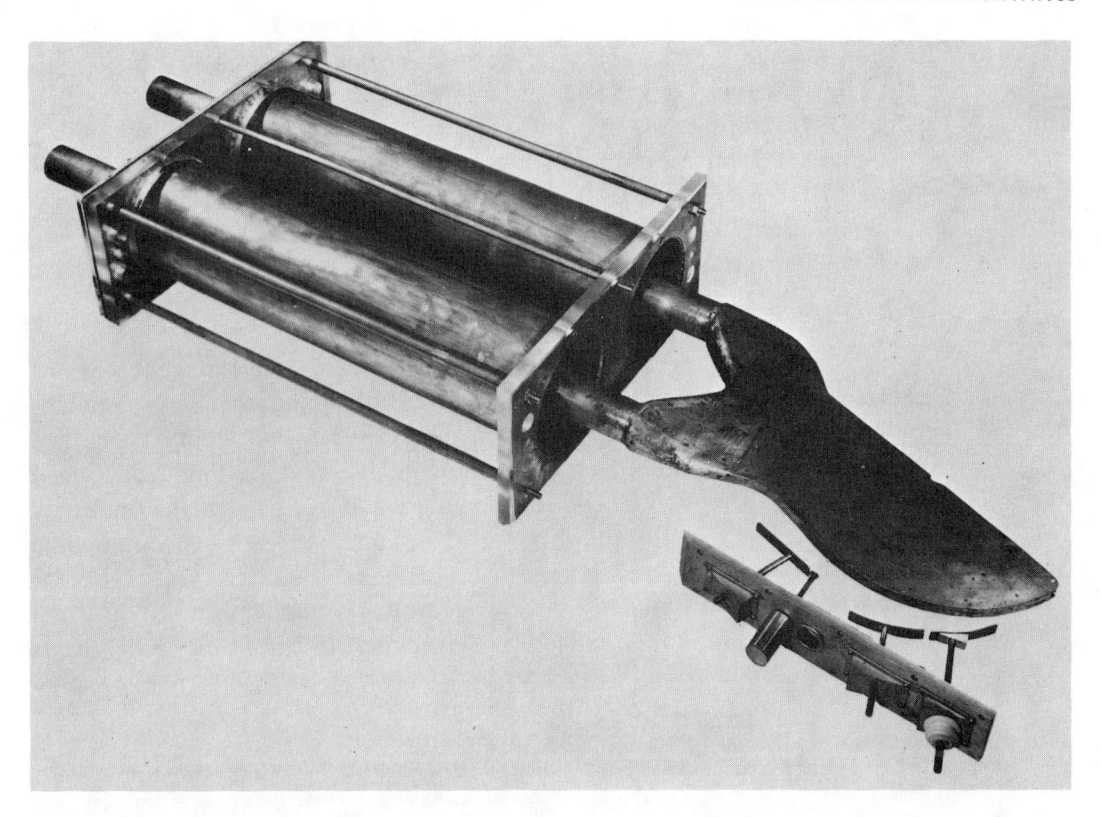

A model of the new dee-structure proposed for the INR cyclotron. The unusual shape of the structure itself is very evident in this photograph.

center that we have heard of elsewhere but have been unable to locate precisely. A one-fourth scale model of the dee and dee-stems has been built and tested. We were impressed by the technical competence of the people who are designing this new machine. They presented us with a detailed report on the design that is available in Chinese.

The present cyclotron has three beam lines leading into the experimental area via a quadrupole doublet and a standard switching dipole magnet. Line 1 is used for activation analyses: Samples are transferred to a counting area via a 2-cm rabbit. This line is also used for radiation damage studies on semiconductors and for isotope production. The beam spot on target is about 15 × 25 mm. External beam intensities (maximum) are 60-70 μA for deuterons and 30 μA for helium ions. Line 2 is used solely for isotope production. Line 3 has a 1.5-diameter scattering chamber, 80-cm deep, with three moveable arms. By brute-force collimation, the beam spot on target is reduced to 3-mm diameter. There is a functioning closed-circuit TV system used for alignment and target monitoring. Beyond the large chamber, there is a smaller one used for PIXE experiments.

In the counting area, we saw two racks (not completely filled) with a 4,000-channel Intertechnique analyzer system with teletype printout. We learned that the Institute staff has built some 4,096-channel analyzers (as elsewhere, essentially copies of the Intertechnique design), as well as Si(Li), Ge(Li), and surface barrier detectors.

Tandem Accelerator Group

The Institute plans to build a 6-MV vertical tandem accelerator. It was not clear that the entire funding for this project has been approved as yet by the Academy of Sciences, but, if so (as appeared likely), the facility is planned to be operational in 1982. Construction of the planned machine will depend very heavily on the facilities of the Vanguard factory in Shanghai and may involve cooperation with the Institutes in Lanzhou (IMP) and in Beijing (IAE).

We were shown detailed drawings of both the tandem and the 7 beam line target room layout. The machine very closely resembles an NEC 8 UD tandem and its 11.8-ft-diameter tank and 16-ft-long column (including some

A layout drawing for the proposed 6-MV tandem accelerator for the INR Shanghai. If this machine receives final approval, it will be fabricated jointly by INR and the Vanguard factory in Shanghai, using techniques developed in a number of Chinese institutions including the Institute for Modern Physics in Lanzhou and corresponding rather closely in some respects to the techniques pioneered by National Electrostatics Corporation in the United States. As shown here, a laddertron-charging system is to be used together with ceramic column and tube sections of the National Electrostatics Corporation variety.

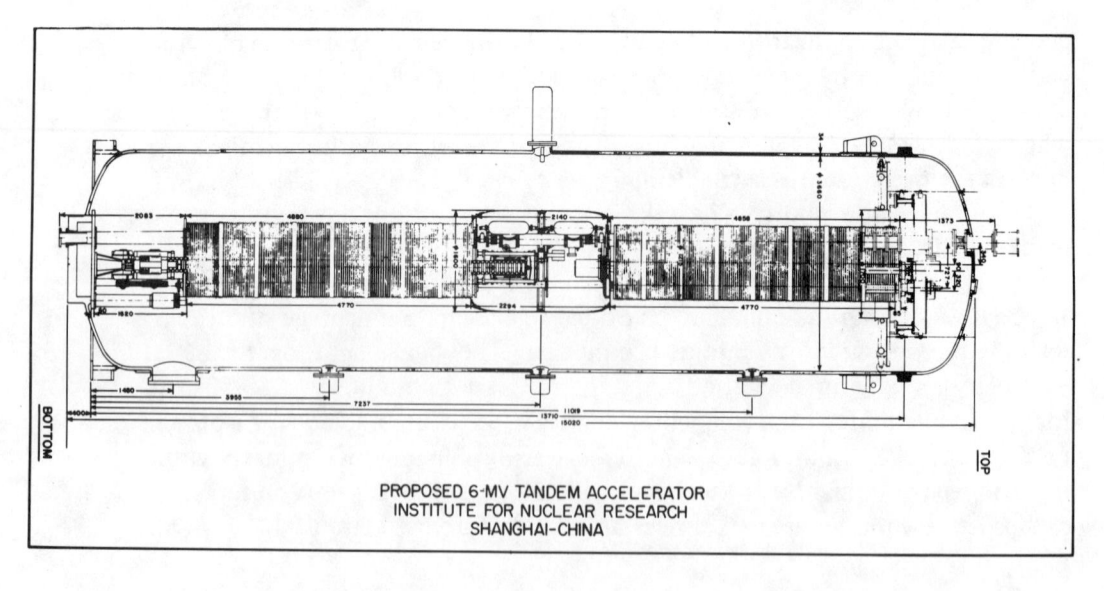

PROPOSED 6-MV TANDEM ACCELERATOR
INSTITUTE FOR NUCLEAR RESEARCH
SHANGHAI-CHINA

Visits to Research Institutes

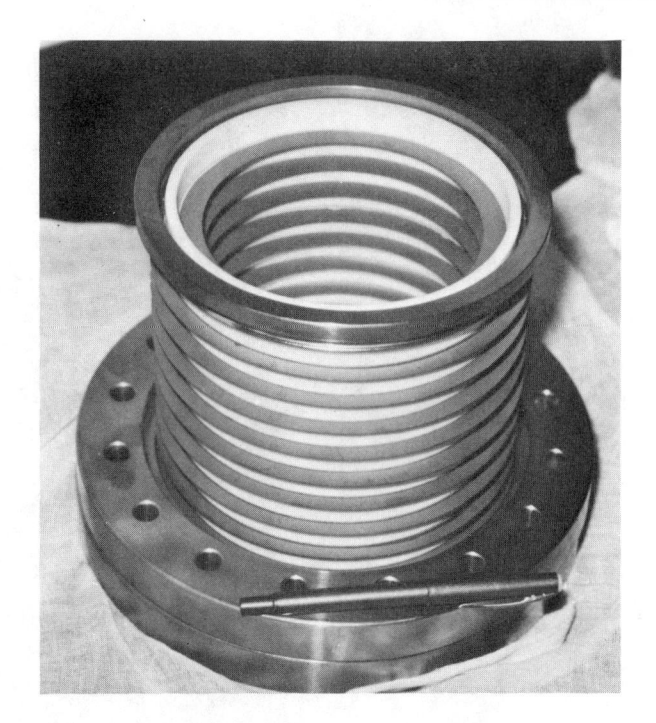

A prototype tube section fabricated at the INR using substantially different techniques from those under study at the IMP in Lanzhou.

dead sections) closely approximates the size of an HVEC FN tandem. The 6-MV rating is clearly conservative and with "state-of-the-art" design should be readily capable of operating at 8 to 9 MV.

The column is vertical, consists of 8 + 8 modular sections constructed from metal-ceramic bonded legs and the 7.5-ft-long terminal is to be fabricated from spun sheet metal (two sections). The accelerator tubes are also of metal-ceramic construction (more about this follows later) equipped with bakeable titanium diaphragms (the electrodes are not inclined). The proposed charging system is a laddertron (presently being developed at the IMP in Lanzhou). Voltage division will be with resistors (not corona tubes), and, although some partial decoupling of the tube and column gradients is planned, the present plans for this decoupling are nebulous. Power will be transmitted from the top of the machine to the terminal via a drive shaft and motor-generator sets (~14 kW). Present planning calls for fiber optic communication with the terminal augmented with lucite control rods. The tank insulating gas will initially be N_2 (80 percent) + CO_2 (20 percent), since SF_6 production is low, if not nonexistent, in China.

Several aspects of the machine design seemed curious to us. We had been led to believe that there was an extensive collaborative effort involving the Vanguard factory, the IMP in Lanzhou, Fudan University, and the INR. But we found, for example, that the two groups involved in tube

The vacuum brazing furnaces used at INR in the fabrication of tube and column sections for study as prototypes of those to be used in the 6-MV tandem.

design, in Lanzhou and at the INR, are following very different paths. The Lanzhou group appears to have very successfully copied the NEC tube, dimensionally and in method of construction, while the INR group appears to have pursued a very different approach. Their tubes more closely resemble the Daresbury ones dimensionally, but differ in that the metal copper-silver to ceramic seal is made by the more conventional technique of (~20/80 percent) brazing—the process carried out *in vacuo* rather than in an argon atmosphere as in Lanzhou. We were shown a few prototype INR tube sections, all of which had been sandblasted to remove surplus braze material. These appeared of high quality, and at least one had been voltage tested under normal operating conditions with internal vacuum and external pressurized insulating gas. Apparently conditioning of the 15-mm pitch titanium electrodes began at about 16 kV/cm, and the final gradient achieved was 33 kV/cm after several hours of operation. The final decision on whether to adopt the Lanzhou tubes or those developed at INR has yet to be made. On the basis of our observations, we would certainly support the former.

We were also very surprised to find that, although such publications as Daresbury progress reports and current issues of *Nuclear Instruments and Methods* are said to be widely available in China, these had apparently not been read, or at least fully comprehended, by personnel at INR. For example, little if anything was known about the highly successful electrostatic shielding of resistors as developed at Daresbury, or for that matter about spark gap protection of resistors. A rather startling surprise was that, while elaborate plans had been made for terminal pumping seemingly with two pairs of titanium T-ball evaporation pumps (each pair mounted in a common housing) plus a centrally located ion pump, the intention was to use gas stripping from the start, and no provision had been made for a foil stripper mechanism. Our firm impression also was that knowledge of long-lived wrinkled foils and those prepared from cracking ethylene gas followed the NEC style—crucial to modern tandem design particularly—has not filtered through the Chinese system. There were several other similar illustrations of this breakdown of information transfer. In contrast, the IMP group in Lanzhou appeared to have studied and understood in detail all the pertinent literature including the most current journal issues.

The prototype negative ion injector consisted of a fairly large 90° magnet preceded by ±30° inflection magnet to accommodate two ion sources. One of the latter was to be a direct extraction trio-plasmatron, presently under development, and the second a sputter source. There appeared to be little provision for high-energy injection, but presumably injection would have to be at an energy of at least 100 keV.

We were again surprised by the apparent lack of communication concerning these design features between the IMP in Lanzhou, the INR, the Vanguard factory, and Fudan University. Although work at all of the above-mentioned institutions appeared to be of reasonable quality—communication—and particularly interinstitutional visits and discussions appeared almost nonexistent. Our very strong recommendations would be that these groups get together more frequently and cooperate on the solution of common problems.

The proposed beam-handling system seemed to us unnecessarily expensive and complex. It consisted of a fixed 90° vertical analyzing magnet followed by a switching magnet located several meters away, the latter capable of deflecting the beam towards seven experimental locations housed in a large common target room. We strongly recommended that consideration be given to rotating the primary 90° magnet about the vertical accelera-

TABLE 2 Tandem Specifications

Pressure vessel	
Internal diameter	3.8 m
Overall length	15.02 m
Operating pressure	~200 psi ($N_2 + CO_2$)
Column	
Number of modules	8
Module length	60 cm
Dead sections	~8 cm
Insulating legs	titanium/ceramic
Equipotenial rings	15/module
Terminal	
Diameter	1.6 m
Length	2.29 m
Power	by drive shaft
Pumping	2 × 2 Ti sublimation + ion pump
Stripper	gas (initially)
Tube	
Construction	titanium/ceramic
Module length	20 cm
Internal diameter	10 or 15 cm (to be decided)
Charging system	Laddertron
Voltage division	by resistors

tor axis and that the possibility of using this rotation to service additional target rooms be explored.

It is perhaps noteworthy that none of the technology and developments (lucite column sections, stainless steel plus pyrex tubes, etc.) of the Vanguard factory, which is presently engaged in upgrading the Institute's 2.5-MV single-ended Van de Graaff to 4.5-MV while also building a similar machine for Beijing University, are to be incorporated in the tandem. The tandem will be of completely new design, and the Vanguard factory will be very much involved. We were told that the government agencies looked on the 6-MV INR tandem as an effective experimental prototype for much larger machines in the future and a test bed for new techniques and systems. Table 2 lists the design specifications for the INR 6-MV tandem.

Negative Ion Source Development

The ion source test facility that we were shown had very recently been relocated and was not completely reassembled. It consisted of a relatively small magnet with a 30° bend and a very large pumping system. The latter was apparently needed to cope with the high gas load of a prototype trioplasmatron direct extraction source, which had just been constructed but not yet tested. No work was in progress on sputter sources, but we were told that such work was planned for the near future.

Visits to Research Institutes

An ion source test-bed developed at INR for testing ion sources, both negative and positive, for use in either the cyclotron or the proposed 6-MV tandem accelerator.

Neutron Generator Group

The Vanguard-built, 200-kV, eight-step cascade, three-phase transformer Cockcroft-Walton has been operating since 1974. An RF source is used to produce a deuteron beam in the 3-5 mA range, and tritiated titanium, water-cooled targets are used for neutron production; the integrated neutron flux obtained is $\sim 10^{10}$/s. This unit has been used primarily for activation analysis work and in agricultural science for the irradiation of seeds in the hope of inducing favorable mutations. A relatively crude rabbit system is in place for sample handling during the following irradiation.

Applications of Nuclear Science Group

In contrast to all the other laboratories we have visited in the PRC, as we have noted above, the INR cyclotron was actually running an experiment when we arrived. In progress was an analysis of samples using proton induced X-rays (PIXE). The target chamber had a slide changer that held 30 samples; the X-rays were detected with a Si(Li) detector imported from France; the modular electronics and multichannel analyzer system were also French. We were shown examples of the research program that employed PIXE. Among them were analysis of the Kirin meteorite for elements above Si, a lunar sample analysis, and a trace element analysis of human blood serum.

The meteoric work was only done on the Kirin meteorite (type H3). The INR group had looked at bulk material, condrules, and the fusion crust; this work has already been published in a Chinese geochemical journal and discussed at a conference that considered the overall findings on the Kirin fall (1976). The idea for the work did not originate within INR but rather from the Geochemical Research Insitute in Guizhou Province. The latter group is active in meteorite research and organizes collaborative analyses of samples by other laboratories throughout the PRC. (Work on Kirin samples were being studied by neutron activation at the IAE in Beijing.)

The lunar sample being studied was a gift from the United States to China. It was apparent from the high Ti concentration observed by PIXE that it was probably an Apollo II soil sample. Part of this sample was also being studied by neutron activation at the IAE in Beijing. These state presentations of lunar material are primarily ceremonial, and little of particular interest is apt to result from such analyses at this late date.

The group doing charged particle activation had their own cyclotron beam line and a pneumatic rabbit system that took the targets to other buildings for analysis. The bulk boron concentration in the Kirin meteorite has been measured in this way; the answer obtained (2-4 ppm) looks reasonable, but it is not clear that enough control experiments have been done to eliminate the possibility of contamination. These techniques have also been applied to boron in silicon—a topic of more applied interest. Similar techniques have also been employed to measure oxygen (both ^{18}O and ^{16}O) in a variety of materials.

INR also has a Mössbauer group that has examined the Kirin meteorite, steel alloys, and Sn in semiconductor materials; all the detectors, electronics, and analyzers were fabricated within the INR. All this work has been published in the local INR journal.

The PIXE group is particularly concerned with obtaining standard samples. For their work on biological samples they would like NBS standards: SRM 1577 (bovine liver) and SRM 1571 (orchard leaves), and some of the delegation members agreed to help in arranging this.

Nuclear Theory Group

We heard presentations of some work on preequilibrium processes, in which an initial Fermi gas is assumed, and semiclassical cascade studies are made to find the time (number of collisions) to reach equilibrium. A second presentation was on the transport theory of fission, and a third one, on work initiated by Professor John Rasmussen of the University of California-Berkeley, who was spending 4 months as a guest at Fudan University, was on π-production in nucleus-nucleus collisions in the range of 100-300 MeV/nucleon. Most of the work used classical, semiclassical or other similar approximations in order to avoid the necessity of a high-speed computer. The group is a small one but appears to have good access to the most recent world literature. The greatest problem faced by the group is its lack of access to a powerful computer system.

Concluding Remarks

Following our visits the delegation reassembled for a plenary discussion with the INR administrators. As usual we were asked for our comments and criticisms. With the preamble that our impressions were necessarily superficial, our comments can be summarized as follows:

1. *On the tandem* good progress is being made and plans look good. A number of suggestions were made during our visit. Overall, we recommended that the INR work more closely with the IMP in Lanzhou and the IAE in Beijing to avoid the necessity of making the same (or different!) mistakes at each place and to speed up the planning. Furthermore, we recommended that it would be profitable to send some members of the accelerator group to annual meetings such as those of tandem operators in the United States (SNEAP) (to be held in October 1979 at the University of Pennsylvania); we emphasized our belief that this attendance would save money in the long run. Middleton agreed to forward formal invitations to this conference to INR and other interested Chinese institutions.

2. *On the cyclotron* we were impressed to see that it appeared to be a well-run machine with a research program well-suited to its characteristics. The proposed conversion seems carefully thought out with attention to details and appropriate modeling. Because of the proposed strange D-shape, it was suggested that perhaps construction of a full-scale model of the radio frequency system would be wise, as would extended visits to foreign laboratories such as ORNL and LBL, where substantial effort has already been devoted to the problems facing the INR group and where bodies of experienced personnel would be happy to discuss detailed questions with PRC colleagues.

3. *On the applications* the work seemed to us to be well chosen. The charged particle activation analysis work would be helped by a variable energy proton accelerator. In the work on lunar samples, it would help to send a member of the group to the United States to learn the present status

of such analyses in the United States and elsewhere in order to avoid obvious duplication and waste effort.

4. *In theory*, our main conclusion was that the work was severely restricted by the lack of an adequate computer.

7
Visits to Industrial Institutions

VANGUARD FACTORY (SHANGHAI)

On June 4th we visited the Vanguard electrical machinery factory (Xianfeng Dianji Chang), which is a branch of the Shanghai Municipal Electrical Machinery Company in the Jiabei section of Shanghai. This larger company is in turn under the direct supervision of the Shanghai Machinery and Electrical Bureau, an arm of the Shanghai municipal government and of the First Ministry of Machine-Building in Beijing. Our purpose in visiting Vanguard was to observe the manufacture of electrostatic accelerators, but in the course of our initial briefing by the Deputy Director of the factory, the Director of the Accelerator Division, and the Deputy Chief Engineer of that Division, we learned that Vanguard is a very large plant with 2,000 workers (of whom 40 percent are female) covering a total area of 97,000 m², established in 1958, and primarily engaged in the building of electric motors. We were told that there are seven divisions in the plant: one for accelerators, two for electric motors—from 1- to 200-kW ratings—and one division each for die casting, punching, repair (manufacture), and maintenance.

The accelerator shop has 100 workers and 20 technical staff, 5 of whom hold the rank of Engineer. Accelerator production began in 1961, but there is no fixed production plan for that division: rather the shop responds to orders from customers very much as in the United States. In the last 5 years, a total of 10 accelerators of various kinds have been produced. The current product line includes 400- and 600-KeV Cockcroft-Walton sets for positive ions; 2-MV electron Van de Graaffs; 2.5-MV proton Van de Graaffs; and they are just completing a 4.5-MV single-ended Van de

NUCLEAR SCIENCE IN CHINA

Senior members of the Vanguard factory brief the delegation on accelerator construction activities. From the left is Zhou Qizhang, Deputy Chief Engineer of the factory; Jiang Zuofa, Deputy Director of the factory; and Pu Huanren, Head of the Accelerator Division.

A schematic illustration of the administrative structure for the Vanguard factory in Shanghai.

ADMINISTRATION of the VANGUARD FACTORY

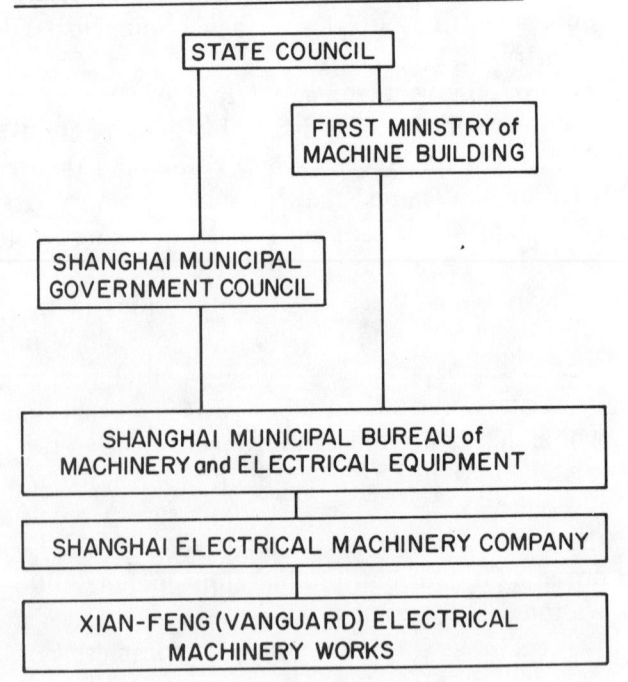

- STATE COUNCIL
  - FIRST MINISTRY of MACHINE BUILDING
- SHANGHAI MUNICIPAL GOVERNMENT COUNCIL
- SHANGHAI MUNICIPAL BUREAU of MACHINERY and ELECTRICAL EQUIPMENT
- SHANGHAI ELECTRICAL MACHINERY COMPANY
- XIAN-FENG (VANGUARD) ELECTRICAL MACHINERY WORKS

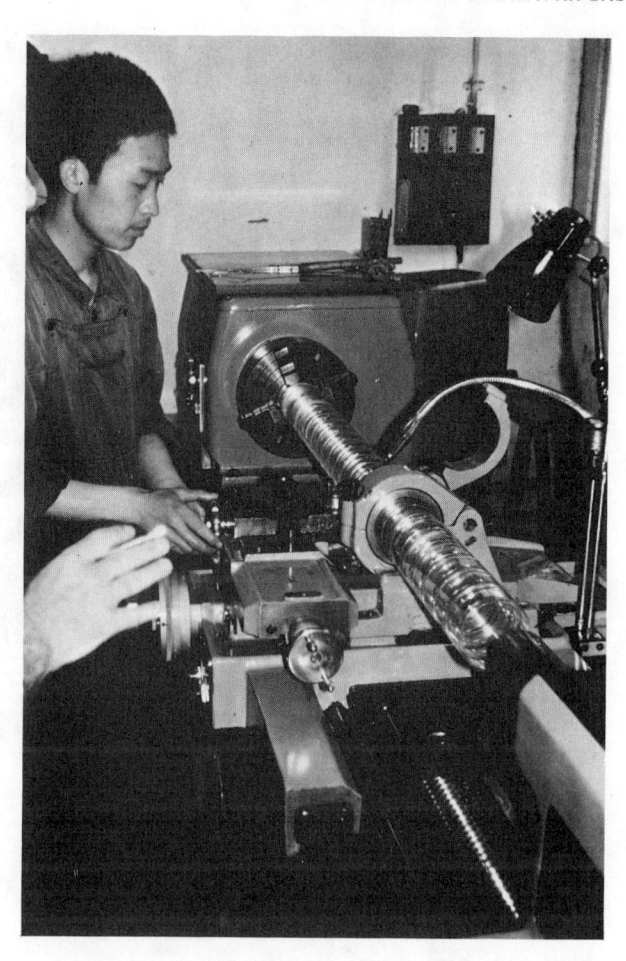

A young machinist in the Vanguard factory uses a high-quality Chinese-made lathe to produce lucite-insulating members. The delegation was surprised to find that the corrugations in these members were being developed freehand by the machinist.

Graaff for the Technical Physics Department at Beijing University, mainly for use with heavy ions from a PIG source. In parallel with this, they are working with Fudan University to supply the necessary components to upgrade the Vanguard 2.5-MV machine now in use at Fudan to 4.5-MV. The factory is also building an 8-MeV electron linac for material testing; no such linacs have been built as yet for medical utilization. We also saw the final test assembly of a 2-MV electron dynamitron with a current of 10 mA. This machine produces 10^6 rad/min at the irradiation point, uses an electrostatic scan to cover a 40-cm-wide production feed belt, and is intended for use in the polymerization of plastics. Others like it, we were told, are used for sterilization of food and medical supplies. The next machine Vanguard expects to build is a 6-MV tandem accelerator for the Shanghai Institute for Nuclear Research. This machine, we were told, will probably use the ceramic

Alex Zucker examines an aluminum pressing that will subsequently form the dome for either a 2.5-MV Van de Graaf or a 3-MV Dynamitron produced in the Vanguard factory. The press used in producing these domes is shown at the left.

tube, column, and laddertron technology being developed in Lanzhou; it is currently scheduled for completion in 1981 or 1982.

Most of our discussion during the initial briefing and question period dealt with details of Van de Graaff construction and testing. It was characterized by very open, candid responses to all our questions, and our impression was one of very solid professionalism throughout. The Chief Engineer spoke excellent English, and this also helped to maximize information transfer. The column of all current Van de Graaffs (2, 2.5, and 4.5 MV) is built of $\sim$ 3-ft-long insulators of plexiglass. We saw some of these insulators being turned freehand. The pyrex accelerating tubes have a constant gradient, with 2.5 cm between the stainless steel electrodes. The tube electrodes and insulating segments are cemented with epoxy and operate at a pressure of 10^{-6} Torr. They appear to be similar in construction to HVEC noninclined field tubes. The accelerators operate with an 80 percent N_2, 20 percent CO_2 insulating gas mixture at a pressure of 16 atmospheres. A 40-cm × 2-mm cotton rubberized charging belt is driven by a 13-kW motor. In the 4.5-MV machine the belt is 40 cm wide and 2 mm thick. The Chinese have the same lifetime and stability problems with these belts as does HVEC. Charge is sprayed on it, without physical contact, from an array of metal needles. The machines are corona-stablized, but none of the electronic control equipment is built by Vanguard. We understand that such equipment is usually supplied by the customer. One set of resistors is used to distribute the voltage gradient on the column. Information is transmitted to and from the terminal through rotating plexiglass shafts. Secondary electrons are suppressed by using small beam apertures in the tubes while the larger, off-center pumping apertures are spiralled to avoid line of sight electon paths over more than a single gap. The voltage stability of the machines is guaranteed to be one part in 10^3. All Chinese positive ion machines apparently use RF ion sources, inductively coupled; beams of 50 μA of protons are standard. Altogether the Vanguard Van de Graaff technology seemed excellent to us, based on U.S. experience.

Vanguard, as noted above, also manufactures 8-MeV electron linacs for materials studies. This accelerator is of the traveling wave type operating at a frequency of 2,985 MHz. Vanguard will not be involved, we were told, with the construction of the IAE-Beijing 100-MeV electron linac. Our inquiries regarding the performance characteristics of these 8-MeV linacs were answered to the effect that these are tailored to the use the particular customer has for them.

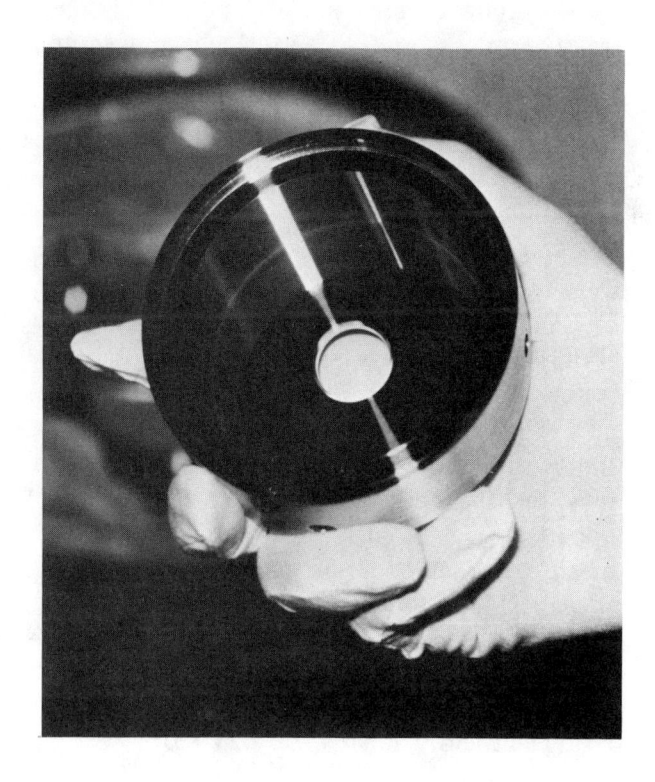

A completed linac diaphragm unit, produced as in the preceeding illustration. The quality of the workmanship is outstanding—so much so that these units require no further grinding or polishing as they come from the production lathes.

We were told that Vanguard has been asked to build the high-intensity 600-kV Cockcroft-Walton preinjector for the 50-GeV machine in Beijing, but we have no further details on its exact specifications. It bears noting, however, that the Vanguard Cockcroft-Walton machines that we saw elsewhere appeared to be of modern design and excellent quality. Vanguard also manufactures beam line equipment such as quadrupole magnets, valves, etc., but they do not manufacture their own vacuum components. Pumps bought are mostly oil diffusion, but some titanium sublimation pumps are coming into use.

We saw machine shops full of high-quality Chinese lathes, some of which were capable of turning 36-inch material. In separate rooms there appeared to be about 10 high-precision lathes. Equally good shapers and milling machines were also in widespread use. Over 75 percent of all machine operators were young women who had received their training at Vanguard. None of the machine tools were tape controlled or otherwise automated, although we were told that this was the next step and that orders had already been placed with machine tool factories in Shanghai where such tape controlled machines were in early commercial production. Curiously enough, rubber O-rings were still made by splicing $\sim 3/8$-inch material together with some kind of cement.

A limited profit motive operates at Vanguard. If the overall factory production is good, and if it sells the equipment it makes, the workers and professional staff get an average 10 percent bonus in pay every month. This bonus ranges from 0 to 30 percent and is given to individual workers according to merit as established in discussions among the workers themselves, but with final recommendations resting with the foreman in each section. Base pay for a beginning employee is about 36 yuan ($\sim$\$24 U.S.) per month; the Director receives slightly less than 4 times this amount. We were told that the 0 percent bonus went to a machinist who produced not a single useable product during the month in question, while the 30 percent bonus went to one who exceeded his quota by a factor of 4! Even total incompetence apparently is not considered sufficient cause for dismissal.

We again noted an absence of safety rules: no safety glasses or safety shoes were being worn. We were told that these were supplied by the factory, but the workers found them inconvenient and chose not to use them; the injury rate is such that 0.4 percent/month of the workers are injured severely enough to report to the local factory dispensary, which has nurses and a full-time physician present. This accident rate is difficult to interpret, because it may include Band-Aid distribution as well as treatment of more serious injuries. OSHA inspectors would have been more than shocked, however, by general shop practices.

The factory runs a "July 21st University"—a full-time 3-year technical school for its workers. It was established in 1974 and has graduated one 3-year class of 25 students; about 40 students are currently enrolled. We have learned that this is a standard practice in the best factories and may well approximate the U.S. technical college, but with vastly more hands-on experience and supervision.

We were repeatedly impressed by the quality of the machined finishes being produced by individual young female lathe and mill operators. Absoutely no mass production activity was in evidence, a situation woefully wasteful of human talent by U.S. standards but viewed otherwise in a society dedicated to 100 percent employment!

Most of all we were impressed by the high standard of production machinery and work in this Vanguard accelerator shop. The finished stainless steel and titanium products looked excellent, and no doubt this accounts in part for the very high morale and industry on the part of the workers that was apparent to all of us. We were shown stockrooms of finished products ranging from valves to accelerator electrodes; in general the finish on these was substantially better than is standard in U.S. products of the same nature. All chrome plating was done in the factory and involved multiple copper-nickel-chrome sequential plating to yield a very superior product. Titanium components for the preinjector to the Beijing 50-GeV accelerator were already in evidence in the store rooms.

We inquired about the cost of the finished products and were told that, for example, the export price of a 2.5-MV Van de Graaff would be 1.5 million yuan (~$1 million U.S.). At Fudan University we learned that Vanguard would charge Fudan 5 million yuan (~$3 million U.S.) for an entirely new 4.5-MV Van de Graaff, but that the 2.5-4.5-MV conversion was costing only 300,000 yuan (~$200,000 U.S.). Both of the prices for complete accelerators are several times higher than the commercial prices of similar machines produced by U.S. industry, but it must be emphasized that all such direct comparisons are suspect given the totally different economic structures in the two countries.

We were told that there is a severe shortage of skilled workers and engineers in China. During the Cultural Revolution, members of management and senior engineering personnel were required to operate machine tools full time. When asked who then did the design work, the reply was "no one"; and when asked what kind of product resulted from this system, the reply was "very bad!" We learned that there is a mandatory retirement at age of 50 for female and 60 for male workers, but no fixed retirement age for engineers and professional employees.

No in-house computer is available for beam dynamics calculations. The physics part of the design is, in general, done by the customer institute. Vanguard does the engineering, production, and testing to specifications.

Other factories apparently specialize in medical X-ray equipment, and there appears to be very little communication between them and Vanguard. This in part reflects the fact that the initial compartmentalization between what we would consider closely related activities begins very high up in the Ministry level in Beijing. And we learned from our request to visit Vanguard that once below that level, the compartmentalization can be zealously guarded! (See Introduction.)

SILK AND DYE FACTORY (HANGZHOU)

In Hangzhou, several members of the delegation had an opportunity to see a large silk factory, while others visited the Dragon Well Tea Plantation. Much of what we saw and heard in the silk factory confirmed earlier impressions gained at the Vanguard factory in Shanghai. This silk and dye factory produces 280 t of raw silk and prints 18,000,000 m of woven silk each year, including 6,000,000 m of its own silk and 12,000,000 m purchased from other Chinese producers. Of this production, 50 percent is for domestic consumption and 50 percent for export (one of the very important sources of hard currency).

The factory occupies a 310,000 m^2 site with 110,000 m^2 of factory floor. Of the 4,700 workers, 67 percent are female and 69 percent live on the factory grounds in housing provided by it. There are three separate workshops housing, for example, 500 reeling machines (extracting silk from the original farmer-grown cocoons), 623 weaving looms, etc. One of these workshops works two 8-hour shifts per day, while the other two work only one shift per day. Currently the factory has 16 fabric designers, 8 for home trade and 8 for export trade.

The average salary is 56 yuan (~$37 U.S.) per month, and the range is from 38 to 108; bonuses averaging about 7-8 yuan per month are paid to about 95 percent of the workers, since the factory consistently exceeds its production quotas. Individual bonuses are again discussed in each workshop and recommended by the shop foremen.

After 5 years of work, employees of the factory can carry their salary with them should they gain admission to higher education. A full school system ranging from elementary to a "July 21st University" is maintained by the factory on its own grounds for use by children of employees and employees themselves. Retirement at 75 percent of final salary is mandatory for women at age 50 and for men at age 60; those who wish may retain their factory housing after retirement. Maternity leave of 56 days is standard for a normal delivery and 72 days (or sometimes more) when complications arise. A factory hospital with full-time physician and nursing staff provides medical care for employees. Aside from the official state holidays, Chinese workers get no vacation. This was made clear to us in our discussions at the Vanguard factory and substantiated here.

Working conditions in large areas of the factory would not be tolerated in the United States. In the loom areas, for example, noise levels are unbelievably high; delegation members, after spending only a few minutes in these areas, found their ears and heads ringing for hours thereafter. We would estimate permanent hearing loss in no more than a week; when we asked why the workers did not at least wear earplugs, we were told that this was impossible since under these conditions the worker could not hear when his or her loom malfunctioned! But we were told that three separate technical committees were working on noise abatement; we gather that this work has been in progress for some time. Even though the weather was unseasonably cool, temperatures were very high in some areas of the factory (over 90°F), and large fans provided the only amelioration.

SHANGHAI INDUSTRIAL EXHIBITION

Few places provide the visitor with such an excellent overview of recent technological developments in China as the Shanghai Industrial Exhibition, located in the magnificent former Sino-Soviet Friendship Palace. Regretfully, reflecting a tight schedule and a limited stay in Shanghai, only Middleton visited the Exhibition—and this was at the expense of a boat tour of the Shanghai harbor.

The Exhibition is devoted entirely to local products, and the extent and diversity of these clearly reflect the fact that Shanghai is one of the main industrial centers of China. The main hall is devoted largely to machine tools and materials and is flanked by smaller halls, one of which is devoted to textile machinery and the other to marine technology (the latter contains a magnificent display of large, highly detailed model ships). Off the main hall are large wings containing an amazing diversity of exhibits of sophisticated industrial equipment (computers, lasers, medical equipment, electronic devices, etc.) and consumer products (quartz watches, cameras, sports equipment, hi-fi sets, color televisions, food products, etc.). A separate spacious hall is devoted to the latest in agricultural machinery and to transportation vehicles—the latter included a 50-ton dump truck.

There is much to interest a physicist, so much so that it is possible to mention here only a few isolated examples. A display of research materials was particularly impressive—this included metallic samples of several square centimeters of almost all the rare earths; crystals of various semiconducting materials, including a slug of polycrystalline silicon of some 3- to 4-inch diameter by about 40 inches in length; and a wide variety of ceramic mouldings and other refractory materials. A nearby exhibit included a bakeable ultra-high vacuum system intended for use with an evaporator. The pumping system consisted of two sorption pumps for roughing and a large bakeable ion pump topped with an all-metal gate valve. During our numerous laboratory visits we could not help noticing the total absence of socket head bolts and occasionally heard the lament that such were not widely available in China. Proudly on display, in the heavy machinery section, of the Exhibition, however, was a large automated machine that churned out socket head bolts at the rate of about 60 per minute.

The general impression created by the Exhibit was that of very impressive technological achievement; clearly some of the most sophisticated machinery and instrumentation may well have represented prototype, but the quality of workmanship and design evident in them augurs well for future indigenous Chinese technology.

During our travels we frequently observed people listening avidly to an English lesson over the radio, and it was not an uncommon sight to see a person in the street reading an English textbook. In spite of this Middleton was taken completely by surprise when he walked by a booth and heard a young lady exhibitor reading aloud in English—she was reading a paperback entitled *A Story about Isaac Newton*! Although making no claim to Newtonian status, Middleton, as an English physicist, received VIP treatment for the remainder of his visit.

8

General Comments on Industrial Development and Miscellaneous Impressions

INDUSTRIAL DEVELOPMENT

Industrial development in China is still recovering from the Cultural Revolution. In 1958—the beginning of the Great Leap Forward—China had announced plans for an extremely rapid economic growth and industrial expansion. Unfortunately some of the optimistic quantities required by the policies of the Great Leap in many industrial areas were achieved only at substantial sacrifice of quality. On top of that, three disastrous agricultural seasons came in sequence, and the Chinese economy was in serious trouble even before the 1960 withdrawal of Soviet personnel, resources, and expertise from China's economy. It was at this point that Chinese leadership fully recognized how essential a stable agricultural base was for all subsequent economic growth. Industries were instructed to reestablish quality at the expense of quantity and were directed to focus upon production relevant to agriculture.

The third 5-year plan, which was to have begun in 1963, was delayed for 3 years and announced in 1966; unfortunately, this coincided with the onset of the Cultural Revolution, wherein emphasis was placed on mobilizing the masses to place class struggle ahead of production goals. By 1967 industrial production had already dropped by 15 percent as compared with the previous year, and the goals of this third 5-year plan were essentially abandoned.

The fourth 5-year plan (1971-1975) again emphasized agriculture and its mechanization, but also included development of a stronger economic and industrial infrastructure. During this period, 13 chemical fertilizer plants were purchased from the United States. Two steel finishing mills were purchased, one from Japan and one from Western Europe, as were a number of other industrial plants.

Following the end of the Cultural Revolution, marked by the deposing of the "Gang of Four," in late 1977, major national conferences were called in industry, agriculture, science, and education for the formulation of national policies in these areas. We have already discussed some of the consequences of the decisions made at these conferences on science and education; that on industry has had equally dramatic consequences.

Instead of a fifth 5-year plan, China announced in 1978 an 8-year plan (1978-1985) with the goal of "building China into a powerful modern socialist country in the next 20 years and by the end of this century." The plan has focused on the "four modernizations"—of industry, agriculture, science and technology, and national defense. While self-reliance is still emphasized in a long-term sense, the new plan acknowledges the importance of importing foreign technology, equipment, and expertise, with some emphasis on the importance of management techniques.

Although our exposure to Chinese industrial practice was minimal, we have been fascinated to see the merging of traditional capitalist and socialist elements that has already taken place. The Chinese have made a very key change in the Marxist maxim "from each according to his abilities; to each according to his *need*," so that it now reads "from each according to his abilities; to each according to his *work*."

Although 100 percent employment—even sometimes at the cost of make-work employment—and a basic salary more or less independent of performance is considered the right of every worker, at the Vanguard factory in Shanghai, for example, very superior productivity results in up to 30 percent salary bonuses; at the Hangzhou silk and dye factory most of the workers are on a piece-work basis, so that their income is tied directly to their productivity; so also was the case at the workshops operated by Zhejiang University.

Almost all Chinese industries of significant size operate extensive training and education programs to improve the qualifications of their workers; and all maintain a very wide range of fringe benefits and employee services, so that in a very real sense a Chinese worker on joining a factory staff becomes a member of a much expanded community—reminiscent of Japanese industrial practice.

The normal working day is of 8 hours (6 days a week), but a luncheon break of 2 to 3 hours is traditional; we were told that this provided time for the worker to go home for lunch. Apart from some half-dozen state holidays per year, workers in general receive *no* vacations unless they are members of university faculties or students. These latter receive 3 weeks in summer and

General Comments on Industrial Development and Miscellaneous Impressions

1 in winter. We were told, however, that unmarried young adults did receive 10-day vacations with pay if that was necessary to permit their visiting parents in a different city. We were also told that there is extensive agitation in industrial circles toward extending vacations to all workers, primarily because the Chinese leaders have become convinced that overall annual productivity will be increased by doing so and that general vacations would probably be granted within the coming year.

After 5 years of work at essentially *any* job, the Chinese worker effectively gets "tenure" and cannot be discharged thereafter without substantial and defined cause.

We suspect, but cannot prove, that in the absence of even rudimentary safety precautions the industrial accident rate must be relatively high.

We were impressed by the attempts to improve the cooperation between industries and universities, in various localities and at the local level; they augur well for the future of both. Although automation is still little used in industry—and is not even desired in many areas because of the workers who would be idled by it—as the Shanghai Exhibition makes clear, such automation is being developed and can be expected to move rather rapidly into industry.

In general we were much impressed by the ability, enthusiasm, and initiative of those whom we met in China who are involved with industry. We believe that the omens are favorable for rapid and effective build up of Chinese industrial capacity given the caveats regarding political, economic, and agricultural stability discussed elsewhere in this report.

MISCELLANEOUS IMPRESSIONS

Energy Development

China is already the world's fourth largest producer and consumer of energy and is blessed with abundant resources of coal, oil, natural gas, and hydroelectric potential.

Currently coal provides about 70 percent of China's total energy consumption; coal reserves are estimated to be in excess of 100 billion tons. Large-scale crude oil production is a relatively recent development, having begun in Gansu Province; production was about 100 million tons in 1978 and is increasing rapidly. Onshore oil reserves are estimated at about 5 billion tons—essentially identical to U.S. onshore reserves. Very substantial offshore reserves have been estimated as well. Currently China ranks thirteenth among world crude oil producers; in terms of natural gas production, China ranks fifth in the world, and, although Chinese natural gas reserves have not been quantified with any accuracy as yet, these reserves are enormous.

An overview of the dam at the Liu Jia Gorge hydroelectric power plant on the Yellow River.

As noted earlier, however, the Chinese appear to have a very rational approach to these fossil fuel reserves as compared to much of the rest of the world. They consider it less than wise to waste the chemical sophistication of these hydrocarbons on simple combustion, and present policy is to conserve them insofar as possible as input to petrochemical and other industrial processes.

Given that 25 percent of U.S. energy consumption is in transportation, and that a very large fraction of this goes into private automobiles, it is important to remember that China does not now have—nor does it envisage in future having—privately owned automobiles. This again reduces Chinese enthusiasm for the burning of fossil fuels.

This attitude is greatly enhanced by the availability of enormous hydroelectric capacity, particularly in the southwest but also along the Yellow and other major rivers. Currently only some 2 percent of the estimated 500,000-MW hydroelectric capacity has been utilized.

Electrical output has been increasing at roughly 10 percent per year during the 1970's, and China now ranks ninth in world electricity production. Total output in 1976 was estimated at 115 billion kWh.

Distribution of energy resources remains a major Chinese problem. Rail capacity is inadequate to move coal as required; pipeline capacity falls far short of demand for crude oil and natural gas movement, although major pipeline projects now have high priority; and the electrical transmission system lags well behind world standards. There is no national grid, for example, and each major section of the country remains relatively isolated in terms of its energy needs.

Improvement of this energy transport system is a matter of urgency for the Chinese; it can be anticipated that as soon as possible the Chinese will export fossil fuels as a source of foreign currency, although we were told that this will be kept to a minimum for the conservation reasons mentioned above. It will be difficult to hold to these in the face of very serious shortages of foreign currency now and in the foreseeable future, coupled with the demand for it not only in high technology areas but in such basic areas as foreign wheat purchase to supplement an already strained agricultural system.

Given the Chinese energy picture, it is not surprising that nuclear energy systems are being developed with what might best be termed "deliberate speed." China has extensive uranium reserves in Xinjiang and elsewhere; nuclear installations are an effective answer to the fact that China's energy resources happen to be very far removed geographically from its population and industrial centers; and in the rapidly increasing environmental sensitivity the Chinese are already looking to nuclear energy as one of the most environmentally acceptable answers to a rapidly growing energy demand.

Very substantial effort is being devoted to the development of different complete nuclear fuel cycles, including reprocessing; and nuclear waste disposal techniques are the subject of very active research and development. China has already ordered commercial nuclear light-water power reactors from France and is considering purchase of heavy-water CANDU systems from Canada. In parallel with these purchases, China is carrying out its own research directed toward development of an indigenous nuclear reactor industry, including fuel reprocessing and waste disposal, but thus far has not settled upon any specific design or fuel cycle as optimum for its purposes.

Research devoted to nuclear fusion energy is in progress, particularly at the Southwest Research Institute in Leshan (near Chengdu) and to a much lesser extent at the Institute of Physics in Beijing and elsewhere. Again, for the reasons noted above, China senses no great urgency in the development of this, or indeed any other, alternative energy source.

The delegation's most direct contact with the Chinese energy situation came during a visit to the Liu Jia Xia hydroelectric plant on the Yellow River, about 100 km from Lanzhou. As China's largest plant of this kind, it has been operating since 1969 and has an installed capacity of 1,250 MW; the gorge and dam site is at an elevation of some 6,000 ft, giving some indication of the residual hydroelectric capacity of the Yellow River. Indeed, new dams are under construction both up and down stream from the one visited.

Five vertical shaft turbine generator sets are installed having individual capacity ratings of 350 MW, 300 MW, and 200 MW for the remaining three generators. The 300-MW unit alone supplies all of Gansu Province, and the remaining power goes into the rudimentary Chinese grid. At the time of our visit, the water level in the reservoir behind the 147-m dam was 40-m below normal, reflecting a prolonged drought over the Yellow River watershed, and in consequence the output was only 20 percent of its total rated value. This corresponds to 120 billion ft^3 of water below normal! In any appraisal of Chinese hydroelectric reserves, it is important to recall this situation; droughts are not uncommon, and the flow volume of rivers such as the Yellow can be highly variable from year to year with corresponding variation in the effective generating capacity.

The plant itself falls administratively under the Ministry of Electrical Power, but this Ministry must consult with the recently split-off Ministry of Water Conservancy and arrive at a mutually acceptable division of available water between power production and irrigation utilization.

Those of the delegation with power plant experience were impressed at this totally Chinese achievement, although some aspects were still somewhat anachronistic. The frequency standard, for example, was still a compensated pendulum clock and frequencies anywhere in the range 49.8-50.2 Hz were deemed acceptable. All control was manual, although we were shown a monitoring system, which appeared to be essentially an automatic stepping switch, that monitored and periodically printed out for diagnosis, up to 500 plant parameter values.

The delegation was allowed to wander freely through the control room, where even a single accidental switch throw could have had impressive consequences; frequently blocked the single operator's view of his operations console; and generally were given much greater access to actual instrumentation than would ever be the case in a comparable U.S. plant.

The primary 330-kV transformers were impressively large, but also impressively noisy as compared to U.S. units; the transformer oil smelled precisely the same; but, with one exception, we saw very little evidence of any automatic fire protection mechanisms. The 330-kV switch gear was installed in a huge cavern hewn from the native rock at the foot of the dam.

The reservoir is silting up—given the enormous amount of loess mud

General Comments on Industrial Development and Miscellaneous Impressions

carried by the Yellow River—at a rate of 5 to 6 m per year. A mobile crane at the top of the dam lifts the penstock strainer gates periodically so that a mechanical device can pick all debris from the strainer openings. The normal operating hydrostatic head is 100 m.

Army personnel, with fixed bayonets, guarded this power plant round the clock.

As noted above, the Chinese hydroelectric potential is the greatest in the world; the entirely indigenous industry (heavy machinery factories in Haerbin) that was responsible for the Liu Jia Xia plant clearly has the capacity to harness much more of this utilized capacity. We were told that such plans have very high priority in all national energy planning for China.

Communications

China lacks an adequate internal communication system. Telephone calls from major east coast cities such as Beijing and Shanghai to North America or Europe we found could usually be completed in less than an hour once the necessary request forms had been submitted to the appropriate hotel functionary. But we were told that calls inside China from Beijing to as major a center as Lanzhou, for example, sometimes required as much as 2 days to complete.

International telephone traffic is largely handled by a satellite-linked, ground-base station purchased several years ago from General Telephone and Electronics. Active negotiations are now in progress whereby the United States would sell a geostationary satellite covering all of China, and the necessary ground stations to complete this system, to the Chinese. This system clearly has a very high priority in the Chinese list of demands for foreign currency purchases.

Each of the major urban centers has a number of AM radio broadcasting stations, and *one* of these is duplicated on the FM band. In contrast to U.S. radio programming, there is relatively little music and a very large amount of talk. Several of the AM stations appear to broadcast identical material. English lessons are now popular and widespread. Within the limited music broadcast, a surprising fraction appears to be Western classics and light classics, together with a small amount of Nashville-type American country music, although traditional Chinese opera remains popular.

Radio sets typically are very large by U.S. standards, and in several of our hotels we found models identical to those in Hotel Dubna in the Soviet Union. Although Japanese sets—Hitachi, Mitsubishi, and Sony—are available in stores, only Chinese models ever appear in store windows. Typical sets have three shortwave bands in addition to AM and FM; since many boast only seven or nine transistors but cabinets worthy of Wurlitzer, the reception quality is not outstanding. Many Chinese told us that they regularly listen to

Voice of America broadcasts as one of the most effective methods of polishing their English.

Television sets, both black and white and color, are still relatively rare but, since the transmission is based on a 625-line system, receive excellent-quality pictures. Chinese television at this time is reminiscent of that in the Soviet Union (who provided and installed the early Chinese equipment) in that very large fractions of the time are devoted to single camera—full-stage coverage of opera, dance, and political affairs. Excellent lectures are apparently given each day—with outstanding graphics and demonstrations—in many areas of science and technology and at least twice each day an English lesson—conversational and grammar—is broadcast.

A number of "high-fidelity" stores appear in all the major centers, but their contents are strikingly different from those in the United States and suggest a very large fraction of do-it-yourself electronic repair and construction in China. Thermionic tubes ranging from subminiature to large 6L6 types are still much in evidence; but so also are transistors and even small-scale integrated circuits, in addition to a wealth of resistors, capacitors, inductors, and the like—with a few of each displayed in a saucer behind glass. Replacement cones for speakers appear to be a favored item, suggesting that loud speaker rehabilitation in the home is also much more prevalent than in the United States.

Beyond all these systems, each city we visited appeared to be well supplied with centrally controlled public address systems having high-power speakers overlooking street corners, squares, and places of public assembly. At apparently random intervals, these blast instructions over the area suggesting that persons should not litter, should not spit in the streets, should remember various aspects of Party training, and the like. It represents an invasion of privacy and noise pollution that would not be tolerated in most countries. At least now, in contrast to even a few years ago, the corresponding speakers in railway compartments (at least those for foreigners) have disabling switches.

Postal service, both internal and external, appeared to be comparable to that available elsewhere in the world; but the Chinese stamps are vastly more attractive than most.

Pollution

Only recently have the Chinese become sensitized to air pollution problems, but active counter measures are already under discussion. In Beijing and Lanzhou a major problem is airborne, very finely divided, loess that blows in off the Gobi and Western deserts and finds its way into even the most tightly sealed normal rooms; at times dust storms transporting this material limit visibility to a few hundred yards, in addition to stripping paint and other finishes from all exposed surfaces.

In the early days of development of the Chinese petrochemical industry, as in most other countries, little attention was paid to air pollution questions. Currently sulphur and nitrogen oxides and a wide variety of other toxic and destructive chemicals are released freely from these plants. We were urged by our Chinese hosts to take photographs of a particularly flagrant example of N_2O_4 release outside of Lanzhou in the hope that our comments at higher levels might help to produce the necessary control legislation. Such control is, at best, still in its infancy.

Most of the heating and cooking fires in individual rooms burn soft coal, and the smoke from these fires produces a pall that frequently hangs heavy over the cities.

We asked about standards of exposure to ionizing radiations and were told that the Chinese have adopted, quite generally, the USNRC-BEIR Committee recommendations.

Although we have no precise data, our visits to several institutions involved in high-power microwave research suggest to us that the Chinese use microwave exposure standards similar to those in the United States, while the Soviet standards are roughly 100 times more stringent.

In general, reflecting pride in country as well as the need to utilize all possible land for productive agriculture, we noted that littering, defacing of exposed surfaces, and in general visual pollution through careless disposal of materials was minimal.

Transportation

Transportation remains one of the major problems confronting Chinese leadership. With about 12,000 miles of track in 1949 at the liberation and only 30,000 in 1976 following the Cultural Revolution, the Chinese railways remain the most important component of the transport system—but they are woefully inadequate to current demands, even for movement of foodstuffs, with the consequence that each major area of China must be much more self-sufficient than would otherwise be the case or than would represent the most effective deployment of Chinese resources.

The highway system in China totals about 435,000 miles, but only about 8,000 miles of this are paved. Traffic is extremely chaotic, with little trace of lane driving and a relatively homogeneous mix of large trucks, small tractors, horsedrawn carts, and bicycles on most streets and highways. The most actively used attachment in any taxi or truck appears to be the horn! Whether by regulation or habit, as the typical Chinese driver moves through masses of pedestrians and cyclists, his passage is punctuated by regular horn blasts; indeed this happens even when no pedetrians or cyclists are in view. The resulting cacophony in major cities is all-pervasive; the concept of noise pollution has not arrived.

There are no private automobiles in China as yet. Each hotel or guesthouse has its own fleet of Chinese-made Red Flags or Shanghai limousines and taxis, respectively. Beijing, in addition, has a taxi fleet. And recently fleets of air conditioned Toyota minibusses have begun to appear. Most Chinese appear to travel in the backs of trucks and jeeps owned by their factory or commune; the major cities also have extensive bus systems, some electrically powered.

The major power source on the farms appears to be a one-cylinder diesel (with the cylinder in an open case filled with cooling water) mounted in cantilever fashion on a single beam supported by two wheels. Power from the large diesel flywheel is transmitted to the transmission and thus to the drive wheels via open, unprotected V-belts. We were astonished that so few Chinese users of these devices appear to have lost fingers in them! These tractors are controlled by a two-handle system, very reminiscent of a traditional single-furrow plow, and are used for everything from cultivating and hauling to taking one's produce and family to market or a Sunday outing, depending upon what sort of trailer or device may be connected to the back end of the support beam. There are clearly millions of these simple tractors now in use throughout the Chinese countryside.

As the tourist industry grows, and it is growing very rapidly, the number of standard design tour busses of Chinese, German, and Japanese manufacture is also increasing rapidly. Gasoline appears to cost roughly the equivalent of $2.00 U.S. per gallon, but since there are no private customers or buyers this price is rather meaningless.

It was of interest to note that one VIP car at Beijing Hotel, however, was a 1979 Oldsmobile 98 sedan—the only new U.S. car we saw. In Shanghai, on the other hand, we saw a remarkable number of 1948 Buicks in excellent condition surviving from just prior to the 1949 establishment of the People's Republic of China. Mercedes Benz automobiles—ranging all the way up to the 600 limousine—seem to remain the vehicles of choice for diplomats.

China makes effective use of its internal waterways for heavy transport, and Shanghai, for example, is clearly one of the world's busiest ports. Much of the canal and river network was destroyed during the Sino-Japanese War, so that in 1949 only about 50,000 miles were usable; this has now been increased to 100,000 miles, and many ambitious extension projects remain in the planning stage.

As yet containerized transport into China is only beginning, both because of a lack of port facilities and because of a lack of subsequent trucking facilities and roads after unloading.

Appropriate to a country of China's vast dimensions (third largest in the world after the U.S.S.R. and Canada), China is rapidly developing its internal air transport system and now has service (frequently sporadic) covering some 70 cities. This schedule has doubled since 1973.

China's internal airline CAAC (Civil Aviation Administration of China) owns 12 Boeing 707's, 35 British Tridents, five Soviet Ilyushin 62's, as well as a number of smaller Ilyushins and a number of small Antonov 24B's. We were told that these latter were now being manufactured in China.

The Chinese airports that we visited tended to be large, uncrowded, and all arranged for suitable welcome of VIP guests. The largest, at Beijing, is dominated, for the entering visitor from abroad, by an heroic white statue of Chairman Mao backlit against a red background. All airports appeared to share their civilian with military utility. Chinese High Altitude Fighters Number 9 were parked in large numbers on the airstrips, while planes that looked substantially more modern—and lethal—were glimpsed in revetments further removed from the airport buildings. We were surprised that there were no restrictions whatsoever on photography either in the airport or in flight; although formal regulations still are in existence, we gained the impression that they are rarely if ever enforced.

We were also surprised to learn that the CAAC 707 and Trident fleet averaged about 1 hour of flight time per day, very much less than is characteristic of such planes elsewhere in the world; we suspect that the current excess capacity reflects both the desire for growth and backup transport for possible military use.

Scheduling is somewhat flexible. On our flight from Lanzhou to Shanghai, for example, our flight left fully 20 minutes before the scheduled time and arrived 1 hour before the scheduled time. On the whole, the Tridents were very comfortable, since they were not crowded and we were able to fold forward the seats in front of us to gain acceptable knee room; the Ilyushin, on the other hand, was very crowded and had rather medieval toilet and service facilities; a standard kitchen refrigerator boasting a top-mounted condenser (General Electric ca. 1940) for example was bolted to the floor in place of one set of three seats. In-flight service, even on 5-hour flights, consisted of tea poured from a battered aluminum tea kettle and small packages of assorted Chinese candies and chewing gum. Cigarettes, however, are no longer distributed with the candy.

Train travel, from Shanghai to Hangzhou, was very comfortable in modern cars with diesel-electric engines and on track bed greatly superior to anything on the U.S. East Coast at least. Much of the railroad travel is still accomplished, however, by marvelous old coal-burning steam locomotives.

Housing

Housing in all the major cities remains in extremely short supply, and all is centrally controlled and allocated in each municipality with each factory or office having its own resident staff trained to cope with the central bureaucracy on behalf of its workers.

Couples having no children or one child typically are allocated a single living room and share kitchen and toilet facilities with one—and usually more than one—other couple. Couples having two or more children are limited to two rooms (the second one maybe windowless) and again are expected to share kitchen and toilet facilities with at least one other family (we were told that this is a not too subtle encouragement for birth control, and it apparently is working well in the cities in limiting population growth); in the country, however, the cohesion of the typical Chinese family and the fact that each is entitled to an individual job and salary results in large family advantages—hence high continuing birth rates. Although precise data are not available (nor do they exist) in China on the total population, the best estimate would appear to be 950 ± 50 million at present, with a net annual increase of 20 million.

The contrast between the heroic structures in Tian An Men Square and the primitive accommodations in which Beijing citizens live only a few blocks from the square is striking. In partial compensation, of the 36 yuan (less than $25 U.S.) that the average worker receives each month in salary, only 2 or 3 yuan are devoted to housing.

New housing projects were seen in various stages of completion throughout our travels. The construction standards appeared reasonable, and good workmanship was evident throughout, in concrete, brickwork, and finish detail. Most of the projects that we saw use prefabricated reinforced concrete structural members and brick facings. In general, we conclude that Chinese construction standards are quite comparable to those in the United States or Western Europe and somewhat superior to those in Eastern Europe. It was not clear, however, that Chinese construction standards adequately reflect the high seismic risk to which the buildings in much of the People's Republic of China are subject.

Construction projects are strange to Western eyes with their mixture of primitive (hand and animal drawn carts) and modern (cranes and large earth movers) techniques. Although individual worker productivity appeared low, progress toward construction completion appeared adequate.

Major apartment building projects dominate the skyline in most of the major cities, reminiscent of Moscow several decades ago. But given the population, its rate of increase, and the primitive state of much of the older housing, the Chinese face a gargantuan task in the housing area!

General Comments on Industrial Development and Miscellaneous Impressions

Health

Our comments on health reflect no expertise, but rather impressions gained, during our travels in China. Throughout the entire trip we saw no single obese or emaciated Chinese citizen, a comment that would be difficult to make elsewhere in the world. Moreover, almost without exception, the enormous number of Chinese whom we saw had completely clear complexions.

Fortunately no members of the delegation required medical assistance during the trip.

Visiting a Chinese pharmacy provides an interesting cross section of old and modern medicine. Antihistamines, for example, are obtained by scraping elk horn (a 6-inch section of such a horn was being retailed at $240.00 U.S. equivalent!), and acupuncture needles and electrical stimulating accessories are everywhere. But the same shelves hold modern antibiotics and the like.

The Chinese smoke much more heavily than do Americans; cigarettes are served everywhere with the ubiquitous tea. We were told that the Chinese were becoming concerned about this on the basis of foreign reports such as that from the U.S. Surgeon General.

Alcohol consumption is very much lower than in the United States, for example, although in Lanzhou we did see derelict alcoholics in small numbers on the major streets. We saw or heard no evidence concerning a drug problem, although we saw rather remarkably healthy plantings of marijuana along the rail line between Shanghai and Hangzhou. We were assured that this was grown for its fibre rather than its hallucinogenic chemical content.

Our general impression was that of a remarkably healthy people.

Consumer Goods and Food

Since the end of the Cultural Revolution, there has been a very striking change in the Chinese production of consumer goods. Most dramatic is the rapid change in clothing styles and colors. Children are now encouraged to wear bright colors; women are beginning to wear brightly colored blouses and skirts; and hybrid versions of both Mao and Sun Yat Sen jackets having Western lapels are appearing in the display windows of the more expensive Beijing and Shanghai shops. Although we saw almost no women wearing cosmetics on the streets, such products are ubiquitous in all the better stores and quite clearly are being purchased extensively. We can only suspect that they will be used much more openly in the near future—at the moment PRC consumers may be practicing at home, and the overseas Chinese stand out clearly in crowds. Within a few years, the drab monochrome characteristic of the Cultural Revolution will be gone, at least in the major cities.

Shop windows display wide ranges of attractive merchandise, and the stores and streets are filled with enthusiastic Chinese shoppers. Fabrics are in short supply, however, and cotton is still rationed with each individual receiving what would be equivalent to about one cotton suit per year—although clearly the ration must cover all clothing, not just suits, and thus suits clearly cannot be acquired each year. Synthetic fibres are not rationed, and one sees increasing use of them by both men and women.

Some families are just now beginning to acquire such luxuries as television sets, refrigerators and washing machines. These also are rationed, on a coupon basis, and waiting periods of up to 2 years are not uncommon.

Bicycles and radios, televisions, and sewing machines are in shortest supply, although they are readily available in the Friendship Stores, and one member of the delegation was able to purchase a bicycle there and have it shipped as a gift to a friend living in China. Assuming that one is fortunate enough to be given one of the small number of bicycle coupons made available to the management of each office (much less than the demand)—and this dispersal of such coupons is one of the prerequisites of management—the recipient may well have to wait over a year to take delivery. And, moreover, a typical worker has a total, we were told, of about 10 yuan per month of disposable income after he pays for food, housing, and other essentials; a typical bicycle costs 150-180 yuan! The bicycles available were rather poorly constructed by Western standards and appear to have frequent mechanical problems. Basically, however, they appear sturdy and the necessary repairs are readily accomplished in the many bicycle shops found in all areas.

Food is also rationed. The average citizen has an allotment of 5 lb of meat per month, 20 lb of rice per month, etc.; we were told that everyone used up all his rations allocation except in the case of rice. Fresh vegetables are brought into the city by farmers to designated locations from whence they sell their produce from large piles dumped on the sidewalks. In the more provincial cities, e.g., Lanzhou, small animals are also butchered directly on the sidewalks and dissected for sale on the spot. Happily, there are essentially no houseflies left in China as a result of an earlier massive eradication campaign. The average Chinese consumption of what they term "grain"—but which includes such items as beans and sweet potatoes in addition to what we would normally include—is somewhat less than 2 lb per person per day.

There appears to be an iodine deficiency in the average diet, inasmuch as one sees rather a large number of cases of prominent goiter in the street crowds; this was much more pronounced in Lanzhou than in the eastern Chinese cities.

Chinese agriculture is widely recognized as the central problem to be faced by the country. China has a population density of almost 2,000 persons per square mile of cultivated areas, whereas the U.S. and the U.S.S.R. have equivalent densities somewhat under 300 persons per square mile. And there is relatively little undeveloped arable land left in China; similarly, the Chinese are already obtaining close to the maximum food yield per unit arable area. As an example, in the Shanghai area in spring they first plant 60-day rice; following its harvest, 120-day rice; and following its harvest, fall wheat that is ready for harvesting the following spring. They already use both chemical and natural fertilizers extensively, so no "green revolution" waits in the wings; every effort is, however, being devoted to improved agricultural productivity, and modest improvements in crop yield could be accomplished with increased mechanization.

As a small vignette, illustrating the efficiency of the Chinese food system, when we asked what happened to the silk moth pupae after all their silk had been unwound from them, we learned that they had been baked by the collecting farmers to kill them immediately after collection and thus prevent their damaging their silk; after unwinding of the silk the pupae were pressed to yield cooking oil; and the residue, after pressing, was used to feed pigs.

Although it appears clear that minimal nutritional standards have been attained in the PRC (a most impressive achievement), to preserve this situation Chinese population growth must be brought under control rapidly or the country will remain at the mercy of natural disasters or climatic fluctuations that can easily produce widespread starvation in any such precariously balanced system. Foreign help probably could not prevent such starvation, inasmuch as the distribution systems are still inadequate to bring food, were it available, to those in need of it. We have found it difficult to assess the success thus far achieved in population control. Clearly the programs have been much more successful in urban than in rural areas given, on the one hand, the space pressures in the cities and, on the other, the obvious advantages, in a full employment economy, of having many members in rural family complexes. We were told, at times, that the population was growing at less than 1 percent per annum; others suggested rates more like 2 percent per annum, which agrees better with external estimates. It is sobering to contemplate that such a 2 percent growth rate means 20 million new mouths to feed each year.

Nowhere is the contrast between the PRC and the United States more dramatic than in the areas of food production. Only 5 percent of the U.S. population of some 220 million are engaged in food production, and these produce a surplus, beyond internal requirements, that helps to feed much of the world. Over 75 percent of the Chinese population of about 1 billion people are engaged in food production, and even this large a fraction barely

NUCLEAR SCIENCE IN CHINA

A Shanghai nursery school class on an outing with its teacher and her assistant. It is now customary for children in this age group to wear very brightly colored clothing.

succeeds in wresting adequate yield from the rather intractable Chinese land to meet internal requirements.

Entertainment

We have already commented upon the general excellence of the dance and operatic performances that we saw during our travels.

The contrast between the beautifully colorful costuming—characteristic of the Tang Dynasty for the most part—and the current clothing was particularly striking. The performance of the "White Snake" that we saw in Beijing was very professional; the very highly stylized male and female voices used by Chinese actors is strange—and piercing—to Western ears; the dance scenes were done in spectacular color and with impressive elan.

This performance was held in a singularly unimpressive Worker's Palace. Here, as elsewhere in China, the most expensive seats cost about

$0.50 U.S. and the least expensive $0.25 U.S. All were filled. And as elsewhere in China, the libretto was projected on a small area beside the stage so that the audience (those who could read Chinese!) could follow it together with action on the stage.

In Lanzhou, the opera "The Imposter Son-in-Law Who Became a Real One" (it translates badly) was again an old traditional but lighter one and played to a full house. So also did a performance (the opening one) of a dance troupe who had a new staging of an old dance drama—"The Silk Road"—based on the legends associated with the Dun Huang Cave Paintings and the fact that Lanzhou was the eastern terminus of the fabled silk road from Europe. It was beautifully done and would be a great success could it be translated to Broadway. During the intermission we had the pleasure of meeting the director, author, and choreographer over tea; this was an occasion when we had no criticisms whatever to provide following the standard request for them!

In Shanghai we saw a performance of the Number One Shanghai Acrobatic Group, which turned out to be something of a variety act including magicians, clowns, trapeze artists, jugglers, tight rope performers, and animal acts (including an adult Panda!). We enjoyed it enormously, but our Chinese hosts insisted that the work of the Number Two Shanghai Acrobatic Group was preferable since they stuck to ancient Chinese acts, whereas the feeling was that the Number One group had been corrupted by Western tourist interests. The criticism is probably valid!

In Hangzhou we saw the opening performance of a variety dance program performed by the Qinghai Province dance troupe. It was substantially less professional than the others we had seen, but may reflect the fact that the troupe members has just completed a long tiring flight—and had been bitten sufficiently by Hangzhou's famous mosquitos to leave large and very visible red welts on all exposed skin!

The Hangzhou Theatre is a new one and superficially is reminiscent of a smaller version of the Washington, D.C., Kennedy Center.

Although we had no opportunity to attend one, movies are very popular. There is a large Chinese production together with widespread use of foreign films—Italian, French, and Yugoslavian to judge from wall posters advertising them. We saw no evidence of American or British films.

Admission rates, here too, are very low; it is a matter of policy apparently that such entertainment is a good thing and costs are underwritten so as to make minimal admission charges feasible.

We were told that there are widespread competitions among the performing groups during the year, and the most highly rated are awarded the great honor of traveling to Beijing to compete in a final competition, for All-

China rating, that becomes part of the National Chinese October celebrations.

Sport events are also extremely popular, and teams throughout China—in a great many sports—go through elimination rounds before the finals in Beijing for All-China rating.

We were much impressed by the serious approach to sports, as exemplified by an incident that coincided with our visit to the Lanzhou Friendship Hotel. A girls' baseball team from Meriden, Conn.—of no particular distinction—had arranged funding to visit China to engage in demonstration games with corresponding Chinese teams. They had played a Lanzhou girls' team just prior to our arrival; immediately after their departure, the hotel filled with a large number of girls' teams from the surrounding provinces in order that they could play the team that had played the Americans and pick up whatever pointers, ideas, or nuances of play that might be available.

The players were outfitted in attractive, colorful uniforms, were in their late teens, and were obviously highly enthusiastic.

In Hangzhou, the most popular sport, understandably, appeared to be walking around Huagang Park and West Lake. In a rather puritanical country, where any contact between the sexes is frowned upon in public, it was pleasant to see young couples walking hand-in-hand.

9

Concluding Remarks

We would conclude by reemphasizing how tentative are all conclusions based on only brief and fragmentary exposure to as vast and diverse a society as that of China.

But because of the warm welcome, generous hospitality, and candid responses that the delegation received throughout its travel, it has returned with the visceral feeling of having obtained a reasonable sample of Chinese achievements and plans.

China has been through a singularly difficult time, has much catching up to do, and her plans are ambitious in nuclear science as elsewhere.

Given a stable political system and continued economic growth, we believe that the plans can be realized—perhaps not on the original optimistic scheduling and not without substantial help from the international scientific community.

We see too possible eventualities that could seriously disrupt or destroy these plans. If Chinese society, for whatever reason, closes in again upon itself to the exclusion of foreign input, products, and assistance, then we believe that plans in science as elsewhere will falter. And if the Chinese are unsuccessful in controlling their population growth, or if a few years of drought seriously damages agricultural productivity, the resulting pressures just to feed its population may force China to modify its plans substantially.

We are hopeful that neither of these scenarios will occur. We have offered to assist our nuclear science colleagues in China both through our own laboratories and through making appropriate contacts in other laboratories throughout the world. It is our expectation that these offers will be taken up—and particularly after the first group of students graduates from the rebuilt Chinese university system 2 years hence we anticipate rapid emergence of China into the world community in nuclear and in many other sciences.

It is our conclusion that extended visits to China by foreign nuclear scientists, apart from those particularly interested in instrumentation or specific applications, would not be particularly productive at present. Rather we have urged our Chinese colleagues to take as much advantage as possible of foreign experience and expertise in the rebuilding of their part of Chinese science to its rightful place in the world community.

Appendix A

Itinerary

May 20 — Delegation assembled in Narita Prince Hotel, Tokyo, for initial planning discussions.

May 21 — *Flight* JAL Tokyo to Beijing, arriving 3:05 p.m. Met by representatives of Chinese Academy of Sciences and Institute for Atomic Energy, transported to Friendship Hotel, discussed proposed itinerary in detail. Delegation, unaccompanied, via taxi to Tian An Men Square.

May 22
A.M. — Formal meeting with Zhao Dongwan, Deputy Director of State Scientific and Technological Commission (SSTC) and associates, at SSTC headquarters for discussion of science policy in China. Formal meeting with Qian Sanqiang, Vice President of Chinese Academy of Sciences (CAS) and associates at CAS headquarters for discussion of science policy in China.

P.M. — Bromley, Kuo, Middleton, Tombrello, and Zucker to Institute of Physics. Hanna, Harvey, Henley, and Kerman to Institute of Theoretical Physics.

Appendixes

EVENING	Banquet in honor of delegation given by Qian Sanqiang at Beijing Duck Restaurant.
May 23 A.M.	Beijing University—following formal introduction, delegation split into two groups visiting teaching laboratories and classrooms and the computer center and library, respectively. Lunch at Summer Palace without hosts.
P.M.	Qinghua University—following formal introduction, visited architecture section, nuclear science activities, and library.
EVENING	Chinese opera "The White Snake" at Worker's Palace, Beijing.
May 24 A.M.	Institute for Atomic Energy—following formal introduction, visited nuclear science facilities. Banquet at Institute. Chef (age 76) out of retirement for the occasion. Host was Wang Ganchang, Director of Institute.
P.M.	Returned to Peking and visited Imperial Palace.
EVENING	Free.
May 25 A.M.	Bromley, Zucker, Middleton, and Tombrello lecture at Institute of Atomic Energy. Hanna lectures at Institute of Physics, Harvey lectures at Institute of High-Energy Physics, and Henley lectures at Beijing University.
P.M.	Middleton and Tombrello lecture at Institute of Atomic Energy, while Bromley and Zucker discuss accelerators and applications of nuclear science, respectively, with Institute staff. Hanna discusses applicatons of nuclear science to condensed matter physics at the Institute of Physics. Harvey discusses high-energy heavy ion interactions at the Institute of High-Energy

Appendixes

	Physics. Kerman lectures and Henley discusses theory with staff at Beijing University.
EVENING	Cabaret entertainment with local citizens in Friendship Hotel.
May 26 A.M.	Bromley and Middleton lecture at Qinghua University, Hanna and Harvey lecture at Institute of Atomic Energy, Zucker lectures at Institute of Physics, Kerman lectures at Beijing University, and Tombrello lectures at the Seismology Bureau's Institute of Geology.
P.M.	Hanna lectures and Harvey holds discussions with staff at Institute of Atomic Energy. Henley lectures and Bromley holds discussions with staff at Beijing University. Middleton holds discussions with staff at Qinghua University, as does Zucker at the Institute of Physics. Tombrello visited Department of Technical Physics at Beijing University.
EVENING	Delegation meeting to assign report writing responsibilities and for initial planning of banquet to be tendered by the delegation June 8.
May 27 A.M.	Visited Great Wall.
P.M.	Visited Ming Tombs.
EVENING	Banquet at Sichuan Restaurant hosted by Wang Gangchang as President of Chinese Physical Society.
May 28 A.M.	Shopping in Beijing—Liu Li Chang quarter and Friendship Store.
P.M.	CAAC flight to Lanzhou via Xi'an arriving 5:15 p.m. Met by Yang Chengzhong, Xie Bowang,

Appendixes

	and associates from Institute of Modern Physics. Transported to Lanzhou Friendship Hotel.
EVENING	Banquet hosted by Yang Chengzhong as Vice Director of the Lanzhou branch of the Chinese Academy of Sciences.
May 29 A.M.	Official welcome to Institute of Modern Physics (IMP) by Xie Bowang, the Secretary of the Committee of the Communist Party of IMP, and by Yang Chengzhong, the Director. Visited nuclear science and accelerator facilities. Delegation split into two groups.
P.M.	Continued visits to nuclear facilities. Received formal presentations on the proposed SFC-SSC cyclotron complex at IMP and on recent nuclear science results at IMP.
EVENING	Dance Opera "The Silk Road" at Lanzhou Theatre based on legends surrounding Dun Huang cave paintings.
May 30 A.M.	Bromley and Harvey lecture to the Gansu Division of the Chinese Physical Society in the auditorium of the Lanzhou Hotel, Middleton lectures and holds discussions with staff at the IMP, Henley lectures and the remainder of the delegation hold discussions at Lanzhou University. Kerman, Tombrello, and Zucker tour Five Spring Hill and White Pagoda Park.
P.M.	Hanna and Kerman lecture at IMP, Zucker holds discussions with IMP staff, Bromley and remainder of delegation visit Lanzhou University. After formal reception, toured Physics Department teaching laboratories; after second formal reception by personnel of Modern Physics Department, toured its facilities. Host was Nie Dajiang, Vice President of Lanzhou University.

EVENING	Chinese comic opera "The Imposter Son-in-Law Who Became a Real One" at the Lanzhou Theatre.
May 31	Visited the hydroelectric generating plant at the Liu Jia Gorge on the Yellow River and took boat trip on reservoir above dam.
June 1 A.M.	Kerman, Tombrello, and Zucker lecture at IMP. Bromley and remainder of delegation, after formal reception by Director, tour Five Spring Park and Museum. Children's Day in China.
P.M.	Detailed discussion of delegation's impressions and recommendations concerning IMP activities with Yang Chengzhong, Xie Bowang, and senior colleagues from IMP. Left for airport at 4 p.m. CAAC flight to Shanghai—left 20 minutes early!—arrived about 8 p.m. Met by representatives of the Shanghai Branch of the Chinese Academy of Sciences and of the Institute of Nuclear Research. Transported to Jing An Guest House.
EVENING	Delegation meeting to discuss report writing assignments.
June 2 A.M.	Bromley, Harvey, Hanna, and Zucker lecture at the Shanghai Science Center. Remainder of delegation visits Shanghai Plant Nursery.
P.M.	Visited Shanghai Museum, shopping at Friendship Store and shops along Nanjing Road.
EVENING	Banquet cohosted by Hu Yungchang, Deputy Director of the Shanghai Branch of the Chinese Academy of Sciences, and by Jin Houchu, Director of the Institute of Nuclear Research (INR).

Appendixes

June 3 A.M.	Visited Yu (Mandarin) Gardens and old section of Shanghai.
P.M.	Boat trip on Huangpu River to junction with Yangtse Chiang and return through Shanghai Harbor. Middleton visits Shanghai Industrial Exhibition instead.
EVENING	Performance of Shanghai Number One Acrobatic Group.
June 4 A.M.	Bromley, Hanna, Harvey, Zucker, and Perrolle to the Vanguard factory where, after formal reception by Director and his senior associates, tour accelerator building division shops and test facilities. Henley, Kerman, Middleton, and Tombrello lecture at Shanghai Science Center. Hanna leaves for Geneva. Kerman and Middleton join Vanguard tour following their lectures.
P.M.	Fudan University. After formal reception by Vice President Xie Xide and associates, toured undergraduate teaching laboratories, lamp research laboratory, nuclear science department. Received formal presentations concerning current research.
EVENING	Chairman's cocktail party for delegation plus Ding and Zhang. Otherwise free.
June 5 A.M.	Institute of Nuclear Research. Delegation split. Bromley, Kuo, Middleton, and Perrolle to electrostatic accelerator section, Zucker and Harvey to cyclotron section, Tombrello to analysis group, Kerman and Henley to theory group. Concluding discussion of impressions and recommendations with Director.
P.M.	By train from Shanghai to Hangzhou. Arriving 7 p.m. in Hangzhou. Met by Cao Xuanling, Director of the Physics Department of Zhejiang

Appendixes

	University, and Liu Jinhua, Vice Director of the Hangzhou Branch of the State Scientific and Technological Commission. Transported to Hangzhou Hotel.
EVENING	Banquet at Hangzhou Hotel hosted by Yang Shilin, Deputy Director of the Zhejiang Provisional Branch of the State Scientific and Technological Commission and Vice President of Zhejiang University. Delegation meeting regarding scheduling.
June 6 A.M.	Visited Pagoda on Zhejiang River, Tiger Spring, Huagang Park, and took boat tour around West Lake returning to hotel.
P.M.	Visited Ling Yin Temple and Friendship Store, Zhejiang University. Formal reception by Yang Shilin and associates. Toured teaching laboratories as well as optical instrument and machine tool shops.
EVENING	Performance of native dances and songs by Qinghai Dance Troupe at Hangzhou Theatre.
June 7 A.M.	Bromley, Harvey, Henley, Kerman, Kuo, and Zucker to Hangzhou silk and dye factory; Harvey and Perrolle to Dragon Well Tea Plantation.
P.M.	Drove to airport, 12:45 p.m. CAAC flight to Beijing. Received by representatives of IAE and CAS. To Qian Men Hotel.
EVENING	Chairman's cocktail party for delegation—otherwise free.
June 8 A.M.	Dawn visit to Tian Tan Temple by part of delegation. Shopping at Friendship Store. To ancient astronomical observatory.

Appendixes

P.M.	Shopping in area northeast of Tian An Men Square. Drinks at Beijing Hotel.
EVENING	Farewell banquet hosted by Bromley at Feng Ziyuan restaurant on behalf of delegation. Twenty-four Chinese guests led by Qian Sanqiang, Vice President of CAS and President of Zhejiang University; Zhou Peiyuan, President of Beijing University; Zhao Zhongyao, Vice Director of the State Scientific and Technological Commission, and Wang Ganghang, Director of the Institute of Atomic Energy and President of the Chinese Physical Society.
June 9 A.M.	Visited Mao Zedong mausoleum on Tian An Men Square after receiving official permission. Toured Tian Tan (Temple of Heaven) and Bei Hai Park. Feng Yinfu, Deputy Foreign Secretary of CAS, hosts farewell luncheon at airport. Kuo remains in Beijing.
P.M.	JAL flight 782 Beijing to Tokyo, arriving 7 p.m.
EVENING	Henley and Kerman continue to Seattle and Vienna, respectively; Zucker and Harvey continue to Tokyo city; Bromley, Middleton, Tombrello, and Perrolle stay at Narita Prince Hotel at airport preparatory to return to U.S. on June 10.

Appendix B

Talks Given in China by the U.S. Nuclear Physics Delegation

MAY 25, 1979 – BEIJING

Institute of Atomic Energy

D. ALLAN BROMLEY	"Heavy Ion Scattering and Interactions: Nuclear Molecular Phenomena"
	"Higher Order Nuclear Reaction Processes"
ALEXANDER ZUCKER	"Research Management at U.S. National Laboratories"
THOMAS A. TOMBRELLO	"Elemental Analysis of Planetary Samples"
	"Sputtering and Radiation Damage"
ROY MIDDLETON	"Tandem as an Ultrasensitive Mass Spectrometer"

Institute of Physics

STANLEY S. HANNA	"Solid State Applications of Nuclear Physics"

Appendixes

Institute of High-Energy Physics

BERNARD G. HARVEY   "Lawrence Berkeley Laboratory Research in Nuclear Physics"

Beijing University

ERNEST M. HENLEY   "Charge Dependence of Nuclear Forces and Tests Thereof"

ARTHUR K. KERMAN   "Time Dependent Theory for Heavy Ion Nuclear Physics"

MAY 26, 1979–BEIJING

Institute of Atomic Energy

STANLEY S. HANNA   "Polarization in Nuclear Physics"

"Giant Resonances"

BERNARD G. HARVEY   "Intermediate and High Energy Heavy Ion Nuclear Physics"

Institute of Physics

ALEXANDER ZUCKER   "Applications of Nuclear Physics to Materials Science"

Qinghua University

ROY MIDDLETON   "Negative Ion Source Development"

Beijing University

D. ALLAN BROMLEY   "University Based Research: Mechanisms and Support"

ERNEST M. HENLEY   "Parity Violation in Nuclei and the Weak Non-leptonic Forces"

ARTHUR K. KERMAN   "Quark Matter Considerations in Nuclear Physics"

Earthquake Bureau

THOMAS A. TOMBRELLO — "Radon Monitoring and Earthquake Prediction"

MAY 30, 1979 – LANZHOU

Lanzhou Hotel (Chinese Society of Physics, Lanzhou Branch)

D. ALLAN BROMLEY — "University Based Research: Mechanisms and Support"

BERNARD G. HARVEY — "Intermediate and High Energy Heavy Ion Nuclear Physics"

Institute of Modern Physics

ROY MIDDLETON — "Negative Ion Source Development"

STANLEY S. HANNA — "Solid State Applications of Nuclear Physics"

ARTHUR K. KERMAN — "Time Dependent Theory for Heavy Ion Nuclear Physics"

ALEXANDER ZUCKER — "Research Management at U.S. National Laboratories"

Lanzhou University

ERNEST M. HENLEY — "Weak Neutral Currents and Parity Nonconservation"

JUNE 1, 1979 – LANZHOU

Institute of Modern Physics

ARTHUR K. KERMAN — "Statistical Theory of Nuclear Reactions"

THOMAS A. TOMBRELLO — "Sputtering and Radiation Damage"

ALEXANDER ZUCKER — "Applications of Nuclear Physics to Materials Science"

Appendixes

JUNE 2, 1979

Shanghai Hall of Science

D. ALLAN BROMLEY	"Heavy Ion Scattering and Interactions: Nuclear Molecular Phenomena"
BERNARD G. HARVEY	"Intermediate and High Energy Heavy Ion Nuclear Physics"
STANLEY S. HANNA	"Solid State Application of Nuclear Physics"
ALEXANDER ZUCKER	"Applications of Nuclear Physics to Materials Science"

JUNE 4, 1979

Shanghai Hall of Science

ERNEST M. HENLEY	"Charge Dependence of Nuclear Forces and Tests Thereof"
ARTHUR K. KERMAN	"Quark Matter Considerations in Nuclear Physics"
THOMAS A. TOMBRELLO	"Elemental Analysis of Planetary Samples"
ROY MIDDLETON	"Development of Negative Ion Sources"

Appendix C

Hotel Accommodations

As a possible aid to future travelers in the PRC, we have included below a brief description of our hotel accommodations, since several of those used by our delegation were not described in standard guidebooks.

Our accommodations were in several instances also in hotels different from those used by earlier delegations reflecting the severe shortage of hotel space currently experienced in China. As a result of an enormous increase in tourism and foreign business trade, the Beijing Hotel was completely unavailable to guests of the Chinese Academy of Sciences. We learned, incidentally, that no Chinese hotel accepts reservations more than 2 days in advance—and then only when the reservations are made in person! The delegation was quartered on its arrival in the Friendship Hotel some 20 minutes by taxi from Tian An Men Square. This was a large, comfortable structure boasting Soviet architecture except for the addition of a typically Chinese roof structure. Service was excellent.

In Lanzhou we again were housed in the Friendship Hotel—like the one in Beijing, built with the assistance of, and originally for, Soviet advisors in China during the period of Sino-Soviet collaboration in the early 1950's. While in Beijing all members of the delegation had single rooms; in Lanzhou, reflecting lesser tourist pressure (Lanzhou was opened to tourists only in January 1979), many of us had suites. Again the service was excellent.

In Shanghai we enjoyed superb quarters in the Jing An Guest House. We were told that until recently this building had been the effective city hall of Shanghai, but in addition housing the mayor of Shanghai and some of his senior muncipal staff. Having recently been completely redecorated and converted to guest house usage, this 9-story building—in a pleasant garden setting—was reminiscent externally of the best of Hilton International and internally, at least on the seventh and eighth floors, of the best of traditional Shanghai hostelries boasting spacious suites, balconies, walk-in closets, enormous bathrooms (having very modern American Standard fixtures), thick rugs, and traditional Shanghai mahogany woodwork throughout. These accommodations were outstanding by any international standard.

In Hangzhou the delegation was housed in the massive Hangzhou Hotel built on beautiful grounds on the north shore of West Lake. It is easy to understand why Marco Polo, on his return to Venice from his first trip to China, said of Hangzhou, "it is without doubt the finest and most splendid city in the world." This was the only hotel we encountered that had central air conditioning; unfortunately, it was turned on only between 10 a.m. and 4 p.m., so that by evening the rooms were extremely hot—and remained so throughout the night. Here, too, it was recommended that we sleep inside mosquito netting tents over the beds; the local mosquitos—apart from being large and voracious—are reputed to carry porcine encephalitis that can be transmitted to humans.

On our return to Beijing we had rooms in the Qian Men Hotel, again a Friendship-type hotel with Soviet architecture (some 5 minutes by taxi from Tian An Men Square). On our arrival some members of the delegation had to share rooms but stalwart efforts by the CAS managed to find single rooms for all on the second night—despite the fact that large numbers of American tourists—traveling as part of a Pan Am tour, and who thought they had reservations at this hotel—received no rooms after some 6 hours of waiting.

In all of these hotels exellent 1-day laundry service was available, food was plentiful and of high quality, and service was excellent. Some housed Friendship shops (where the prices are the same as everywhere else in China but items are more apt to be available), while all had service counters where certain items were available only for foreign currency (Johnny Walker Red Label Scotch at $8.00 U.S. per 25 oz; Coca-Cola at $3.00 U.S. per bottle!).

Appendix D

Names of Hosts and Scientists at Institutions Visited

BEIJING

State Scientific and Technological Commission (SSTC)—May 22, 1979

赵东宛   Zhao Dongwan
                 Deputy Director, SSTC

魏兆麟   Wei Zhaolin
                 Head, Fifth Bureau, SSTC

黄坤益   Huang Kunyi
                 Foreign Affairs Bureau, SSTC

Chinese Academy of Sciences (CAS)—May 22, 1979

钱三强   Qian Sanqiang
                 Vice President, CAS

金力生   Qin Lisheng
                 Deputy Secretary-General, CAS

王淦昌   Wang Ganchang
                 Director, Institute of Atomic Energy (IAE)
                 Vice Minister, Secondary Ministry of Machine-Building

Appendixes

李 寿 枬　Li Shounan
　　　　　　Deputy Director, IAE

冯 囡 复　Feng Yinfu
　　　　　　Deputy Director, Foreign Affairs Bureau, CAS

李 明 德　Li Mingde
　　　　　　Foreign Affairs Bureau, CAS

Beijing University—May 23, 1979

周 培 元　Zhou Peiyuan
　　　　　　President (met later on June 8)

王 竹 溪　Wang Zhuqi
　　　　　　Vice President

胡 济 民　Hu Jimin
　　　　　　Chairman, Technical Physics Department

曾 谨 言　Zeng Jinyan

　　　　　　Zhang Qiren

陈 佳 洱　Chen Jiaer

Qinghua University—May 23, 1979

张 维　　Chang Wei
　　　　　　Vice President

张 礼　　Chang Li
　　　　　　Deputy Chairman, Engineering Physics Department

陈 世 猷　Chen Shiyou
　　　　　　Lecturer, Engineering Physics Department

王 支 礼　Wang Zhili
　　　　　　Lecturer, Engineering Physics Department (Accelerators)

陈 泽 民　Chen Zemin
　　　　　Lecturer, Engineering Physics Department
　　　　　(Accelerators; Nuclear Physics)

薛 禹 易　Xue Yuyi
　　　　　Lecturer, Engineering Physics Department
　　　　　(Nuclear Physics)

李 道 增　Li Daozeng
　　　　　Lecturer, Architecture Department

Institute of Physics—May 22, 1979

施 汝 为　Shih Ruwei
　　　　　Director

管 惟 炎　Guan Weiyan
　　　　　Deputy Director

陆 学 善　Lu Xueshan
　　　　　Deputy Director

Institute of Theoretical Physics—May 22, 1979

何 祚 庥　He Zuoxiu
　　　　　Deputy Director

赵 万 云　Zhao Wanyun
　　　　　Particles and Fields

赵 恩 广　Zhao Enguang
　　　　　Nuclear Theory

朱 熙 泉　Zhu Xiquan
　　　　　Nuclear Theory

Other researchers (not met) and their specialities

彭 桓 武　Peng Huanwu
　　　　　Director

Appendixes

胡 宁　Hu Ning
　　　　Deputy Director, Particles and Fields, Gravitation

戴 元 本　Dai Yuanben
　　　　Particles and Fields

郭 汉 英　Guo Hanying
　　　　Gravitation

周 光 召　Zhou Guangzhao
　　　　Particles and Fields

邹 振 隆　Zou Zhenlong
　　　　Gravitation and Astrophysics

黄 祖 洽　Huang Zuqia

于 敏　Yu Min

张 元 仲　Zhang Yuanzhong
　　　　Particles and Fields, Gravitation

李 根 道　Li Gendao
　　　　Mathematics

安 瑛　An Ying
　　　　Particles and Fields

陈 时　Chen Shi
　　　　Particles and Fields, Gravitation

吴 詠 时　Wu Yongshi
　　　　Particles and Fields

张 历 宁　Zhang Lining
　　　　Mathematics, Gravitation

朱 重 远　Zhu Zhongyuan
　　　　Particles and Fields

李 小 源　Li Xiaoyuan
　　　　Particles and Fields

Dong Mingde
  Mechanics, Particles and Fields

Hu Renan
  Mechanics

Liu Yufen
  Gravitation

Hao Bailin
  Statistical and Computational Physics

Yu Lu
  Statistical Physics

Zheng Weimo
  Statistical Physics

Lu Qi
  Numerical Mathematics

Institute of High-Energy Physics—May 25, 1979

Hu Ning
  Director

Zhao Zhongyao
  Deputy Director

Zhu Hongyuan
  Head, Theoretical Group

Zhang Zongye
  Theoretical Group

Institute of Atomic Energy—May 24-25, 1979

Wang Ganchang
  Director

Li Shounan
  Deputy Director

Appendixes

Wang Dexi
  Deputy Director

Dai Chuanzeng
  Deputy Director

Ding Shengyao

Weng Peikun

Zhuo Yizhong

Chen Yongshou

Yang Minzhang

Ding Dazhao

Yang Zhen

Wang Chuanying

LANZHOU

Institute of Modern Physics—May 29-June 1, 1979

Yang Chengzhong
  Director

Xie Bowang
  Secretary of the Communist Party Committee

Zhang Enhou
  Deputy Director

王 樹 芬　Wang Shufen (f)
　　　　　　Director, Applied Physics Lab

陳 奕 愛　Chen Yiai
　　　　　　Director, Electronics and Detector Lab

尹 仲 禮　Yen Zhongli
　　　　　　Vice Director, Electronics and Detector Lab

戴 光 曦　Dai Guangxi
　　　　　　Vice Director, First Research Lab, Nuclear Physics Division

劉 迠 业　Liu Jianye
　　　　　　Vice Director, First Research Lab, Nuclear Physics Division

張 敬 叶　Zhang Jingye
　　　　　　First Research Lab

張 守 謹　Zhang Shoujin
　　　　　　Director, Separated Cyclotron Division

魏 宝 文　Wei Baowen
　　　　　　Vice Director, Separated Cyclotron Division

張 銘 麟　Zhang Minglin
　　　　　　Vice Director, Separated Cyclotron Division

喬 庆 文　Chiao Chingwen
　　　　　　Vice Director, Separated Cyclotron Division

郭 箕 第　Guo Qidi
　　　　　　Vice Director, Tandem Division

許 士 元　Xu Shiyuan
　　　　　　Vice Director, Cyclotron Labs

李 学 寬　Li Xuekuan
　　　　　　Vice Director, Cyclotron Labs

Appendixes

蒋 维 横   Jiang Weimo
               Vice Director, Cyclotron Labs

刘 嘉 玫   Liu Jiawen
               Foreign Affairs Office

Lanzhou University—May 30, 1979

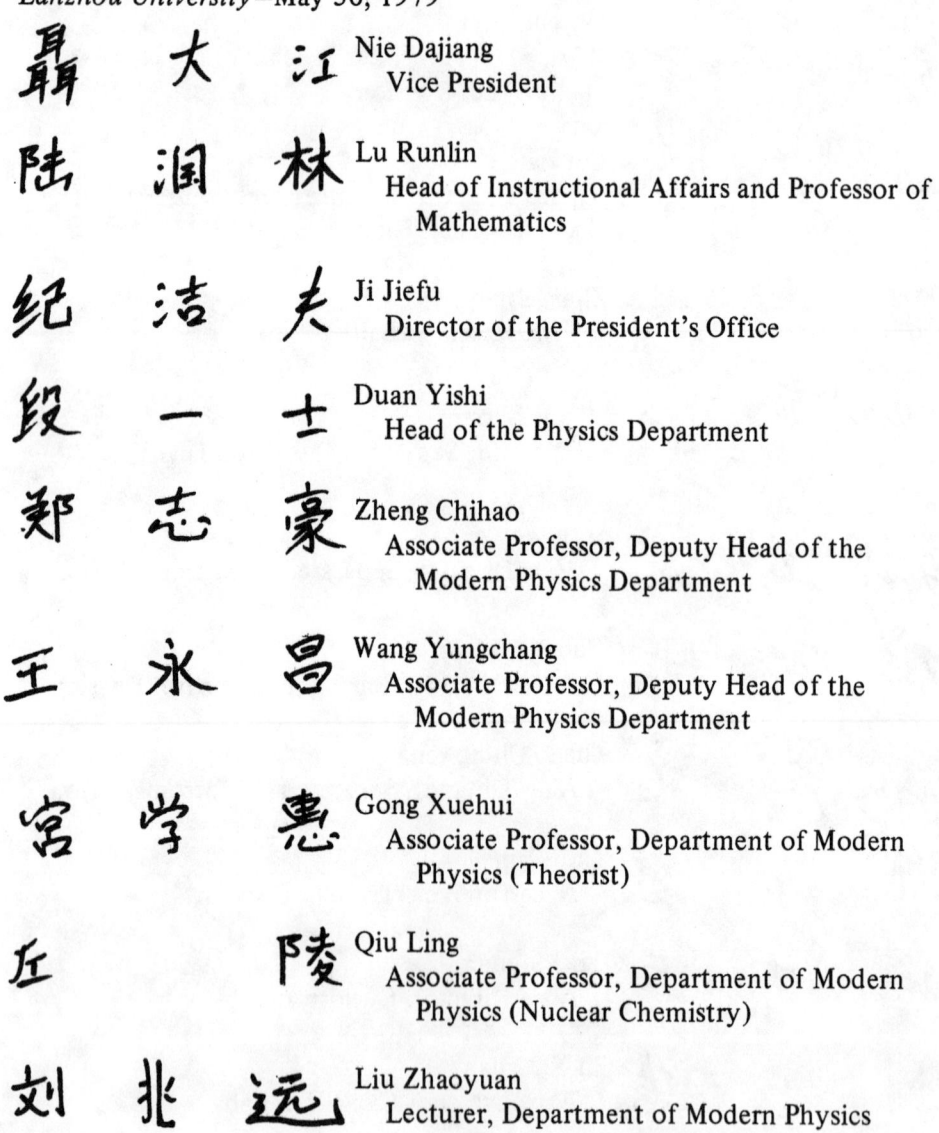

聂 大 江   Nie Dajiang
               Vice President

陆 润 林   Lu Runlin
               Head of Instructional Affairs and Professor of Mathematics

纪 洁 夫   Ji Jiefu
               Director of the President's Office

段 一 士   Duan Yishi
               Head of the Physics Department

郑 志 豪   Zheng Chihao
               Associate Professor, Deputy Head of the Modern Physics Department

王 永 昌   Wang Yungchang
               Associate Professor, Deputy Head of the Modern Physics Department

宫 学 惠   Gong Xuehui
               Associate Professor, Department of Modern Physics (Theorist)

左 陵   Qiu Ling
               Associate Professor, Department of Modern Physics (Nuclear Chemistry)

刘 兆 远   Liu Zhaoyuan
               Lecturer, Department of Modern Physics

Appendixes

SHANGHAI

Hu Yungchang
    Deputy Director, Shanghai Branch, CAS

Institute for Nuclear Research—June 5, 1979

Jin Houchu
    Director

Zhang Jiahua
    Deputy Director

Cheng Xiaowu
    Director, Nuclear Physics Division

Jiang Dazhen
    Nuclear Physics Division

Jin Hansheng
    Nuclear Physics Division

Li Yungjian
    Nuclear Physics Division

Yan Xiuying
    Electronics and Detector Division

Mao Yu
    Accelerator Division

Zhang Weizhong
    Accelerator Division

Zhou Shiyuan
    Accelerator Division

Lai Weiquan
    Accelerator Division

Fu Teqi
    Theoretical Physics

Appendixes

Fudan University—June 4, 1979

谢希德　　Xie Xide (f)
　　　　　　Vice President

杨福家　　Yang Fujia
　　　　　　Head, Nuclear Physics Department

Other senior members of the Physics Department (not met) and their specialities

王福山　　Wang Fushan
　　　　　　Acting Department Chairman, General Physics

蔡祖泉　　Cai Zuguan
　　　　　　Electric Light Sources

周同庆　　Zhou Tongqing
　　　　　　Optics and Spectroscopy

叶蕴理　　Ye Yunli
　　　　　　Optics

周世勋　　Zhou Shixun
　　　　　　Theoretical Physics (Multibody Quantum Statistics)

方俊鑫　　Fang Junxin
　　　　　　Solid State Physics and Dialectric Physics

李郁芬　　Li Yufen
　　　　　　Laser Physics and Chemistry

华中一　　Hua Zhongyi
　　　　　　Vacuum Physics, Electronic Physics

章志鸣　　Zhang Zhiwu
　　　　　　Spectroscopy and Optical Information Processing

李仲卿　　Li Zhongqing
　　　　　　General Physics

Appendixes

唐璞山　　Tang Pushan
　　　　　　Semiconductor Microelectronics

倪光烔　　Ni Guangton
　　　　　　Theoretical Physics (Basic Particle Theory)

王　迅　　Wang Xun
　　　　　　Semiconductor Physics, Surface Physics

凌燮亭　　Ling Xieting
　　　　　　Radio Electronics

孙　鑫　　Sun Xin
　　　　　　Theoretical Physics

Other senior members of the Nuclear Sciences Department (not met) and their specialities

卢鹤绂　　Lu Hefu
　　　　　　Theoretical Physics

顾元壮　　Gu Yuanzhuang
　　　　　　Accelerator Theory and Technology

秦启宗　　Qin Qizong
　　　　　　Radiation Chemistry and Laser Chemistry

Vanguard Electrical Works—June 4, 1979

蒋佑法　　Jiang Zuofa
　　　　　　Deputy Director

濮焕仁　　Pu Huanren
　　　　　　Deputy Director, Head of Accelerator Division

周启章　　Zhou Qizhang
　　　　　　Deputy Chief Engineer

王恒东　　Wang Hendong
　　　　　　Head of the Technical Section

Appendixes

HANGZHOU

楊 士 林   Yang Shilin
   Deputy Director, Zhejiang Science and Technology Commission (and Vice President of Zhejiang University)

姜 尚 文   Jiang Shangwen
   Zhejiang S&T Commission Staff

刘 俊 华   Liu Junhua
   Zhejiang S&T Commission Staff

Zhejiang University—June 6, 1979

钱 三 强   Qian Sanqiang
   President (met in Beijing)

楊 士 林   Yang Shilin
   Vice President

曹 萱 龄   Cao Huanling
   Head, Physics Department

Appendix E

Technical Materials Received in China by Members of the Delegation

At the major institutions visited by the delegation, its members were given packets of descriptive materials, reprints, preprints, and the like. While these collections were not elaborate by American standards, they do represent a significant advance in the exchange of scientific materials over the situation reported by many previous American delegations that have visited China in recent years. For illustrative purposes, titles of materials received are listed below.

INSTITUTE OF ATOMIC ENERGY, BEIJING

Descriptive brochures (in English)

"The Experimental Model of the Electron Linac"
"On the Several Researches for Fast Neutrons Using a Time of Flight Spectrometer"
"The Measurement of Fission Cross Section"
"Some Work on the Large Liquid Scintillation Counter"
"Activation Analysis with Accelerator"
"Activation Analysis with Reactor Neutrons"

Abstracts (in English)

"D + ^{6}Li, α + ^{6}Li and α + ^{7}Li Three Body Reactions at Low Energies"
"Study of the Gamma-Ray Spectra and Production Cross Sections in Fast Neutron Reactions"

Appendixes

"(α,p) Pre-Equilibrium Emission Studies at E = 18 Mev"
"Search for Intermediate Structure of Nuclear Reaction Induced by Low Energy Deuterons"

Paper (draft, in English)
"The Transport Process of the Nuclear Reaction"

INSTITUTE OF MODERN PHYSICS, LANZHOU

Preprints (in English)

"Production and Identification on Neutron Deficient Isotopes ^{118}I, ^{117}I and ^{115}I," Sun Xijun, Guo Junsheng, Cho Chicheng, Pan Zongyou, Guo Yingxiang

"Separation of Am, Cm, Cf and Y by Cation Exchange with Alpha-hydroxy Isobutyric Acid," Li Wenxin, Gun Zihui, Niu Fang, Sun Huangjiang, Yang Zhenguo

Reprints (with English Abstracts)

All are from *Gaoneng Wuli Yu He Wuli* (*Physica Energiae Fortis et Physica Nuclearis*) and all the authors are from the IMP in Lanzhou. Their names are romanized as shown in English on the reprints.

"Heavy Ion Researches in Lanchow," Nuclear Physics Research Laboratory. Vol. 1, No. 1, November 1977.

"The Effect of Nuclear Distortion in Deep Inelastic Scattering," Wu Kuo-Huah, Zhong Ji-Quan, Ge Ling-Xiao. Vol. 1, No. 1, November 1977.

"α Particles Emitted in the Reaction of ^{12}C on ^{209}Bi," Shen Wen-Ging, Xu Shu-Wei, Wang Da-Yan, Xie Yuan-Xiang, Guo Zhong-Yab, Li Zu-Yu. Vol. 1, No. 1, November 1977.

"The Measurement of Complete Fusion Cross-Sections for the Reactions ^{12}C + ^{27}Al, ^{12}C + ^{209}Bi and ^{14}N + Pb," Sun Chi-chang, He Yi, Shen Jiu-sheng, Chen Hou, Chen Ke-liang. Vol. 2, No. 2, March 1978.

"The Measurement of the Excitation Function of Isotopes of Fr and At, Produced in the Bombardment of ^{12}C on ^{209}Bi," Guo Jun-sheng, Sun Xi-jun, Xu Xiao-ji, Wang Jun, Liu Hong-ye. Vol. 2, No. 2, March 1978.

"Angular Distributions of Fission Fragments and the Shapes of the Saddle Point of Compound Nuclei," Liu Gou-xing, Wang Zhi-gou, Yin Shu-zhi, Hao Bingan, Yuan Shuang-gui, Xia Xing-shuo. Vol. 2, No. 3, May 1978.

"A Semi-Classical Analysis on the Reaction ^{12}C + ^{209}Bi at Bombarding Energies Slightly Above the Coulomb Barrier," Xu Shu-wei, Ran Qi-hui, Ma Hong-fan. Vol. 2, No. 6, November 1978.

"Study of the Deep Inelastic Scattering of ^{12}C on ^{27}Al," Wu Zhong-li, Zhu Yong-tai, Xia Guo-zhong, Liu Bu-sheng, Li Fa-wei, Fan Guo-ying. Vol. 3, No. 2, March 1979.

"The Interplay on Nuclear Deformation and Pair Correlation Nuclear Phase Diagram," Xu Gong-ou, Zhang Ying-ye. Vol. 3, No. 2, March 1979.

LANZHOU UNIVERSITY

(All materials in Chinese, except last item.)

"Non-crystaline Silicone and Solar Cells," Chen Guang-hua and Wang Yinyue, Lanzhou University, Physics Department. January 1979. (Preprint)

"The Negative Ion Property of Low Temperature Deposited SiO_2," Shop No. 7 of the Forever Red [Yong Hong] Instrumentation and Materials Factory and the Senior Project Team, Semiconductor Division, Physics Department, Lanzhou University. *Scholarly Journal of Lanzhou University*, December 1975.

"The Technical Factors That Affect the Field of IC Chips," Zhao Pixin, Ningguang Electrical Works and Li Siyuan, Lanzhou University. *Scholarly Journal of Lanzhou University*, June 1977.

"The Importance of Alloying Techniques in the Production of IC's," Ningguang Factory Senior Project Team, Semiconductor Division, Physics Department, Lanzhou University and Shop No. 2, Ningguang Electrical Works. *Scholarly Journal of Lanzhou University*, September 1977.

"A Physical Chemistry Model of Au in the Interface of SiO_2-Si," Li Siyuan and Zhang Xiuwen, Lanzhou University, Physics Department. March 1979. (Preprint)

"The Problem of Interaction Among Impurity Defects," Li Siyuan and Li Shousong, Lanzhou University, Physics Department. February 1979. (Preprint)

"A Study of the Low Current Transistors in Low Power Operational Amplifliers 8Fc75-0," Shop No. 7 of the Forever Red [Yong Hong] Instrumentation and Materials Factory and Senior Project Team, Semiconductor Division, Physics Department, Lanzhou University. *Scholarly Journal of Lanzhou University*, March 1979.

Appendixes

"The Electronic Process in a Non-crystaline Semi-conductor," Chen Changhua and Wang Yinyue, Lanzhou University, Physics Department. March 1979. (Preprint)

"SV(2) Gauge Theory and the Electrodynamics of N Magnetic Monopoles," Duan Yishi and Ge Molin, Lanzhou University, Center for Theoretical Physics. November 1977. (Preprint)

"The Scaler Property of Electron-proton Deep Inelastic Scattering," Duan Yishi and Ge Molin, Lanzhou University, Physics Department. *Scholarly Journal of Lanzhou University*, June 1974.

"On Gauge Field Theory," Duan Yishi and Ge Molin, Lanzhou University, Physics Department. *Scholarly Journal of Lanzhou University*, June 1974.

"A Gauge Theory of Cabbibo Angles," Kuang Yuping, Ma Zhonggi, Hsu Baiwei, Yang Xuping, Lanzhou University. *Acta Physica Sinica* 24, July 1975.

"The Generator Coordinate Method and Nuclear Collective Motions," Hsu Kung-ngou, Lanzhou University. *Scientia Sinica* (in English), Vol. xvii, No. 5, October 1974.

INSTITUTE FOR
NUCLEAR RESEARCH, SHANGHAI

"Plan for Modifying the 1.2 MeV Cyclotron" (in Chinese), March 1979.

Copies of the journal, *He Jishu (Nuclear Technology)*, issues 1 (February) and 2 (May) for 1979. (in Chinese)

FUDAN UNIVERSITY

Copies of *Fudan Xuebao (Fudan Journal)* (natural science edition), issue 1 (March) for 1979. (in Chinese)

FUNDERBURG LIBRARY
MANCHESTER COLLEGE

WITHDRAWN
from
Funderburg Library